THE FIVE-HUNDRED-WORD THEME

3rd
edition

THE FIVE-HUNDRED-WORD THEME

LEE J. MARTIN
AND
HARRY P. KROITOR
Texas A&M University

PRENTICE-HALL, INC.,
Englewood Cliffs, New Jersey 07632

Library of Congress Cataloging in Publication Data

Martin, Lee J.
   The five-hundred-word theme.

   Includes index.
   1. English language—Rhetoric.   I. Kroitor,
Harry P., 1924–   joint author.   II. Title.
PE1408.M3866 1979   808.04'2   77-19061
ISBN 0-13-321588-1

10 9 8 7 6 5 4 3 2 1

Printed in the United States of America

PRENTICE-HALL INTERNATIONAL, INC., *London*
PRENTICE-HALL OF AUSTRALIA, PTY. LIMITED, *Sydney*
PRENTICE-HALL OF CANADA, LTD., *Toronto*
PRENTICE-HALL OF INDIA PRIVATE LIMITED, *New Delhi*
PRENTICE-HALL OF JAPAN, INC., *Tokyo*
PRENTICE-HALL OF SOUTHEAST ASIA PTE. LTD., *Singapore*
WHITEHALL BOOKS LIMITED, *Wellington, New Zealand*

CONTENTS

getting started: discovery, specific focus, thesis

36

maintaining unity and coherence

64

writing paragraphs

96

vii
contents

6

putting the parts together: the whole paper
155

7

research and the long paper
171

TWO

REVISION—MECHANICS AND STYLE

207

8

mechanics: grammar, punctuation, spelling

209

9

revising your paper—diction

260

10

revising your paper—sentences

286

PREFACE TO THE FIRST EDITION

This book offers the freshman composition student the basic knowledge necessary to write a short theme of the type most often required in beginning composition courses. I have made two assumptions: that most students will profit little in college by further formal study of "mechanics" of the language, and that students need above all an orderly approach to the problem of organizing and writing a short paper that makes a logical point and supports it. Such an orderly approach is the subject of this book.

I have used the five-hundred-word theme because in this length a student can best learn and practice basic principles that apply to all writing. *Never do I intend to imply, however, that themes assigned should be exactly five hundred words.* I do intend that they should be close to this length. A shorter paper gives the student little opportunity to develop his subject; a longer one becomes burdensome for both student and teacher without offering any particular advantage to the beginning writer.

I have stressed organization. Indeed, the diagrams in the book present a pattern for organizing the short theme—a pattern for the beginning student to follow one step at a time until he has learned and practiced the basic principles of composition. *I would not expect him to stay in the mold after his first semester of college composition, but I would expect him to apply the principles taught here to all his writing.*

I am deeply indebted to my wife Harriet, who supplied a number of the exercises and offered invaluable editorial help.

L.J.M.

PREFACE TO THE THIRD EDITION

to the student

You already know how to write. Keep this thought secure as a reminder that you already have skills to develop into effective communication techniques. However, everyone needs practice in writing papers that clearly make one logical point and adequately support it. Everyone, even professionals writing for money. By stressing a preplanned picture-outline, this book presents one way to tackle the problem successfully.

Throughout, this revised edition reminds you that the basic pattern it describes in the early chapters is a successful way to *begin,* that writing according to a clear plan doesn't have to destroy creativity, that effective writing requires sharply focused thought and a specific, controlled attitude toward your subject. It also reminds you to try other methods of organizing and developing your papers, to build beyond basic patterns after mastering them. Equally important, the new chapter on research and the long paper shows you how the techniques learned in writing the short paper apply to the longer research paper. The basic patterns are the same.

Following basic patterns, then, is your starting point. However, if you haven't assumed a specific attitude—toward your subject and toward your reader—your papers may still be ineffective. In fact, many of us never think of the audience we are writing for, and the result is a kind of "writing in a vacuum" that keeps us from sounding like human beings. Your writing should take on strength and life if you practice the two basic skills this book emphasizes— clearly explaining a main point with supporting evidence, and honestly projecting a convincing attitude with self-confidence. The first part of the book (Focus, Discovery, Organization) stresses primarily the first skill. The second part (Revision—Mechanics and Style) shows you that there's more to writing than merely following a formula, and it provides a review of grammar, punctuation, and spelling.

TO THE TEACHER This book presents a method, not a theory. Without any major changes in approach or method, the third edition emphasizes and expands some of the material often overlooked in previous editions. I have expanded the material on writing thesis statements and have included new diagrams to illustrate the discovery process, the funnel effect, logical division, and controlling attitude. I have revised the discussion of unity and coherence, tying it to the new material on controlling attitude. And, in response to numerous requests, I have added a new chapter on research and the long paper, showing that it uses all the techniques learned in writing a five-hundred-word theme.

The methods presented in the book are *starting* points, not rigid patterns to be followed slavishly or indefinitely. To emphasize this point, throughout the text I have suggested alternative approaches for experimentation. The definition of exposition used includes writing with an argumentative bias. By "writing with conviction" I mean honestly convincing yourself first and extending this tone of conviction to include a specific audience. The result is, I think, a book with greater flexibility and greater rhetorical depth than found in the previous edition, *without* any loss in instructional value to the student.

Still aimed at freshman composition students, the book gives them explicit thinking and writing instructions to follow. Its assumptions and methods are basically those of rhetoric as it has been known for over two thousand years: Discovery and invention, arrangement and organization, and, through revision, an introduction to some of the problems of tone and style. In addition, however, the third edition provides some material from traditional, structural, and transformational grammar to help teachers with students who need work in basic expression.

I am pleased to have this continued opportunity to expand work begun with Dr. Martin some years ago and to reaffirm my confidence in a book whose conciseness, directness, and clarity have won for it the support and respect of hard-working teachers at many schools.

H.P.K.
1978

THE FIVE-HUNDRED-WORD THEME

FOCUS, DISCOVERY, ORGANIZATION

Part 1 of this book introduces the *rhetoric* of communication. Rhetoric can be defined simply as the *art* of *discovering* the *most effective* means of *communication* in a *particular situation*. To say that rhetoric is an art implies that it is a *skill* you can learn. It implies also that you, as communicator, *choose* the most effective organization, words, sentences, and paragraphs for the messages you want to send. As the sender of a message, your aim is to get the receiver to say, "I understand," "I agree." To achieve this, you must first develop the skill that is the main focus of Part 1—the ability to explain a main point clearly and support it with specific evidence.

With this basic aim in mind, Chapter 1 stresses the importance of writing to prevent misunderstanding, especially in expository writing. Chapter 2 emphasizes organization, distinguishing between deductive and inductive approaches. Chapter 3 presents the discovery process of rhetoric ("invention"), showing you how to discover something to say, how to focus the reader's attention through a good thesis statement with a sharp controlling attitude, and how to discover support for the thesis. In Chapter 4 you will learn that the controlling attitude of the thesis statement is only half the key to unity, and that directional signals can effectively guide a reader through your writing. The developmental paragraphs you will study in Chapter 5 provide additional rhetorical skills, while Chapter 6 asks you to bring all the skills together. Then in Chapter 7 you will be given the challenge of writing a long paper, a research paper requiring the application of all the skills learned in the previous chapters. By the end of Part 1, therefore, you will know many of the basic techniques of the *art of rhetoric*; later you will learn more about tone and style.

writing
to prevent
misunderstanding

like most skills, effective writing can be taught in principle and improved by practice. The first part of this book (Focus, Discovery, Organization) presents the basic principles you need to write a simple five-hundred-word paper—principles involved in any kind of writing. And it provides practice in using these principles in the exercises following each chapter. It introduces the parts of the short paper one at a time and lets you practice each before going to the next. It also shows you how to put these parts together as a whole paper sharply focused on a single, well-supported point. The second part (Revision—Mechanics and Style) provides practical guides to revision, including some ways to make your paper more convincing, since successful communication requires not only the controlled presentation of specific ideas but the projection of the right attitude as well.

WHY SHOULD YOU LEARN TO WRITE MORE EFFECTIVELY?

Why should you learn to write more effectively? The basic answer is simple: *survival.* If you learn to communicate accurately and effectively so you can't be misunderstood, you'll improve all your grades in school, get a better job when you graduate, and earn more money in the process. Effective leaders are effective communicators. And leadership positions demand higher salaries. It is logical, then, to learn effective communication.

Effective communication is an exact, two-way process in which a *sender* gets a *receiver* to understand and, perhaps, to agree with a specific *message.* As the following two cartoon illustrations suggest, receivers can misunderstand even the simplest statement if it lacks specific details or is incomplete. And senders of messages don't always project what they *think* they are projecting. One of the writer's biggest jobs, therefore, is to learn to think as a reader, anticipating questions and providing details to prevent misunderstanding. To accomplish this, you must consider the entire communication situation. Think of your readers and ask yourself, "Will they understand what I'm saying?" Don't give them a chance to jump to the wrong conclusion; lead them inescapably to the message you have in mind. This is the first and most important reward of learning to write more effectively. You won't go around wondering, "Why don't people understand me?"

The most obvious advantage of improving your writing is that you can put your ideas into an understandable, convincing, valid form. Like many students, you probably have good ideas but have trouble expressing them. Composing a paper is one way you can learn to state your ideas specifically and to show the evidence you have

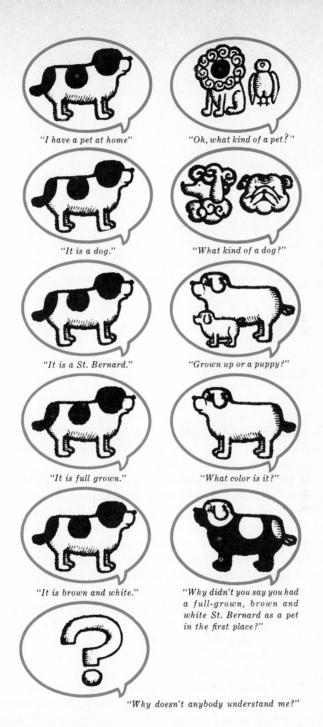

Source: Reprinted with permission of Benziger Bruce & Glencoe, Inc. (Beverly Hills, California), a Division of Macmillan Publishing Co., Inc., from *Communications* by Donald Fabun. Copyright 1965, 1968 by Kaiser Aluminum and Chemical Corporation.

SOURCE: *The New Yorker Album of Drawings, 1925–1975* (New York: The Viking Press, 1975). Copyright by New Yorker Magazine.

to support those ideas. Unless you write them down, however, your ideas are likely to remain half-formed, and when you try to express them, you may find you're not successful in communicating exactly what you mean.

Think of the endless opportunities you have for effective communication. They provide the challenge of choosing—choosing the right ideas, choosing the right words, choosing the right sentence patterns, choosing the right paragraphs, choosing the right organization. Suppose, for example, that your best friend has decided to run for a class office and you think he or she has the qualities to make an outstanding student government officer. Suppose that your friend asks you to present these qualities to the student body by writing a letter to the college newspaper. How would you go about explaining these qualities so that the readers of the newspaper would believe in your friend as you do? Practicing the techniques of expository writing as we'll define it will make it much easier for you to express and support your ideas clearly and concisely in any situation. And by carefully revising your diction and sentence structure to fit the attitude you have in mind, you will add strength and conviction to your paper. You'll be able to get your reader to say, "I understand, I agree."

Having communication skills at your command will help you gain confidence in your own ability to function as an individual—and to carry your own weight in any social or business situation. Suppose, again, you have decided to try to get a job next summer in one of the national parks or in a summer camp as a counselor. You would have to write a letter outlining all your qualifications for this job, and you would have to sell yourself to the person doing the hiring. You would actually be doing two things: (1) *describing your qualifications with supporting evidence*, and (2) *projecting a convincing attitude of self-confidence.* To do those things well on paper you must be confident of your presentation of yourself to your prospective employer.

Similarly, in your school work a knowledge of the techniques of expository writing will greatly increase your chances for better grades in any courses that require writing. Writing an essay examination or a paper requires you to organize facts and apply the techniques of revision that will strengthen your presentation and make it convincing. The more effectively your present your ideas and the knowledge you have, the more your writing will improve and the better your grades will be.

Perhaps most important to you, however, as a citizen of our democracy, is the ability to write logically and to recognize logical thought when you read or hear it. The techniques of expository writing require you to use all the evidence you can collect to support the ideas you want your reader to understand or accept. As you collect evidence you should be able to judge the logic of your ideas. If the evidence disproves your ideas, then you should discard or alter them. But if the evidence shows that your ideas are probably right, you are then justified in presenting and supporting them. Knowing this, you should also become more cautious about accepting generalizations *others* make, unless they support them with valid evidence.

This cautious approach to ideas is necessary for the survival of democracy as we know it; as long as people demand proof in support of ideas, no one person or group can lead an entire nation down an undesired or wrong path. Open debate, the critical examination of ideas and their proof, has always been fundamental to our democratic national character, enabling it to thrive despite wars, political corruption, and domestic battles over issues such as ecology and pollution.

WHAT YOU MUST BRING TO WRITING

Effective writing isn't easy; it demands patience and discipline. Don't expect to sit down and produce a successful paper in the time it takes you to write down five hundred words. Maybe a few experienced writers can do this, for their very experience enables them to choose the proper word and to frame sentences exactly; but even established writers find writing hard work and know the value of revision. Beginning writers soon learn that if they are to produce work that they can be proud of and that will communicate their intentions precisely, they must work hard and revise thoroughly.

Effective writing also requires self-discipline—in word choice, in sentence patterns, in paragraph development, in organization. You'll need to learn how to write unified, coherent paragraphs that convey each supporting idea unmistakably. You'll need to learn economy and effectiveness in wording. Most important, you must learn how to stick to a single, limited subject so that you finish the paper with a definite, preplanned point you have developed and supported. Before you write the first word, you must discipline yourself to think through your subject thoroughly and to decide on a definite attitude toward that subject. And even though the act of writing will itself generate new ideas as your paper grows—ideas you will want to add if they fit your purposes—your starting point will be those ideas you discover before you begin writing.

The thought you bring to writing is most important; without it you cannot write at all, for writing is the communication of thought. You must think through your subject *before* you start to write, selecting or rejecting ideas that occur to you. And you must write logically. For instance, you may have to discard some of your prejudices—those ideas and opinions you hold without logic and evidence to back them up—because they are based in emotion rather than in fact. Although everyone thinks emotionally at times, the emotional has only a limited place in most writing. You must have an open and inquiring mind, as free from prejudice and unsupported opinion as you can make it, so that you can accept fact where you find it and can develop the habit of using only fact to support generalizations.

What you must bring to writing, then, is the desire to become educated. You must want to develop the ability to face fact without coloring or slanting it to fit a set of prejudices, to communicate soundly supported ideas to others either in speech or writing, to lose any narrow provincialism, and to consider all ideas, particularly those that go beyond restricted interests. This ability will help you become mature and objective; learning the techniques of effective communication in writing will hasten this process. And most important, when you speak or write you will be less likely to be misunderstood.

THE KIND OF WRITING YOU ARE EXPECTED TO DO

You already know much about the basic *kinds* of writing found in most books. If you've written a letter telling someone of a personal experience—a dance, a date, an accident you had, a fishing or hunting experience—then you were practicing a basic kind of writing. More likely, you probably *told* someone a story or a joke, or tried to prove a point or explain an opinion. Look at these communication events closely, and you'll see that you regularly use four basic "approaches." Most simply stated, you *tell, show, argue,* and *explain*; you are using *narration, description, argument,* and *exposition.* Though this book is primarily about *expository* writing, you need to understand the four basic kinds of writing and use them when they fit your communication aims.

telling—narration

To tell a story is to narrate events, to give an account of how something happened, step by step, minute by minute. *Narration presents an orderly sequence of events in time:* how you caught your giant fish (or best date), had your worst kitchen accident, shot your first deer, rescued your pet toad from a trespassing serpent, or fell flat on your face in gym class. Though used primarily in fiction, narrative paragraphs often work exceptionally well in exposition or argumentation to illustrate a point. Your aim: to get your reader to say, "I see," "I understand."

showing—description

To present a picture, to show your reader how something looks, feels, tastes, or what it sounds like is to describe. *Description presents an orderly, part-by-part picture of something in space*—your room, the main street, your campus, a city, a guitar, your cafeteria, a tree, a building, or your pet toad. In an expository paper, you can often use paragraphs of descriptive detail to support or develop a general statement. Your aim: to get your reader to say, "I see," "I understand."

arguing—argumentation

To get your reader to *accept* a belief or take a specific action, you use argumentation. When you argue, you try to *prove* something. You don't argue to deceive your reader, nor merely for the sake of arguing. *Argumentation* presents valid *proof to persuade someone to accept an opinion or idea and to do something.* Some writers consider exposition to be a form of argument; in fact, often you'll find it very hard to keep these two kinds of writing from overlapping. Your aim: to get your reader to say, "I understand," "I agree," "I will act."

explaining—exposition

The kind of writing you will be expected to do most of the time—in school and on the job—is *exposition.* Expository writing is the straightforward *explanation* of something—a process, an object, an idea, an event. It analyzes or accounts for something by presenting specific information to support the explanation given. For example, if you want to establish the idea that organizing political clubs on your campus would in *some ways* benefit the students, you would be using exposition. You would be explaining and supporting an idea. If, however, you wanted to *prove* that organizing political clubs on your campus *would benefit* students, you would have shifted into argument. The kinds of support needed in these two approaches, and the kinds of agreement expected from the reader, are basically different. Can you see why? Exposition is probably the most common kind of writing, since it includes explanations of such things as following a road map, making a cake, rebuilding a motor, writing a theme, driving a car, and other *processes. The main purpose of exposition is to present information to explain, analyze, or account for a process, an object, an idea, or an event.* Any writing—no matter what combination of kinds is used—that has as its *primary* purpose *to make a subject clear by presenting specific information,* we will consider expository writing. Your aim: to get your reader to say, "I understand," "I see your point."

Depending on his communication aims and needs a writer will select or combine the four basic kinds of writing, as he tells a story, describes, argues, or explains. The organization pattern for his whole paper *and* for its individual paragraphs will depend on the kind of writing he chooses to do, since each kind of writing has a specific purpose for the selected information it presents. Some common organization patterns and their most likely application in the basic kinds of writing are shown on page 11.

The expository papers you will write will contain some narration, description, and argument. The organization patterns for the information within your papers (or for individual paragraphs) will include some or all of those listed on page 11.

You will begin by concentrating on expository papers of approximately five hundred words, though eventually you will experiment with longer papers. In addition, you'll practice writing single paragraphs of more than one hundred words to gain skill in using the various organization patterns of support development. These paragraphs shouldn't be written as ends in themselves but as parts of clearly organized and well-developed papers. If you study and follow the principles set down in this book, carefully examining the illustrations and exercises, you should be able to conceive and write a clearly organized and well-developed paper of five hundred words. And because the principles of effective exposition apply to any writing situation—to

ORGANIZATION PATTERN	APPLICATION—KINDS OF WRITING
Logical order	Inductive or deductive order, in exposition, explanatory exposition, and argumentation
Cause-to-effect or effect-to-cause order	Logical order, in exposition, argumentation, and explanatory exposition
Familiar-to-unfamiliar order	To explain complex, new ideas, processes, or objects, in explanatory exposition
Climactic order	To present information in order of increasing importance or intensity, in narration and argumentation
Anticlimactic order	To present information in order of decreasing importance or intensity, in argumentation and exposition
Chronological order	To present events as they occur in time or in sequence in a process, as in narration
Spatial order	To present information in a natural, "physical" order, from left to right, bottom to top, near to far, inside to outside, in description
Whole-to-part or part-to-whole order	To present information systematically by moving from individual components or parts to the whole object (or concept), or from one aspect to the entire picture, in description

business letters and reports, scientific papers, essay examinations in school, even to personal letters—these principles will help you in all that you write. Communicate accurately and effectively, and people won't misunderstand you.

exercises

A. Study the cartoon showing the little "flower girl."
1. Decide on an appropriate *caption* (title) for the cartoon, using a word, a short phrase, or a very short statement (not more than ten words).
2. Rewrite your brief caption as a fully developed sentence that clearly expresses *your* understanding of the cartoon.
3. To support your caption and your statement about it, write a series of short, one-sentence observations based on the cartoon's details. For example, one sentence might be: "The children are smiling." Or, "A record player sits on the shelf to the left."
4. Compare your captions and observations with those written by your classmates.

B. Write a paragraph titled "Some Communication Booby Traps," or "Why Misunderstanding Is Easy."

REVIEW TERMS

Here are some of the more important terms used in this chapter. Understanding these will make the next chapter easier.

A. Exposition, expository, communication, communication situation, sender, message, receiver, evidence, facts, validity, proof, unified, coherent, narration, description, argumentation, a process, organization pattern, inductive, deductive, chronological, climactic, spatial

B. Diction, paragraph, sentence, sentence pattern

2

seeing the whole paper

@ lthough everyone has something to say, too many people have trouble saying it. And putting thoughts into written form seems to add to the trouble. Faced with presenting our thoughts to someone else, we hesitate. Where should we begin? How much should we include? Which ideas are most relevant to the point we're trying to communicate? Does the order of presentation matter? Many of these questions and much of the hesitation will disappear if you have a definite plan in mind. The best plan is one that helps you get started and organizes your thoughts so that they move logically and systematically from the opening statements. And this applies to every paper you write: It must have a beginning, a middle, and an ending, each designed with the purpose of the whole paper clearly in mind.

ORGANIZING THE PAPER: BEGINNING, MIDDLE, ENDING

You can't begin to write an effective paper unless you have a fairly specific idea of the product you want to create. What is it? What does it look like? To begin with, your product will be a short expository paper of approximately five hundred words. The basic diagram for deductive organization will help you visualize the whole paper by showing the *logical* relationship of each part of the paper to all the other parts and to the whole. Study it carefully. Each block in the diagram represents one paragraph of the paper, which to begin with will be arbitrarily limited to four very functional paragraphs.

beginning

The first block shows the *introductory paragraph*. The line across the bottom is used to suggest that the final sentence of the paragraph is the *thesis statement* of your paper, the one main point you will develop and support. This end position for the thesis statement is quite arbitrary; you could also place it at the beginning of the introductory paragraph or at the end of the whole paper. Or you may omit the statement entirely; you can imply it in a way that makes readers determine for themselves the logical point the evidence supports. Depending on your choice, the resulting organization pattern will be *deductive* or *inductive*. *Deduct* means "to lead away from," *induct* means "to lead in." If you choose deductive organization, you will "lead the reader away from" a thesis statement presented somewhere in the beginning paragraph and *explained* in the rest of the paper. If you choose inductive organization, you will "lead your reader

14

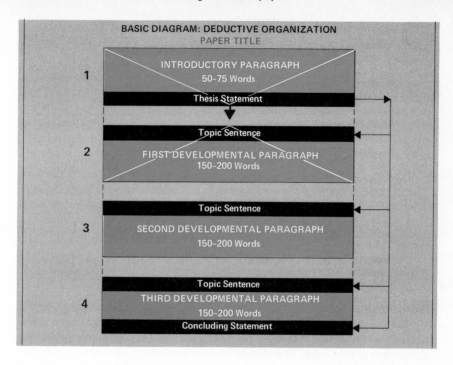

BASIC DIAGRAM: DEDUCTIVE ORGANIZATION
PAPER TITLE

1 INTRODUCTORY PARAGRAPH
50–75 Words
Thesis Statement

2 Topic Sentence
FIRST DEVELOPMENTAL PARAGRAPH
150–200 Words

3 Topic Sentence
SECOND DEVELOPMENTAL PARAGRAPH
150–200 Words

4 Topic Sentence
THIRD DEVELOPMENTAL PARAGRAPH
150–200 Words
Concluding Statement

into" the paper, perhaps by asking a question or suggesting a line of investigation *to be followed* in succeeding paragraphs, with an accurate conclusion at the end of the paper.

deductive organization

The relation of the thesis statement to the rest of the paper, where you place it and how you phrase it, influences the organization pattern of the paper and the way in which you present explanatory, supporting evidence. If, for example, you give the thesis statement in the beginning paragraph of the paper, as shown in the basic diagram, and then follow it with supporting evidence in each paragraph, you will be reasoning logically from a *general* statement (thesis) to *particulars,* details that explain or illustrate it. In effect, you have already examined the particulars and reached a "conclusion," which is then represented by the thesis statement. Each developmental paragraph then repeats the pattern, providing a general statement in the topic sentence, with supporting details in the sentences following it. Consider, for example, the following description, the beginning of a developmental paragraph with a topic sentence as the opener.

Sheila is also a sharp dresser. She pays careful attention to color coordination, usually wearing colors that harmonize or contrast effectively. She never wears badly wrinkled jeans, usually changing them daily for a neat, fresh look. Her skirts and blouses look as if they've just come off the ironing board. . . .

In some ways similar to a deductive method of reasoning, this organization pattern is the one you will use in your first writing attempts.

Placing the thesis statement at the end of the introductory paragraph has several advantages: It lets you use the first sentences of the paragraph to set the general tone of communication between your reader and yourself, to establish a kind of common ground; it prevents you from confusing or misleading your reader with information placed between a first-sentence thesis statement and the first paragraph of the body; and it facilitates coherence because it positions the thesis close to the body of the paper, creating a link with the topic sentence of the first developmental paragraph.

inductive organization

If, however, you omit the thesis statement until you reach the end of the paper, you would be presenting details or *particulars* first, building toward the general *idea* represented by the "thesis" at the end of the paper. This organization pattern, presenting facts or evidence first, reasoning from individual instances to a general or universal statement, is the *inductive* approach. It makes the introductory paragraph almost unnecessary or forces it to serve only the more traditional purposes of getting the reader's interest and establishing suitable tone or common ground to gain reader acceptance.

With this inductive approach the thesis statement functions as a conclusion, an inference based on specific evidence presented. This approach is similar to the scientific method of examining a number of specific examples *to answer a question.* If, for example, you wanted to investigate the safety of children's toys, your question might be, "Are children's toys safe?" Or, "Are children's toys unsafe?" Or, "How safe are children's toys?"

You would actually look at as many toys as possible, examine each for potential safety hazards, describe the hazards discovered in each toy, and then accurately summarize your discoveries in a conclusion. This concluding paragraph would present the *results* of your investigation and then answer the question asked at the beginning of the paper. Your last two sentences in this paragraph could say, "Though many of the toys examined were found to be safe, at least half of them have potential safety hazards that could lead to injury. Clearly, not all toys are safe." This conclusion *accurately* states what the evidence supports. It doesn't say, for example, "Children's toys are unsafe," implying that *all* toys are unsafe. Nor does it say, "Most children's toys are unsafe." It concludes clearly that *of those toys examined*, a *specific number* were found to be unsafe.

With a deductive organization pattern, this conclusion, in a slightly different form, would appear as a *thesis statement* at the end of the introductory paragraph. With the inductive organization pattern, the thesis statement is *replaced* by a question presented at the beginning, investigated throughout the paper, and then *accurately* answered in a concluding paragraph.

Here is a diagram to help you picture inductive organization. To answer this paper's question *reliably*, you would have to study

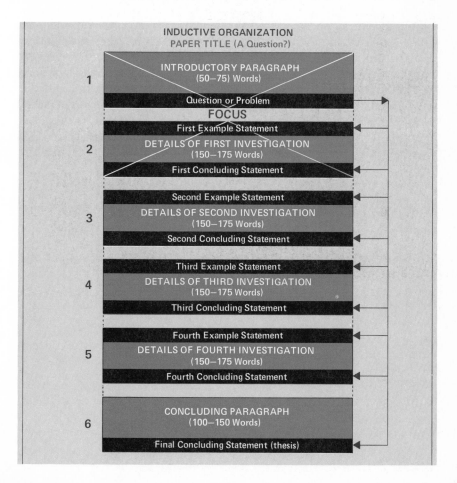

far more examples. The question/problem statement functions as a thesis statement, example statements function as topic sentences in each paragraph, and concluding statements are added throughout. A full concluding paragraph summarizes the findings of the investigation. This is a much longer paper than the basic five-hundred-word theme.

Clearly, how you conceive and plan the beginning of your paper is crucial to successful organization and development of the whole. The beginning paragraph reflects your *approach* to the subject and guides your readers by providing them with adequate clues to follow. For the first papers you write, put the thesis statement at the end of the introductory paragraph; after you have mastered this approach, you should try others.

You will learn more about the introductory paragraph later. In your first papers concentrate on the main functions of this paragraph. It can serve as a kind of "map" or "blueprint" for the rest of the paper by suggesting the order of presentation (the organization pattern) for the ideas in the rest of the paper. This order may be suggested by the thesis sentence itself, or it may be implied elsewhere in the introductory paragraph. Either way the "blueprint" can be a valuable guide to readers as they move through the developmental paragraphs that follow. Your first paragraph, therefore, is very important: It contains a thesis statement, it establishes tone and common ground, and it provides a "blueprint" for the ideas following it.

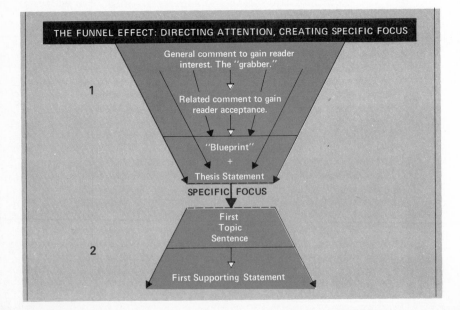

THE FUNNEL EFFECT: DIRECTING ATTENTION, CREATING SPECIFIC FOCUS

1. General comment to gain reader interest. The "grabber."

Related comment to gain reader acceptance.

"Blueprint" + Thesis Statement

SPECIFIC FOCUS

2. First Topic Sentence

First Supporting Statement

The importance and effect of this introductory paragraph can be represented visually, as in the diagram of the "funnel effect." The diagram shows that the introductory paragraph has a *funneling effect.* It directs reader interest and acceptance, its "blueprint" *controls the direction* of the whole paper, and its thesis statement creates a *specific focus* immediately echoed by the first topic sentence in the First Developmental Paragraph.

middle

In the basic diagram, in the block representing the paper's second paragraph and labeled First Developmental Paragraph, the first sentence is the *topic sentence.* Again, this position is arbitrary. The topic sentence can come in the middle or at the end of the paragraph, or it can be implied. But for the first few papers you write, place all topic sentences, specifically stated, at the beginning of developmental paragraphs. The topic sentence is to the paragraph what the thesis statement is to the whole paper; it is the *one point* the paragraph makes. But it is even more closely related to the thesis statement; it is one reason the thesis statement is valid. The remainder of the paragraph, about 150 to 200 words, is evidence presented to establish the soundness of the topic sentence. Once you have written this paragraph, you will have one tightly reasoned unit supporting the main point of the paper. In the first papers you write, you will include two more such units; however, *there's no reason why a paper shouldn't have more than three developmental paragraphs, or only two.*

The topic sentence in the Second Developmental Paragraph is the second "proof" of the thesis, and the material presented in the paragraph supports this second topic sentence. When you have completed this paragraph, your support of the thesis statement becomes much stronger. You have given two reasons to show that the thesis statement is valid, and you have supported each reason with logical *evidence.*

The final paragraph, the Third Developmental Paragraph, should be the strongest in support of the thesis statement. Make the most important reason—the one you think will clinch the point—the topic sentence of this paragraph. Give it strong support in the remainder of the paragraph, and you will leave readers with the understanding you want them to have. Once you have them at this point, hit them with the concluding statement as the last sentence in the whole paper.

ending

In the basic diagram, your paper's last sentence is also the last sentence of the Third Developmental Paragraph. However, depending on your choice of organization pattern and the length and complexity of your paper, this sentence may have to be expanded into a complete concluding paragraph, separated from the Third Developmental Paragraph.

As the diagram suggests, in your first papers the *concluding statement* will simply restate the thesis statement so that you finish by reminding the reader that this is the point you have made in the paper. Because it is better not to make the point in the exact words used at the beginning of the paper, change the wording enough so that the concluding statement will serve as an "echo" and have a greater effect on readers as it concludes your strongest paragraph.

Whether you are writing a simple concluding statement or a more complete concluding paragraph, don't tell the reader you are ending your paper. Such statements as "In conclusion it can be seen that . . ." or "To sum up . . ." are trite and unnecessary. Although a formal concluding paragraph is usually unnecessary, summing up is often desirable in a much longer paper. Also, certain kinds of papers may require recommendations or questions for further consideration. But in a five-hundred-word paper, the concluding statement does the necessary summing up, sparing you and your readers the tediousness of a bloated concluding paragraph that often adds nothing to the paper.

A kind of picture-outline, the basic diagram represents only *one* convenient pattern for writing a five-hundred-word paper. But it can serve as your formula, or recipe. *If your subject requires variation, then alter the formula; add or delete a paragraph.* You will know how because you will have learned the basic pattern and will be able to see the whole paper. But until you do learn the basic pattern, follow the diagram we have just examined.

The writer of the paper "Unleashed Danger" followed the basic diagram exactly, without dullness and without letting the "formula" shout too loudly at readers. To help you follow the pattern, the thesis statement, topic sentences, and concluding statement are in color.

UNLEASHED DANGER

If you are a dog lover don't read this. Tend to your dogs instead: Train them, restrain them, kennel them. But don't let them run loose near my house—unless you want a bruised and battered dog, with fear in his heart and a permanent whimper in his voice. Not that I dislike dogs. Not at all. I have been known to affectionately pet puppies of all kinds. I bow to no man in my respect for all ages, sizes, and breeds of well-disciplined dogs but I hate the havoc that unleashed dogs cause. Their habit of wet—marking their romping trails is upsetting, and the surprises they leave for bare feet on a lawn are disgusting. Far worse, however, dogs on the loose terrorize cyclists and pedestrians, create traffic hazards, and damage gardens. Clearly, their unleashed presence on streets and sidewalks is a dangerous nuisance.

Although barking dogs may not bite, they can scare cyclists and pedestrians half to death. I don't know which is worse, the little yappers or the big barkers. If you're riding a bicycle the yappers are mostly a nuisance, though they are threatening enough to force you to zig—zag dangerously on the street. It is a brave cyclist who can ignore the barker whose flashing teeth are nipping at the handle bars. I have seen school children panic on their bicycles when a barker leaps out at them, forcing them to turn wildly to avoid being bitten and sometimes even causing a youngster to fall onto the road. Or suppose you are walking at night and one of the yappers rushes out, snapping and snarling only inches away from your heels. I tend to freeze in my steps, cuss quite a bit, and wish I had a big stick. Or a big gun. Or a middle—sized tiger.

Both yappers and barkers are traffic hazards. Motorists and cyclists and pedestrians, conditioned by dog—lovers to think of these brutes as people, automatically react to protect them. Just watch a jaywalking dog saunter across a busy highway in some suburban town. Cars swerve, brakes screech, accidents occur. The unsuspecting driver thinks the dog is patiently waiting for a break in the traffic, or for a light to turn green, perhaps. Then without warning man's best friend heads across. The sickening thud of flesh against metal is a sound that will haunt any driver for weeks——if he escapes traffic in the adjoining lane as he tries unthinkingly to avoid the dog. Equally hazardous are those dogs that dart onto the road they think they own, barking at everything rolling by. Once a little yapper so worried me that I ran my car into an innocent fire hydrant. Throw together one dog, a few cyclists, and several cars and the results can be tragic. Or watch a young pedestrian trying to coax his reluctant mutt across a car-filled street. Frightening. And dangerous.

What makes me blow up, however, is that unleashed dogs damage gardens. If you are a gardener then you probably react as I do after some night—marauding barker with size thirteen feet has stomped through your flower bed or tomato patch. The first time I saw a three—inch—deep depression in the soft soil I reached for my shotgun, certain some wild beast had chosen my yard for a den. Just as irritating is the systematic territory marker who has chosen a corner of the front hedge and the base of the yard lamp as routine targets——with Master only feet away, half—sharply calling, "No, no Spot!" Spot isn't listening. But what really makes me irate is when I'm crossing the lawn barefooted on a Sunday morning to get the newspaper and I step into some marker's calling card. I don't think I'd actually shoot the scoundrel if I caught him, but I might make him walk barefoot on my lawn for a few days. Yappers, barkers, markers are fine as puppies, or firmly on a leash, or in a kennel; on the loose, however, they're definitely a menace.

Note that this paper makes just one main point, dogs on the loose are a dangerous nuisance, stated at the end of the introductory paragraph and preceded by a kind of "blueprint" of supporting reasons. Although these reasons answer the implied question *why* and focus attention through the use of *because,* the best thesis sentences don't actually use the words "why" or "because." Then, to convince the reader of the validity of the main point, the middle part of the paper explains the reasons in the order mentioned in the introduction, one in each of the three developmental paragraphs. The topic sentence of each paragraph restates a reason.

The first topic sentence, italicized in the second paragraph, makes the point that dogs on the loose are a dangerous nuisance because they can scare cyclists and pedestrians half to death. The remainder of the paragraph establishes this topic sentence as valid by suggesting some dangerous consequences of being scared. It mentions that cyclists are forced to zigzag on the road, that school children panic and turn wildly, and that a person walking at night will freeze in his steps.

The second topic sentence, italicized in the third paragraph, directly states that barking dogs on the loose are traffic hazards. To support this statement the writer says that people automatically protect dogs by swerving to miss them, which can be dangerous; to avoid dogs drivers may run into things; and on busy streets youngsters trying to coax their dogs across become a frightening and dangerous hazard.

The third topic sentence, italicized at the beginning of the fourth paragraph, presents the writer's strongest feelings—that dogs damage gardens, destroying flowers and vegetables by making deep depressions in the soil, marring hedges and yard objects by spotting them, and messing on lawns. This paragraph is the most personal and probably the most emotional one in the theme, suggesting that the writer's chief gripe is personal. The concluding statement, italicized at the end of the fourth paragraph, restates the thesis statement and echoes the paper's title.

Although this paper could be strengthened in many ways, the writer has made his point and supported it with evidence based on his own experience and observation. One criticism that could be made of this paper is that it overuses "I" in attempting to sound personal and to keep the reader interested. But even very serious papers sometimes use "I," as you can see immediately if you check the introductory paragraphs on pages 105, 107 and 281–82. However, your instructor may ask you to avoid using "I" in your first papers (it's not easy to do well). This doesn't mean you have to be impersonal and dull, as the freshman introductory paragraph on page 279 shows.

A more straightforward approach that boldly asserts the subject (without using "I") can be seen in the more formal introductory paragraphs on pages 106 and 283. In the exercises at the end of this chapter there are additional examples of papers that present their subject directly without using "I."

The use of the first person in this paper is only one of a number of devices used to personalize it and to project a *feeling* of informality and humor. For example, who is addressed in the first sentence? Is this *audience* consistently addressed throughout the paper? What would happen to the effect if all the *contractions* were removed? Did you notice that the paper contains a number of purposeful sentence

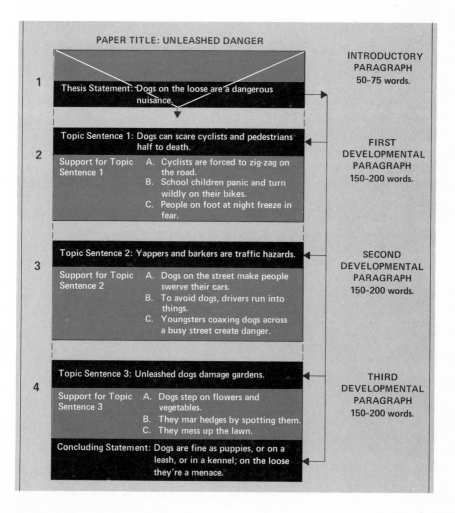

PAPER TITLE: UNLEASHED DANGER

1   Thesis Statement: Dogs on the loose are a dangerous nuisance.

INTRODUCTORY PARAGRAPH
50–75 words.

2   Topic Sentence 1: Dogs can scare cyclists and pedestrians half to death.

Support for Topic Sentence 1
A. Cyclists are forced to zig-zag on the road.
B. School children panic and turn wildly on their bikes.
C. People on foot at night freeze in fear.

FIRST DEVELOPMENTAL PARAGRAPH
150–200 words.

3   Topic Sentence 2: Yappers and barkers are traffic hazards.

Support for Topic Sentence 2
A. Dogs on the street make people swerve their cars.
B. To avoid dogs, drivers run into things.
C. Youngsters coaxing dogs across a busy street create danger.

SECOND DEVELOPMENTAL PARAGRAPH
150–200 words.

4   Topic Sentence 3: Unleashed dogs damage gardens.

Support for Topic Sentence 3
A. Dogs step on flowers and vegetables.
B. They mar hedges by spotting them.
C. They mess up the lawn.

THIRD DEVELOPMENTAL PARAGRAPH
150–200 words.

Concluding Statement: Dogs are fine as puppies, or on a leash, or in a kennel; on the loose they're a menace.

fragments? What effect do they have? Also, the writer uses several perfectly *balanced* sentences without conjunctions: "Train them, restrain them, kennel them" is a good example. How do these sentences affect you? And notice the effect of certain carefully chosen *descriptive words*: "pet puppies," "romping trails," "yappers," "big barkers," "nipping at the handle bars," "man's best friend," "mutt," "size thirteen feet," "half-sharply," and "Spot." Why do you suppose the writer chose to call the marker a "scoundrel"?

All these devices contribute to the *personal, informal, humorous tone* of the paper. As suggested on pages 25, 101, and 156, and explained on pages 277–78, tone is an important quality used by a writer to gain *reader interest* and *acceptance* and to project the *writer's voice.* Even solid supporting statements logically presented may fail to get complete *understanding* and *agreement* from the reader if the tone is unsuitable. You will find a preliminary exercise on changing the "writer's voice" (tone) on page 108.

The organization of papers such as "Unleashed Danger" can be shown in another type of diagram, one that inserts the supporting points for each topic sentence. The result is a picture-outline that clearly shows the paper's main points and their logical relation to each other and to the support given for each point. With this framework of thesis statement, three reasons to uphold the thesis statement, support for the reasons, and a concluding statement, you could have written the five-hundred-word paper on the nuisances of dogs on the loose. A diagram such as the one on page 23 can be used to test the validity of either the preliminary outline or the first draft of other, similar papers.

Now study the paper below and decide whether it is better than the one about dogs, using, if you wish, the check sheet given on page 158.

THE PRACTICAL COLLEGE MARRIAGE

Two really can live as cheaply as one, but as any struggling coed and her haunted husband can testify, those two had better prepare for a painful existence, but practical. The money that the folks were glad to send their young one must now serve two. The lessons this pair learns are the most practical in the world, though. They know before the honeymoon is over that, although they'll cry a lot, they'll learn to slice their output and savor their income. They learn to be practical about entertainment, about the care and mending of garments, and about the nourishing qualities of peanut butter.

Entertainment is not what it used to be. In the old days, Mary took for granted two or three movies a week and dancing at least on Saturday night. Mom and Dad didn't mind paying that little bit, as long as their college daughter kept up her grades. Now in their room—with—kitchen—privileges apartment Mary and Jim get along fine––but movies are out, and they wouldn't dream of trying to squeeze a dancing cover charge out of what little Dad sends and they can earn. For entertainment, Jim can help with the dishes, and they can walk together, hand in hand, to the library for a blissful evening of research. It's a terribly practical pursuit, actually.

The clothing situation gets serious. Neither Mary nor her Jim would dare gain weight, even if their home—cooked meals were that tempting. They dressed well in their single days, and they still do, but alas, in the very same garments that looked so much better last semester. Shoes get resoled now, instead of replaced, and the shine on Jim's "good" suit is more noticeable. It isn't as though he had to keep up with his fraternity brothers any longer. Camaraderie with that carefree group is nice to remember, but meeting with the boys is no longer practical. Mary watches fashions, but she does not buy the fads. She found out in a hurry that it is not the practical way to dress.

Their menu does not vary much, and there is no longer the balanced touch of the dormitory dietician. They watch out for yellow and green vegetables, of course, and a potato a day with some kind of protein. But the old zip is gone, and with it went between—class cokes and Sunday at the Garden Steakhouse with the rest of the English majors. They are grateful, naturally, to the famous scientist who developed peanut butter. Even if it does stick to the palate and begin to grow old too soon, Mary and Jim buy more peanut butter, because it's very practical. But when it's all over and the children are grown, Jim and Mary will look back on these days as some of the best in their lives, because look at the great lessons they learned.

Compare this paper with the basic diagram for the five-hundred-word paper, and you will see that this paper follows the diagram exactly but is not a slavish, mechanical, line-by-line copy of it. *Nor should it be. Translating the basic diagram into a paper truly your own requires decisions in tone, in diction, in sentence structure, in selection and organization of ideas.* Note how this writer establishes a friendly, informal tone in the first few sentences by choosing words to suggest a friendly attitude: *really, coed, haunted, folks,* and *they'll* are good examples. This writer, however decides not to use "I," creating a somewhat less personal tone than that created by the writer of the paper on dogs. You don't have to write a stiff, formal paper just because you are following a preplanned picture-outline. A little creative thinking will help you write a fresh, personal paper. Eventually you'll want to experiment with patterns of organization quite unlike the basic diagram you are studying here and with papers considerably longer than five hundred words. You may want to try inductive organization, and you will want to practice expanding your developmental paragraphs by fleshing out your supporting reasons, perhaps as E. B. White has done in the paragraph given on page 148.

exercises

I. Analyze the following papers for organization. Answer the questions at the end of each paper to aid your analysis.

A. MISPLACED GOALS IN EDUCATION STIFLE THE INQUIRING MIND

1. Lack of encouragement of creativity in the present school system discourages a real search for knowledge. Importance continually placed on following a certain form has given students a misplaced set of values.

2. Even though following directions is important, too often students are graded solely on how well they do this. In spite of their original thoughts, their grades may be low because they left too small a margin, wrote on the bottom line, or numbered the pages in the wrong corner. Following a rigid form of roman numerals, students lose sight of the content of the material. If they have researched the subject, they might lose all credit because they have not tagged their sources properly. Professors should emphasize the thought shown in students' work rather than rigid adherence to a given form.

3. Thinking things through for themselves, students might come up with ideas other than their professor's. Grade school and high school have taught them that this is not advisable. Students who can most nearly duplicate the teacher's instruction are regarded most highly. If the teacher will "lay it on the line," then it can be easily duplicated. Such narrow goals restrict students, making them conform to the ideas already set out for them. Stepping outside the expected way of working a problem, finding a different meaning to a passage in literature, or bringing some original idea to class is too often penalized.

4. Memorization of details clutters the mind with facts that are never assimilated. World geography consists of a detailed compilation of isolated facts on individual countries. "How many square miles is Uruguay?" and "What is its population?" are asked rather than "How has its location in South America affected its economic growth?" The value of associating the past with the future is lost in history classes where twenty dates are given—students are asked to write who was president and vice-president.

5. With elementary and secondary education goals set on teaching students to follow strict forms or to reproduce an instructor's or text's words and memorize details without connecting them, it is easily understandable that students today apparently lack an inquiring mind. Any deviation from the usual they wish to do must be done outside their classwork.

6. To encourage original thought educational goals must be realigned. Importance must be placed on the entire content of the material and its broad implications. Reslanting history to increase the value, using geography in studies of modern economics and politics, looking into physics proofs rather than just formulas will help stimulate thought. A broadening of teachers' views will broaden the scope and responsibility of students. More scholastic freedom and more creative goals will reawaken the inquiring mind.

questions for analysis of paper A

This exercise answers its own questions so that you can understand what you are expected to do in analyzing the organization of the paragraphs.

1. What is the thesis statement of Paper *A?*

    Answer: The thesis statement is the first sentence: *Lack of encouragement of creativity in the present school system discourages a real search for knowledge.*

2. How does the second paragraph support this thesis statement?

    Answer: It gives and supports one reason for the validity of the thesis statement. It makes the point that students are frequently graded on how well they follow form rather than on how deeply they think.

3. What is the function of the second sentence in the introductory paragraph?

    Answer: This sentence does not belong in the introductory paragraph. It should be the first sentence of the second paragraph, because it is really the topic sentence of that paragraph. All the second paragraph is a discussion of the subject given in the second sentence of the introductory paragraph. Nowhere else in the paper is *following a certain form* discussed. The introductory paragraph should be expanded to about fifty to seventy-five words, with the thesis statement at the end. Rarely can a single sentence function effectively as a whole paragraph.

4. How does the third paragraph support the thesis statement?

    Answer: It gives and supports a second reason for the validity of the thesis statement. It makes the point that too frequently students are rewarded for simply parroting the teacher's ideas and are penalized if they put forward the result of their own thinking.

5. Which sentence is the topic sentence of the third paragraph?

    Answer: The last sentence in the paragraph is the topic sentence. It probably would be better placed as the first sentence.

6. a. Which sentence is the topic sentence of the fourth paragraph?

    b. What is the function of this paragraph in the paper?

    Answer: a. The first sentence in the fourth paragraph is the topic sentence.

    b. The fourth paragraph gives and supports a third reason for the validity of the thesis statement. It deplores the emphasis on insignificant details.

7. What is the function of the fifth paragraph?

    Answer: The fifth paragraph sums up the points that have been made in support of the thesis statement. The paper would be more effectively organized if most of the material in the fifth paragraph were part of the revised introductory paragraph and if a concluding statement were placed at the end of the fourth paragraph. (This weakness in organization, especially demonstrated by the inadequacy of the introductory paragraph, is probably caused by the writer's failure to think through his subject before starting to write. He probably devised his support for the thesis statement as he wrote from paragraph to paragraph. Then when he got to the end he could see what his support was and summed it up there. It takes a skillful student to succeed at the organize-as-you-write plan. This student was not quite skillful enough.)

8. Does the sixth paragraph support the thesis statement? Does it belong in the paper? Why or why not?

Answer: The sixth paragraph does not support the thesis statement because it does not give and support a reason for the validity of the thesis. In fact, this paragraph does not belong in the paper because it introduces a second subject by attempting to explain what should be done about the situation. The subject of this paragraph could be explored and supported in another paper, not here.

9. Where should this paper end?

Answer: The paper should end with the fourth paragraph.

B. EDUCATORS THAT DISCOURAGE THINKING

1. There is no doubt that today's public school students are lacking in creative thinking. They find it far less trouble to develop a sort of mnemonic memorizing mind that follows but never leads. Therefore, most students prefer to memorize and leave tiresome thinking for later.

2. Classroom discussion is different. There students are often willing to shine forth orally, but never, never in writing. They would rather be asked to respond with a *T* for True and *F* for False on a simple and clearcut objective exam than be asked to think an issue through and discuss it in writing.

3. Students are inclined to drag their feet when it comes to showing their teacher, via clear and thorough essay-type discussions, that they have a full understanding of course content. But this is hardly the fault of the student, at least not in the high school that I attended. In fact, from the elementary level up to Grade 12, we were trained to memorize, and we soon learned that perfecting the practice of spouting out the outlined truths, with no time out for understanding and tying together of isolated facts, was the way to the best grades. We worked out the formula for success and we learned to like it, in the way any child learns to adapt to the security of a system.

4. If the nation is to continue to survive and even to progress, then such trends as this must be halted. Such lazy testing is developed for lazy grading, and the obvious answer is that teachers must begin to care enough to improve their methods. Teachers must be taught before they can teach; otherwise, the inquiring minds of our potential leaders will never be freed from the regimented, "fill-in-the-blank" type of nonthink-

ing. It could even be that there is more truth in the ancient admonition: If you can't do it, teach it; if you can't teach it, teach others to teach it.

questions for analysis of paper B

1. The thesis statement of this paper is the last sentence of the first paragraph: *Most students prefer to . . . leave tiresome thinking for later.* The writer makes only one point in the remainder of the paper to support this thesis. What is it?

2. The second paragraph consists of only two sentences and does not give or support an idea. Could these two sentences be integrated into any other paragraph in the paper? If so, which one? If not, why not?

3. The third paragraph is the only one that can be called a developmental paragraph. What topic sentence does it develop?

4. What is the purpose of the fourth paragraph? Does it contain material that might be used in the third paragraph? Is there another subject here that might be used as a topic sentence in support of the thesis statement? What is it?

5. Since the paper gives only one reason for the validity of the thesis statement, make up two more reasons that might be supported in developmental paragraphs. (The writer of this paper can handle the language fairly well. From all indications, however, he wrote this paper without much planning. The result is that the paper does not fully support its thesis, some ideas and paragraphs are left undeveloped, and the whole ends with a vague *such trends as this must be halted.*)

C. WHY STUDENTS NO LONGER INQUIRE

1. Today's high school students are not interested in "why." They prefer to be led to simple answers already set down for them, as they have always been led. They do not seek out solutions to problems of economics or geography or literature. In fact, one of the standard slogans at testing time at my high school was always: "We don't know the questions, just the answers." All we knew was what our teachers told us: just the facts. These we memorized, because memorizing is all that was ever required of us.

2. It seems to be a workbook world, and such a teaching method teaches nobody anything. In chemistry labs across the country, students are handed tubes and burners and a problem to "solve." But they are shackled by the workbook at their elbows. Mix so-and-so much of A with this-and-that amounts of B. You get *C.* Here's what happened, and why. Student react with yawns. The experiment got them nowhere. They discovered nothing, and arrived at no conclusion but that one concluded for them.

3. When these same students are given something tangible to work toward, they show their mettle. What did the word *slave* mean to Ancient Sparta? What was the real relationship between Philip and Alexander, and how do you know? Where's the proof of romanticism in Wordsworth's

ode? How can that teacher call a triangle *beautiful?* Such questions stir students to think and to research. They are challenged. They want to know, and they will find out.

4. When students are introduced to an unanswered problem, they cannot help working up an interest in finding an answer. They want to assume responsibility. Even if they arrive at only a half-right conclusion, at least they have had the freedom of investigating. They might, in their struggles, hit upon an original idea. How nice to have understood the question, to have cared enough to try for an answer, to have contributed to the world's knowledge.

questions for analysis of paper C

1. What is the thesis statement of Paper *C?*

2. What is the purpose of the rest of the introductory paragraph? Does this paragraph indicate any reason for the validity of the thesis statement? If so, are these reasons developed and supported in the remainder of the paper?

3. The first sentence of the second paragraph is the topic sentence. What did the writer do in the remainder of the paragraph to establish this point as a valid one? Has the writer offered enough evidence to establish the point? What might be done to make the topic sentence valid?

4. Does the third paragraph support the topic sentence? Look at it closely. Does it give and support a second reason for the validity of the thesis statement? If so, is the evidence offered in support of the topic sentence enough to establish it as valid? If not, what is the purpose of the third paragraph?

5. In what way is the fourth paragraph related to the thesis statement? What is its purpose in the paper?

D. THE CASE AGAINST HIGH SCHOOL FOOTBALL

1. High school football is an outrageous waste. The game is too expensive: in dollars and cents, in hours and minutes, in morale, and in physical well-being. When gym equipment and coaching salaries grow more important than academic progress and class work waits upon athletes, when the student's sense of academic and competitive values is distorted, and fine young bodies are deliberately exposed to physical violence, then football does indeed cost too much.

2. Seldom does the total gate receipt for the season, even with the added dimes and quarters from concession stands, smooth out the balance. School administrators and their staff pay top prices for dummies, pads, cleated shoes, and face guards; their boys need and deserve the best possible protection out there on the field of danger. Turfs, sturdy bleachers, and weather-conditioned gymnasiums are theirs to maintain (with a giant slice of the school board's carefully balanced budget). And the hiring of the go-gettingest coach available is one of the greatest expenses the school faces. But all that is the simple, red-and-black side of the ledger.

3. Though not quite so obvious to the outsider as dollar cost, the existing situation makes it almost shameful for students to neglect their team in favor of class work. When there are posters to put out, tickets to sell, or athletic banquets to be arranged, students are often expected to make the time, even during a class period, if the heat is on, to back the team. They can hardly be expected to pay more attention to their Biology III notebooks than they pay to the Homecoming Game; why, it's practically a breach of faith! So they set aside the biology assignment and the Latin translation, and the three chapters in the Hardy novel due tomorrow, so they won't be late for the pep rally. After all, Miss Hopkins and those other teachers must realize (they've heard it all week over the intercom) that Coach Jamison and his boys need all the spirit that can be whipped up if they're to ring up another victory for Consolidated High.

4. However, the song that resounds across the campus for the week is not an echo of the old softie that insists "It is not that we win or lose, but how we play the game!" None of that mush for the up-to-date pigskin elevens. It's no more who we play, but who we beat. The coach shouts out his determined promises, then the bugles blare for the captain Himself, the biggest imaginable Man on Campus. So long to the fellow with the *A* average and to all the other wearers of the letter sweater, the mark of the scholar. And often the school's reputation is built on its team's winning streak, not on the number of serious students who go on to excel in their college studies. As a result, the football-centered school distorts the value of competition, substituting "beat the opposition" for "compete honorably." Still, all this is to say nothing of the deliberate exposure to physical dangers, even death, to which public schools subject their students in the glorious name of football. We'd rather not dwell on the number of boys who either don't make it at all or who are carried out between quarters to a life of lameness, of back or brain. Besides those caught in the crossfire on the gridiron, too, are those who wreck (or die) in automobile or school bus collisions en route to the Big Game.

5. There's no winner in high school football. When the count is taken of money, time, energy, and suffering spent on "the game," both teams have lost, no matter how many times the boys first downed, touched down, touched back, or kicked goal. The real score (obscured by the glaring numbers on the great electric scoreboard) reads NOTHING to NOTHING.

questions for analysis of paper D

1. Outline Paper *D* so that it fits the basic diagram for a five-hundred-word paper. Arrange and label your outline as follows:

   Thesis Statement: . . . .

      Topic Sentence 1: . . . .

         Supporting Statement A: . . . .

         Supporting Statement B: . . . .

         Supporting Statement C: . . . .

       . . . .

Topic Sentence 2: . . . .
    Supporting Statement A: . . . .
    Supporting Statement B: . . . .
    Supporting Statement C: . . . .
Topic Sentence 3: . . . .
. . . .

2. Does the introductory paragraph contain a "blueprint"? List these anticipatory ideas in the order in which they appear in the paragraph. Does this paragraph follow the diagram illustrating the "funnel effect" (see page 18)? Is the second paragraph clearly tied to the introductory one?

3. Examine paragraph four for unity. Does every sentence comment on the distortion of competitive values? Do you think this topic is sufficiently developed? Suggest several possible solutions to the problem.

4. What is the purpose of paragraph five? What does it replace in the basic diagram? Does it succeed? Why?

E. LAW AND ORDER

1. Often we are subjected to a cry for "law and order." U.S. ̣ ̣dents have made that one of the major issues in their campaigns for the White House. In their speeches, governors and mayors and congressmen also call for "law and order." Newspaper editorials remind us that we are becoming a lawless nation. Certainly, we know that our country is undergoing radical changes. New philosophies are being presented; fresh ideas claim our attention. And if we are to continue as a representative democracy, we must maintain an orderly system for granting change.

2. No honest American is opposed to "law and order." We all understand that the democratic processes require calm evaluation of new proposals. I would, for example, be the last person to advocate civil disobedience as a laudable method of gaining just ends. Our nation, although it grew out of an act of civil disobedience, has established orderly channels that effectively preclude the need for lawlessness.

3. But many Americans are worried that our country can devolve into anarchy. They are worried about militant minorities. They are bothered by student unrest. They fear corruption in government. They feel that certain Supreme Court rulings have unfairly tied the hands of the police in their attempts to protect society from organized crime. And those Americans, too, are sincere.

4. Yet I feel the issue of "law and order" is spurious. Those who have adopted this cry are motivated by fear and influenced by propaganda. In effect, I am arguing that sincere people are worried, and politicians are trading upon that fear.

5. There are those who say that crime in America has increased in direct proportion to the increase in the budget of the FBI. This view, although an exaggeration, does contain an element of truth. For today we have much better methods of reporting crimes. Furthermore, some actions now are considered crimes that in recent years were dismissed as

"youthful folly." Finally, we know that an increasing urbanization *must* result in increasing crime.

6. I believe, however, that the new emphasis on "law and order" masks the innate prejudice of white Americans against increasing cries for justice by oppressed minority groups: blacks, Indians, Chicanos, the poor, college students. In other words, when some Southern politicians scream for "law and order" what they really mean is "keep the niggers down." When some traditional Republicans say "law and order" what they really mean is "preserve the conservative establishment."

7. Propaganda helps produce the image of lawlessness. Lurid stories about murder and rape sell newspapers and keep viewers watching television. And the mass media may not really understand how they contribute toward increasing the fears of the "average American." Reporters insist on reporting the news, whether it is an armed robbery or a student demonstration or a riot in a ghetto. What they sometimes overlook are the causes behind the events they are reporting.

8. Two things are obvious: America must maintain its established institutions of democracy and freedom. But America must also maintain its traditional open-mindedness. We must not be misled by those who would use our concern to further their own ends.

9. It is probably true that disorders have increased in America. As more people become educated, they recognize that America still has plenty of unsolved problems. Sociologists have theorized that a new generation, faced with the prospect of instant atomic-missile destruction, believe that our nation can no longer afford leisurely evolution. "Freedom Now" is their rallying cry.

10. Let us, then, beware those who would use "Freedom Now" as an excuse for destruction. But let us also beware those who would use "law and order" as a barrier to legitimate cries for help.

questions for analysis of paper E

Paper *E* has been included because it departs in many ways from the basic diagram you have been studying. The purpose of this exercise is to help you discover some of these differences and to compare them with the pattern you already know.

1. a. What is the chief difference between the title of this paper and the titles of the other papers used as illustrations in this chapter?
   b. Without omitting the words *law* and *order,* can you phrase a better title? Why do you consider yours better?
2. a. What is the purpose of the fourth paragraph of this paper?
   b. Could the basic idea of this paragraph be stated earlier in the paper without a loss of effect? What *is* this effect?
   c. What is the relation of this paragraph to those preceding and to those following it? To the title?
3. a. What purposes do the first three paragraphs serve? To what part of the basic diagram you have been studying do they compare? Could they be combined into one paragraph? What effect would this have?

    b. Why has this student writer chosen to devote so much space to the first three paragraphs? Does this decision strengthen or weaken the paper?

    c. Which general references in these paragraphs could be made more specific? Explain how.

4. Is this paper *expository* or *argumentative*? Or both? Why?

5. a. What ties together paragraphs four, eight, and ten?

    b. Would it be possible to combine eight and ten? Try writing one version.

6. a. Which of the paragraphs would you call developmental? Why?

    b. What kind of support and evidence does the writer present? Explain.

    c. Do you consider this paper convincing? Why?

    d. In what ways does the writer try to make this paper convincing? Does the writer seem to have a specific audience in mind? How would you characterize the general feeling (tone) of the paper: Formal? Informal? Serious? Quiet? Judicious? Argumentative? What is the basis for your opinion?

7. Try to draw a diagram to represent the relation of this paper's parts to one another. Could this diagram be made to fit the four-paragraph diagram you've been studying? Do you think a closer adherence to the basic pattern would improve the paper? Explain why.

II. To discover how well you manage a five-hundred-word paper, write one to fit the basic pattern studied in this chapter. Choose as the starting point for your thinking one of the following:

A. Communication booby traps for senders.

B. Communication booby traps for receivers.

C. When I'm with a group of students, I'm not myself.

D. The pot problem.

E. Writing essay exams makes me panic.

F. Essay exams handicap me.

G. The dating game is a waste of time.

H. I couldn't get along without _____.

I. Women don't need equal rights with men.

J. Today's young people have too much (not enough) responsibility.

K. Grades are an obstacle to real learning.

L. Premarital sex is (is not) desirable.

III. Practice discovering reasons to support any opinion you adopt. Here are some suggestions.

A. If you could be any animal you wanted to be, which would you choose? Make a list of supporting reasons.

B. If you could be any person (real or imaginary) you wanted to be, whom would you choose? Supply reasons.

C. Suppose you have a chance to write to your school principal (or president) and ask to change something about your school that really bothers you, what would it be? Make a list of one-sentence statements explaining *why* you want this change.

D. Choose something (or someone) in your class to describe, and then describe it in a systematic way using specific details. Call it "*X*" and see if you classmates can recognize what you've described.

E. Make a list of one-sentence statements to support the following statement: "Teen-age courting is like a roller coaster."

REVIEW TERMS

Understanding the meaning of the following terms will help you master the material in this chapter.

A. Expository, logical, beginning, middle, ending, paragraph, introductory paragraph, developmental paragraph, thesis statement, topic sentence, deductive, inductive, organization pattern, tone, common ground, conclusion, concluding statement, concluding paragraph, evidence, grabber, blueprint, reader acceptance, focus, direction, validity, writer's voice

B. Sentence, contraction, balanced sentence, fragment, grammatical fragment, rhetorical fragment, descriptive, diction, informal, conjunction

getting started:
discovery,
specific focus,
thesis

Writing is a creative act. It is an active *process* through which you put together feelings, attitudes, thoughts, and words in a way that makes it impossible for someone to misunderstand you. It's a complex process, however, and I like to think of it as probably man's greatest invention. Each time you communicate, you "invent" a message that projects part of your experience, part of your *self.* You must *choose* the part you want to communicate. But what part? How do you choose? In a sense, then, writing is a problem-solving process tied to your relation to the people and the world around you. Long before you actually set down words on paper, you are automatically involved in trying to figure out what to say and how to say it. You're involved in a creative act of *discovery.* Let's call it the "prewriting process."

DISCOVERY: THE PREWRITING PROCESS

The success of your papers depends in great part on how actively and fully you exercise the prewriting process. As you've already seen, part of your prewriting concentrates on solving problems in organization. But the most important part of prewriting is the discovery of thoughts, of feelings, of the means of communicating real messages to real people. For good writers, the process of writing is always an act of discovery. As they put down words—enjoying the game of selecting, adding, rejecting—they *discover* words that fit exactly the thoughts and feelings they are trying to communicate in a specific situation.

If you have trouble getting started, it may be because you aren't letting this discovery process work for you. Or you may not be allowing enough time to enjoy and play with your feelings and thoughts and the words that fit them. Last-minute, one-shot writing lacks this sense of play and discovery; it carries with it, instead, a feeling of fumbling, of false starts hastily covered up with uncomfortable words, of fuzzy thought in worn-out language. If you are a fumbler or a last-minute writer, learn to discover your exact thoughts and feelings before you try to set them down—that's what getting started is all about. Then continue this discovery process as you plan, outline, and write the paper.

As you write, new ideas will come to you. Like the more experienced writer, you should discover that the writing process itself generates new ideas, adding to those you've already decided on. Don't hesitate to include these new thoughts, for they are an important part of the creative writing process. Equally important, however, is an additional discovery you should make—that your in-class papers must somehow become those "real messages" and that you, your classmates, and your teacher are the "real people" involved. Writing for specific readers in real situations is the essential requirement of any writing process.

Some of the exercises you'll be asked to do later in this book will make you more aware of this person-to-person relationship in writing and will help you overcome the artificiality often found in classroom themes. For example, you will be asked to write to a specific audience—a close friend, your parents, your teacher in an informal mood, someone younger than you, an elderly retired person, someone in Congress. And you will also be asked to play a role, writing as if you were someone other than yourself—a local city official, a sports writer, a television newscaster, your mother, your teacher, your best friend. As a result, you should discover new things to say as well as new ways of saying the things you already know. You should discover that language and thoughts and people are always part of the writing equation.

How much time you take to think, plan, and write will depend on the difficulty of the subject, your knowledge of the subject, and your experience with it. Good writers always take the prewriting time they need—hours, days, perhaps weeks—before choosing a specific idea and the writing strategy to go with it. You may not have this much time, but you probably have more discovery time available than you are aware of—while eating, showering, shaving, combing your hair, brushing your teeth, or walking to class. And especially while you're in the library. You must set aside some thinking or reading time specifically for this discovery process, jotting down ideas that occur to you.

To get you started quickly and efficiently, this chapter will ask you to think about and to practice the following discovery processes:

1. Discovering a *single, limited subject*
2. Discovering the *specific point* you're going to establish *about* this limited subject
3. Discovering how to write a *complete thesis statement*
4. Discovering *support* for the thesis statement
5. Discovering how to write a complete *purpose statement*

DISCOVERY: CHOOSING, LIMITING, FOCUSING

At the beginning of a writing course, your instructor may assign a specific subject for a five-hundred-word paper and clearly define the paper's purpose. But he may simply give you a general subject or send you to the library to find your own. To cut down on false starts and unnecessary fumbling, you'll need to practice discovering single, limited subjects you can discuss adequately in five hundred words.

1. discover a single, limited subject

You already have many subjects you can write about. Believe this, for it will greatly improve your self-confidence. For example, you've had unique experiences to write about and use as evidence in support of your assertions. You have observed people, places, and things; you have formed opinions and impressions; you know smells and sounds and colors and textures. You have been in school for a dozen years, storing information. You have read billboards, newspapers, and books; you know television and the movies. Most important, you have formed some definite and strongly held opinions you can support in writing. Of course, you may find (as we all do) that you have some opinions and ideas you can't justify logically when you try to write them down. But you do have a good supply of material; all you have to do is discover it by letting your memory play.

Suppose you have chosen five possible subjects for your paper.

1. The Life of Abraham Lincoln
2. Dates I Have Had
3. My College
4. My High School Graduation
5. Battles of the Civil War

Any of these general subjects could be used for a paper, depending on its length. For the first and fifth subjects you would probably use material you had learned in school or from your reading, or possibly from research in the library. The others would come from your own experience and observation; you would discover the material by giving your mind time to think.

But none of the subjects, as stated, is suitable for development in a five-hundred-word paper. Since many volumes have been written about Lincoln's life, you couldn't possibly write five hundred significant words about Lincoln's *whole* life. Similarly, the second subject, as it stands, can't be used as the subject of a five-hundred-word paper, since you probably can say nothing meaningful about *all* your dates in so short a paper. You will do better if you choose one date, or an episode in one date, and then say something significant about it. The third subject presents the same problem. Any college has numerous "parts"—faculty, students, dormitories, courses, sports, student union, and so on—but you can't possibly write convincingly about all of these under a general subject heading. Not in five hundred words. However, if you chose "My College" as your subject, you'd be obligated to do so. At first glance, the fourth subject seems fairly limited—your high school graduation. But even a little thought will show you that *graduation* is another multiple subject in disguise, including many related events—commencement exercises, the senior prom, preparations for graduation, problems preventing graduation, embarrassing moments. Again the subject is too general. Obviously the last subject is unsatisfactory too. No one can say anything meaningful about *all* the battles of the Civil War in a short paper. In fact, in a short paper you couldn't write meaningfully about *all* aspects of even *one* battle. You will need to think further and more exactly before you start writing.

Notice that two words provide the key to your problem: *single* and *limited*. To explain an idea, a physical object, a process, or an event in a short paper, you must learn to "divide" your general subject to make it manageable. You can discover a single, limited subject by logically dividing a general subject through the process of analysis.

Suppose your instructor asks you to write a five-hundred-word paper on one of the following subjects:

Accidents	Drinking	Neighborhood
Advertising	Education	Newspapers
Aggression	Farming	People
Ambitions	Flight	Pets
Animals	Freedom	Planes
Birds	Friends	Pollution
Books	Girls	Population
Boys	Guns	Prejudices
Buildings	High Schools	Recreation
Cars	Hobbies	Schools
Clothes	Hostility	Solids
Clubs	Jobs	Space
Colleges	Laws	Sports
Community	Liquids	Television
Congress	Magazines	Travel
Dating	Movies	Vacations
Dogs	Music	Voting

Don't panic. *Choose.* Reject any notions that you have nothing to write about. You *do* have material to use in writing good papers. You've accumulated a great deal of knowledge in your lifetime (or else what have you been doing all this time?). You have had a variety of unique experiences, you have made observations of all sorts, you have formed strong opinions.

With proper limitation, you could easily write a five-hundred-word paper on any of these subjects, and if you put your mind to work, you could discover many more. None of these, for instance, would let you use much of the knowledge you've picked up in your study of literature or history or science. A quick mental tour of these studies should suggest many possible general subjects—wars, battles, great men, novels, plays, poems, chemicals, animals, air, gas, and geese are a few. Discovery is a game; play it with a positive attitude and you will find getting started much easier than you think.

Once you have chosen a general subject (or it has been assigned to you), the job is barely begun. Although you *can* write a short paper on a general subject, the odds are overwhelming that it will be weak because you will not have planned carefully enough or limited your subject to one you can discuss in relatively few words.

Limiting is the process of dividing a general subject into its parts, selecting one of these parts, and then further limiting it. Suppose that from the list of general subjects above you decided to write on *high schools.* First, think of possible *divisions* of this subject, as suggested in the diagram illustrating how to divide all general subjects.

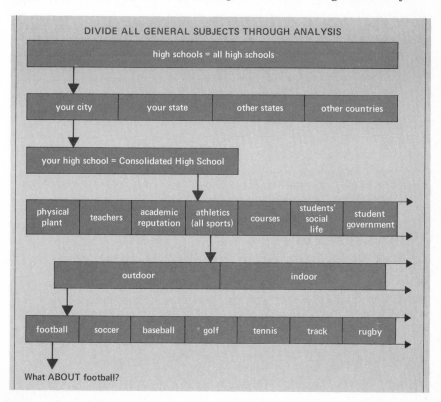

Almost always a *general* subject implies a great many limited, *single* subjects. The diagram represents a process of *logical analysis* ("dividing"), through which a broad, complex, general subject can be divided into manageable units ("parts"). It is essentially a questioning process, since its success depends on the repeated, thoughtful application of a question:

Does this subject include related narrow subjects?

Although this question can be restated in many ways, some version of it must be applied to every subject you examine: Can this subject be divided? What does this subject imply?

Take a careful look at the diagram. Follow the thinking process through all its stages:

1. Can the subject *high schools* be divided into logical parts?

    Without a qualifying modifier, most general subjects imply *all* aspects, *everything* about the subject (rather than one aspect or some parts). *High schools* means "all high schools," so that the answer to the question is obvious: Of course the subject can be divided.

    If you look at the list of subjects given on page 40 you'll see that most of them imply the modifier *all*: *All* accidents (in the home, on highways, in school, everywhere); *all* television (types of programs, production of programs, advertising, kinds of TV sets, cost, and so on); *all* aspects of education; everything about a neighborhood (physical, social, economic, linguistic, etc.).

    List all the parts of *high schools* you can discover; choose *one* that interests you and again think about it.

2. Can the subject *high schools in my city* be divided into logical parts?

    Without necessarily listing all the schools in your city, you could choose one (presumably your own) to think about.

3. Can the subject *Consolidated High School* be divided?

    Clearly, it can. List all the parts you can discover; choose one that really interests you and again think of it. If you chose *athletics*, it would become the subject for further analysis.

4. Can the subject *athletics at Consolidated High School* be divided?

    Again your answer must be yes, and again you divide the subject, thinking of *outdoor* and *indoor sports*; if you prefer outdoor sports, you try to think of all the outdoor sports played at your high school (Consolidated), and list them.

5. Can the subject *football at Consolidated High School* be divided further?

    It can be "divided" only into logical subjects dealing with *football* at Consolidated High; it cannot be divided into new subjects. At this point you probably have a *single, limited* subject; it cannot be divided into *new* related subjects. (We'll see shortly that *varsity* and *intramural* football could be used sharpen the focus.)

As this process of analysis suggests, almost always a general subject implies a great many *single, limited* subjects. This was the problem with the five general subjects discussed earlier in this unit. The subject *The Life of Abraham Lincoln*, for example, can be logically divided into personal background, preparation for politics, election to the presidency, Lincoln's stand on slavery, the countless problems brought on by the Civil War, his Gettysburg address, his assassination, and more. Each of these, though more limited than the general subject, can be divided still further into more specific ones—opposition to his election, his tactics to gain election, the immediate results of his election, and so on.

To have unity, your paper must have one limited subject to develop in one direction. However, when you come to write a thesis statement you'll often be tempted to include more than one subject because *in your mind* they seem closely tied together. Here's an example:

> Our student election is not being run properly and we must do something about it.

Here are two thesis statements. The first condemns existing procedures and the second urges action to revise the faulty procedures. The sentence is composed of two independent clauses (two sentences, if you wish) joined by the coordinating conjunction *and*. The two parts of this compound sentence have equal importance because both have exactly the same grammatical construction. But you could include both parts in an acceptable thesis statement if you subordinate one part to the other and make it less important:

> Since our student election is not being run properly, we must do something about it.

Adding the subordinating conjunction *since* changes the first part of the sentence into a dependent clause, allowing the independent clause to carry the main statement as a single subject: We must do something about (the improper procedures in our student election). You can see now that the dependent clause that begins the sentence can be reduced to a phrase and incorporated into the independent clause:

> We must correct improper procedure in our student election.

Improper procedures in our student election	must be corrected.
Limited Subject Area	Predicate Area

Each of these thesis statements has a single, limited subject: *Improper procedures in our student election.* Each also has a specific focus (controlling attitude): *must correct,* and *must be corrected.* This specific focus or controlling attitude is the predicate area of your thesis statement. Discovering this attitude is the subject of the next section.

Before writing on any subject, you must practice the process of logically dividing general subjects to discover single, limited subjects. And you must avoid the temptation to include more than one subject in a thesis statement merely because they seem closely tied together in your mind. Together, these two skills will assure you of success in the crucial first step in the prewriting discovery process.

> To discover a *single, limited* subject is to choose for your paper only *one* subject that cannot be significantly divided further; it is the key to *unity* of thought.

exercises

A. Study the diagram showing you how to divide the general subject *high schools* by logical analysis.
   1. Instead of *athletics,* take three other parallel subjects and narrow them by further division to single, limited subjects. (You might try *physical plant, students' social life,* and *student government.*)
   2. Using the diagram as a guide (don't be afraid to change it), divide the following general subjects for each: *television, drinking, pollution, liquids.*
B. Compare your response to Exercises A-1 and A-2 with those of other students in the class. How much variation is there? Discuss the differences and possible reasons for them.
C. Everybody talks about freedom. Here's your chance:
   1. Without too much thinking, write three or four sentences about freedom. Quickly.
   2. Now take time to divide the general subject *freedom* into as many first-level subdivisions as five minutes will allow. (No need to carry the division all the way down to the final, limited level.)
   3. With Exercise C-2 complete, again write three or four sentences about freedom.
   4. Compare your responses to Exercises *C*-1 and *C*-3. List the major differences between your two comments on freedom. Comment on the value and some of the uses of logical division.

2. *discover a specific focus—controlling attitude*

Having completed the process of logically dividing your general subject, the next step is to choose one of the single, limited subjects for further thought and analysis. Always choose a subject you know and are really interested in. You are then more likely to write a paper about it that sounds authoritative and convincing. Returning to the analysis of *high school* and, finally, *high school sports*, you decide against soccer, baseball, golf, tennis, track, and rugby and choose football. Your single, limited subject is *Football at Consolidated High School.*

You must now discover the specific point you're going to establish *about* this single, limited subject. You must strengthen the unity of your paper by giving it a specific *focus* or *direction* by deciding on a *controlling attitude.* You must discover what to say *about* your chosen limited subject. But how? The process can be very simply stated:

Ask a question about the limited subject, then answer it.

"But what question shall I ask?" you will say. Let's see how this process works by examining some methods used by professional writers.

One way to discover what to say about your limited subject is to ask the basic questions often used by journalists reporting events: *Who? What? When? Where? Why? How?* However, in their simplest form, these questions can usually be used successfully with only relatively few events—a good example would be a specific automobile accident. But a question approach will work if the questions are carefully phrased. For example, if you applied these general questions to the limited subject *Football at Consolidated High School* you might come up with the following specific questions.

> *Who* are the players? *Whose* role is most important?
> *What* is football? *What* are the basic rules?
> *Where* is football played? *When?*
> *How* is football played (at Consolidated High)?
> *How* well is football played (at Consolidated High)?

The basic journalistic questions are really a simplified version of a discovery method used by writers over two thousand years ago to find supporting arguments. Somewhat modified, this method can be successfully applied to find out what to say *about* limited subjects. Using this method as a basis, the *discovery questions* on p. 46 have been devised and grouped in a chart according to the kind of subject being discussed. While each question probably works best with the subject class it was designed for, with a little modification each could be asked about almost any subject. And you could probably design additional questions of your own. The important thing is to practice asking questions *about* your limited subject; the aim is to discover as many *controlling attitudes*, as many *directions* for your subject,

DISCOVERY QUESTIONS*

SUBJECT CLASS	EXAMPLES OF GENERAL SUBJECTS	DISCOVERY QUESTIONS
A. Events Actions	accidents, car accidents, fires, election to presidency, graduation, a touchdown, a lousy date, failure in math, a murder, an explosion, a battle, a picnic, the game of football	1. Specifically what happened? 2. What caused it? 3. What were the consequences? 4. How was it related to other events? 5. How was it unlike or like similar events? 6. How could the event have been changed or prevented? 7. What values or costs were involved? (See no. 3.) 8. Who was involved?
B. Concepts Terms Ideas	freedom, fear, fact, truth, war, peace, democracy, lie, law, detente, pollution, tyranny, love, professional, immoral, obscene, prurient	1. How do most people define it? 2. How do *you* define it? 3. How has it influenced people's lives? 4. How is it similar to concepts associated with it? 5. How could it be improved or changed? 6. What value does it have, and for whom? (See no. 3.)
C. Objects Things Persons	cars, colleges, dogs, teachers, Jack Smith, building, house, ice, container, cup, box, gun, water, rain, phone, computers, knives, ships, girls, Agnes Gooch, acorns, Abraham Lincoln, American presidents, Democrats, athletes, football players	1. What are its physical characteristics? (dimensions, texture, shape, color) 2. What are its parts and how do they fit together? 3. What are its uses? 4. Who uses it? 5. What other object is it similar to? 6. How is it unlike things resembling it? 7. Where did it come from? 8. Who made it? 9. What value does it have, and for whom? (See nos. 3 and 4.)

*Adapted from Edward P. J. Corbett, *Classical Rhetoric for the Modern Student,* 2nd ed. (New York: Oxford University Press, 1971).

as possible. You will then have many alternatives from which to choose the *one specific direction* for your paper. Now let's apply some of the questions to the limited subject *Football at Consolidated High School* and study the results.

Play the game of discovery by finding questions that provide useful and significant information about your limited subject:

FOOTBALL AT CONSOLIDATED HIGH SCHOOL

1. What value does football have and for whom? (A–7, C–9)
2. What value does football have for the players?
3. What value does football have for the school?
4. What value does football have for nonplayers?
5. What does football cost the high school? (A-7)
6. How could football at CHS be improved or changed? (B-5)
7. How is football unlike other team sports? (A-5 C-5,6)
8. Who are the most important players on the CHS team? (C-2)
9. Who is the football hero at CHS? (B-3)
10. What emphasis is placed on football at CHS? (A-3, B-3,6, C-9)
11. What safety equipment is used? (C-2)
12. How do other students treat football players? (B-3)
13. How do teachers treat football players? (B-3)
14. What experience do you get playing on the CHS team? (C-9)
15. How well do students support football at CHS? (B-3)
16. How does football at CHS affect the players' academic standing? (B-3)

Using discovery questions to come up with a list similar to this one is the most important prewriting skill you can learn. By answering the questions on your list, you should be able to discover many possible controlling attitudes, *one* of which you would then choose to write about. The *one* controlling attitude you choose will become the predicate area of your thesis statement, as you will soon see. And what you say about the limited subject in the predicate area is the most important part of the thesis statement, for it is here you *express your view,* the controlling attitude to be explored and supported in the rest of the paper. This attitude will be the key to the content of your paper. Consequently, you must be certain that your attitude can be supported and that readers cannot misunderstand it.

After you have used the discovery questions to determine which controlling attitude you want to use, you will still have to learn the following guidelines before you can phrase an acceptable limited predicate area.

a. The predicate area must also be limited.   Even though you've gone through the process of limiting the subject of the thesis statement, you may find when you write your statement that it's still too broad to deal with. It probably needs limiting in the predicate area. Consider this thesis statement:

The United States is the best of all countries.

Proving this thesis would be easy if you were planning to write several volumes, but you cannot do it in a short paper. The predicate area of this thesis, *is the best of all countries,* obligates the writer to prove that the United States is better than *any* other country. To fulfill this obligation, the writer would have to consider the economic, moral, religious, political, and social conditions in every country of the world and then contrast them to those in the United States. This is not possible in five hundred words. Similarly, a statement such as

Lee was a greater general than Grant.

cannot be established without considering the campaigns of each general and then comparing them. Neither is this a job for a short paper.

b. The predicate area of the thesis statement should present an argumentative attitude toward the subject.   If you are to establish a main point, or adequately support a thesis, your paper must be partially argumentative. After all, you are trying to explain to the reader that your point is a sound one. Your paper will have no purpose other than to support the validity of this main point, which you will argue by presenting all the logical reasons and sound evidence you can muster. Your thesis statement must be the trumpet's call that sounds the challenge—you on one side, your reader on the other. You will try to get your reader to say, "I understand" *and* "I agree," giving your paper an argumentative attitude. So be bold about it; issue your challenge clearly and forcefully, as if you were engaging in debate. Use no weak phrases such as "to me" or "in my opinion" in your thesis, nor anywhere else in your paper, for they leave with your reader the impression that you are merely stating an opinion and are apologetic about supporting it. Step from the crowd and write something like these thesis statements:

> The high school student needs more responsibility.
> Lady Macbeth is more masculine than feminine.
> Watching television encourages violence.
> Freshman English is a farce.
> Charles Dickens found American life bewildering.
> The mind must be exercised.

Only if your thesis statement reflects a specific controlling attitude toward a single, limited subject, phrased with directness and conviction, will you grab your reader's interest. And even if the instructor is your only reader, he will like your paper better simply because you caught his attention and challenged his thought.

But a striking thesis statement alone will not win you a good grade; the thesis still has to be properly developed and logically supported. Select a thesis you can believe in and support. If you don't believe what you say, neither will the reader, and *you are writing to convince your reader.*

c. The predicate area must say something meaningful. A thesis statement about which there can be no controversy, about which everyone agrees, can hardly result in a paper that anyone will want to read. If, for instance, you try to write a paper using a thesis like

Travel by plane saves time.

or

Good conservation practices help the farmer.

you aren't going to get much of a reaction from your reader except "Ho-hum. So what?" And justifiably. For these statements are trite and too general to be truly meaningful.

d. The predicate area must say something exact about the subject. Look at this thesis statement:

Football is an exciting game.

The predicate area is made up of the phrase *is an exciting game.* If you are to write a paper on this thesis, its content must be controlled by the key word *exciting,* because it gives your paper its single direction. There is no other emotion or feeling you can write about in your paper. But what exactly does *exciting* mean? It's hard to define and does not *lead* the reader sufficiently. What might be exciting to one person might leave another cold. And there is the problem with such a predicate area—it does not get to a precise point. It is not exact. It allows the writer to say almost anything as long as it is in any way associated with football. Consequently, the writer can ramble and support no specific point in the paper. To improve this statement, assert a specific controlling attitude about one variety of football:

Even touch football <u>is dangerous.</u>

You can see that the same difficulty exists in this thesis statement:

Macbeth makes fascinating reading.

If you are assigned a paper on *Macbeth,* make an exact point about the play:

Macbeth's early recognition of guilt	increases his conflict.
Single, Limited Subject	Specific, Limited Predicate

When you can't find something to say about your limited subject, turn to the discovery questions for help. Make a game of the process. Stretch or modify questions to fit your needs. And be sure to write down every question in a form that clearly applies to your limited subject. Now you can delete those questions that least appeal to you, one by one, until you finally end up choosing the *one* you best understand. You're on your way. You are ready to write a complete thesis statement, combining the limited subject with the specific focus you've decided to use.

3. write a complete thesis statement

A good thesis statement is vital to your paper because it clearly presents the main point you are going to make and support. It controls the focus and direction of your paper. Without it your paper will probably lack unity; with it the paper will have a controlling attitude that restricts your limited subject, focusing attention on what the paper is about.

The thesis statement should be written as a sentence with an argumentative bias—the controlling attitude. Like all sentences, it has a *subject area* and a *predicate area.* As in all sentences, the subject area of the thesis statement announces *what* will be discussed (the grammatical subject of the sentence). And, as in all sentences, the predicate area says something *about* the subject. Here is a diagram showing all the elements in a thesis statement:

Complete Thesis Statement
(A Complete Sentence)

Limited Subject + Modifiers	+	Verb + Completers + Modifiers
Limited Subject Area (*One* Limited Subject)		Limited Predicate Area (Controlling Attitude)

You have just studied the process of dividing a general subject to discover a single, limited subject you can adequately discuss in five hundred words. And you have also practiced using discovery questions to determine a controlling attitude (focus) for the limited subject. Now let's put this information to work.

Any of the sixteen questions you discovered above contains the basic information you need for the thesis statement. Let's choose the third question as our starting point:

What value does football have for Consolidated High School?

You can see that the question contains the two elements you need:

Single, Limited Subject	Predicate Area (Focus)
Football at Consolidated High School	value

Since most schools have both varsity and intramural football, you will sharpen your limited subject by choosing one of them. The resulting limited subject now reads: *Varsity football at Consolidated High School.* And since the question asks *what value football has,* you need to consider some possible answers:

It *has little* value for the school.
It *has limited* value for the players. (Question 2)
It *has* value for the school.
It *has no* value for nonplayers. (Question 4)
It *has no* value for the school.

Since your limited subject concentrates on the *school,* discard the second and fourth ideas (you'll probably be able to use them later). Suppose you choose the last statement. Here's a first try at a thesis statement:

At Consolidated High School, varsity football has no value.

This thesis statement fits the diagram model, but its predicate area, "has no value," could be more exact and more argumentative. You need to think about it further. Since your paper will argue that varsity football has "no value" for the school, you could make it even more argumentative by making a suggestion based on the "no value" attitude. You could write several thesis statements:

Varsity football	at Consolidated High	should be discontinued.
Limited Subject	Modifier	Limited Predicate

Varsity football	should be discontinued at	Consolidated High.
Limited Subject	Verb +	Completer

Although both sentences communicate the same idea, they differ grammatically. But the difference is merely a matter of emphasis; both are acceptable thesis statements. Notice that the statement "has no value" is still lurking in these two sentences: *should be discontinued* (because it has no value). If you play with this relationship, you could easily discover a number of additional *controlling attitudes:*

> should be severely limited (because it has no value)
> should be separated from school activities (because it has no value)
> should be restricted to seniors only (because it has no value)
> should be cut from the school budget (because it has no value)

You might even come up with the following thesis statement:

| Varsity football at Consolidated High | is an outrageous waste. |

Limited Subject   Modifier   Limited Predicate

The two diagrams below review the process of framing a thesis statement presented so far. The first represents the process in general terms; the second uses a specific example to illustrate the process.

In the first diagram, the general subject might be one already suggested, "My School." For illustration, assume that your school

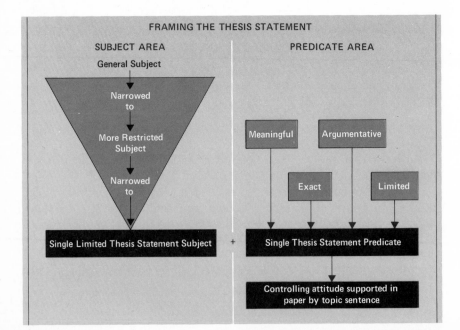

is Glory University. To restrict this general subject to a more manageable one, you must then list the divisions of that general subject
you will be able to write about from your observation and experience.
To discover these divisions, you would use the process of logical analysis
that you have already practiced. Then you would choose your limited
subject. Would you choose sports, professors, dormitory life, registration day, academic work, or the student union? Because you have
probably been through it recently, you might pick *registration day.*
You now have a limited subject for the specific thesis statement of
your five-hundred-word paper. To complete the statement, you must
form the predicate area by saying something about the subject. At
this point in the process you would use the discovery questions to
explore the many controlling attitudes available to you. The attitude
you choose, of course, will depend on your own experience. You might
say that you found registration day frustrating or tiring or confusing
or inefficient or pleasant or efficient, or none of these. To illustrate,
let's say that you found it confusing. You now have a thesis statement
in its simplest form:

Registration day was confusing.

In reaching a specific thesis statement you have gone through
the process of selection shown by the second diagram (on page 54).

The large block on the left indicates the general subject, "Glory
University." The smaller blocks in the middle of the page represent
six of the many limited subjects that are a part of the general subject.
The shading of the fourth block shows that only one part, *registration
day,* has been selected as the limited subject of the paper. The blocks
on the right of the page show some of the many controlling attitudes
you might have discovered about the limited subject, *registration day.*
The shading of the block labeled *confusing* indicates the selection
of a specific controlling attitude toward the subject. Now, the content
of the paper is restricted to the subject matter represented by the
two shaded blocks. *Material from no other block should be used in
writing the paper.* The paper may only demonstrate that registration
day was confusing. The key word controlling the content of the paper
is *confusing.* Any material that does not establish the validity of
that key word does not belong in the paper.

Now you have a thesis statement: *Registration day was confusing.*
This statement, however, is not a particularly good expression of
the thesis. First, because the paper is to concern Glory University
as its general subject, mention it in your thesis statement:

Registration day at Glory University was confusing.

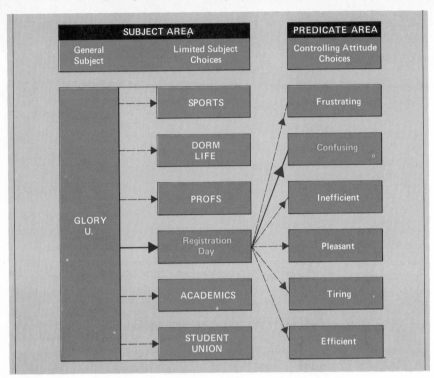

Everything being equal, a complex sentence, one that contains a dependent clause, will probably serve best as a thesis statement, depending on the context of the introductory paragraph. So try a complex sentence:

Although I had memorized every step I was to take, registration day at Glory University was confusing.

This sentence can be improved by making the verb active. Revise it to this version:

Although I had memorized every step I was to take, registration day at Glory University confused me.

The dependent clause of this thesis statement lets you lead up to the central issue by commenting, perhaps, on some of the "steps" you had "memorized." As suggested in Chapter 2 in the diagram of the "funnel effect" (p. 18), this lead-in comment appears in the first few sentences of your introductory paragraph. And changing "was confusing" to "confused me" specifically focuses reader attention on your *personal* experience, explicitly excluding discussion of any *general* confusion at registration that didn't directly involve *you.*

exercises

A. Here are some thesis statements. Decide if they are suitable for development in a short paper by examining their subject and predicate areas; list reasons for accepting or rejecting each thesis area.
   1. My trip to Houston was the most educational vacation I've taken.
   2. The politician's speech was boring and full of clichés.
   3. Social fraternities encourage scholarship.
   4. Basketball intrigues me.
   5. Body contact sports can sometimes be dangerous.
   6. Women do not drive as well as men do.
   7. People cause automobile accidents.
   8. Water skiing is more fun than any other sport I have tried.
   9. Intercollegiate sports benefit the university and build spirit in the student body.
   10. High school football benefits the school and builds spirit in all students.
   11. College sports offer many advantages to the student.
   12. College sports shape the character of participating students.
   13. Intercollegiate sports shape the character of participating students.
   14. Although intercollegiate football builds spirit in the student body, its chief function is to advertise the university.
   15 The mind must be exercised.

B. Rewrite in acceptable form those thesis statements in Exercise *A* that you consider unsuitable for development in a short paper.

C. Rewrite the following general subjects to make each a single, limited subject:
   1. Interesting people I have known
   2. My summer vacation
   3. Shakespeare's *Julius Caesar*
   4. Hunting
   5. Oil

D. Think about the limited subjects you devise in Exercise *C* and invent a specific controlling attitude for each.

E. Combine the limited subjects and limited predicates of Exercises *C* and *D* into acceptable thesis statements.

F. Examine the three cartoons on pages 5, 6, and 277. Devise at least two thesis statements for each cartoon, capturing the basic underlying idea as you interpret it. Be prepared to defend both subject and predicate areas of your statements.

4. discover support for the thesis statement

So far, the discovery prewriting process has taken you through three learning experiences: You've practiced how to find a single, limited subject; you've learned how to state a specific point about the limited subject; and you've practiced analyzing and writing complete thesis statements. You have two more skills to learn: how to discover support for the thesis statement, and how to write a complete purpose statement.

Once you have written a good thesis statement, you must find logical reasons to support the controlling attitude it contains. Suppose, for instance, you've decided to use this thesis statement:

Interschool football should be discontinued at Consolidated High School.

Your aim is to complete the predicate area of the statement, *should be discontinued at Consolidated High School* because. . . . If you have trouble getting started, try scanning the discovery questions listed earlier in this chapter to find questions you can ask about this subject. Here are some possibilities:

How has it (interschool football) influenced people's lives?
What value does it have, and for whom?
Who uses it?
What costs are involved?
How has it influenced people's lives?

Answers to these questions should lead you to consider the individuals directly or indirectly influenced by interschool football: participants and nonparticipants, students as well as others who may or may not derive any real "value" from the game. Further logical analysis should reveal that all of the following people could be considered: the players themselves, all the other nonparticipating students, the teachers, the spectators (including parents), the coaches. To argue that interschool football *should be discontinued* is to suggest that some (or all) of these people would probably be better off without the game. Why? Perhaps the game results in serious injuries to the players, or interferes with the teachers' classroom work. Is the game too costly? In what ways? And who ultimately pays the bills? In effect, you are trying to complete the statement, *the game should be discontinued because*. . . . With or without the discovery questions, the word *because* directs your search for evidence to support the attitude you have asserted in the thesis statement. And if you actually believe the thesis statement, you should be able to list a number of *reasons* for your belief. Your list might be something like the following:

Interschool football should be discontinued at Consolidated High School because:

1. The school loses money on interschool football.
2. The average student is unable to participate in the game.
3. Players are seriously injured each year.
4. Students lose class time in activities supporting the team.
5. Students' attention is taken away from academic subjects.
6. Students lose study time attending pep rallies.
7. Trips to neighboring cities are dangerous.
8. The importance of the football player is overrated.
9. Football is likely to teach players the wrong set of values.
10. Too much attention is given to football at the expense of scholarship.
11. The coach seems more important than other teachers.
12. The cost of building and maintaining the stadium is high.
13. The value of the school is likely to be judged by the success of its football team.
14. The winning coach is paid a premium salary.
15. Winning at all costs becomes too important.

Inspect this list and you can see that certain reasons may be grouped together because they are closely related. This process of grouping is called *classification,* a key to sorting and managing information. It is the reverse process of logical *division,* which you used early in this chapter to discover limited, manageable "parts" of general subject areas. Now that you are at the other end of the process, you use classification to sort your ideas systematically. You will soon discover that some of the reasons you have listed at random may have to be left out and others may have to be modified so that you can get the grouping that best points to your thesis statement. Also, after you begin the actual writing of the paper, new reasons probably will occur to you and some of your attitudes may change. Don't hesitate to add the reasons to your list or to make other changes you feel are needed. The following *sentence outline* is one way to arrange your reasons:

I. The cost of interschool football is prohibitive.
   A. The school loses money on interschool football.
   B. The cost of building and maintaining a stadium is high.
   C. The winning coach is paid a premium salary.
II. Scholarship is forced to take second place to football.
   A. Students lose class time in activities that support the team.
   B. Students' attention is taken away from academic study.
   C. Students lose study time attending pep rallies.
   D. Coaches seem more important than other teachers.
III. The effect of interschool football on the student body is harmful.
   A. It builds the wrong set of values.
      1. Winning at any cost becomes too important.

    2. The importance of the star football player is magnified out of proportion.

    3. The school is judged by the success of its football team.

  B. Students are placed in unnecessary danger.

    1. Players are seriously injured each year.

    2. Students driving to out-of-town games invite tragedy.

Study how this arrangement uses classification to group together related ideas. Since Statements 1, 12, and 14 are about *money, stadium cost,* and *coaches' salaries,* they have been brought together by the topic sentence stating that *cost* (subject) *is prohibitive* (predicate). Statements 4, 5, 6, and 11 comment on the relation of *football* to *scholarship;* the topic sentence for these is a rewording of Statement 10: *scholarship* (subject) *is forced to take second place* (predicate). The remaining statements comment on *harmful effects* on students in two ways, represented by the words *value* and *danger.* A new topic sentence is devised to state that the *effect* (subject) is *harmful* (predicate); Statement 9 functions as the first subheading (*builds the wrong set of values*), under which Statements 15, 8, and 13 fit neatly; a second subheading is invented (*placed in unnecessary danger*) to serve as the lead-in for Statements 2 and 7. Which statement was omitted? Why?

    The process you have just studied clearly has two basic steps:

1. Discover reasons to support your thesis statement
2. Classify related reasons into major controlling categories

Classifying your reasons into major controlling categories should suggest topic sentences for *developmental paragraphs* in a short paper, or *section* headings for a long paper. But whether your paper is short or long, classification is the process that gives you the information needed to write a good *purpose statement,* a kind of blueprint, anticipating the whole paper and guiding the reader systematically through it.

5. *write a complete purpose statement*

You have your supporting reasons, and you have classified them into logical subject categories representing your three developmental paragraphs. Now you can write a *purpose statement.* Your instructor may ask you to turn in a purpose statement for each paper you write, since a carefully worded statement will help you see the main components of your paper. A good purpose statement includes all of the following:

A single, limited subject
A specific controlling attitude
The word *because* (stated or implied)
All the supporting reasons (major subject categories)

Although the purpose statement does not usually become part of the paper proper, it does contain all the ideas that will appear in your introductory paragraph. A purpose statement for a paper using the material arranged above from the thesis on football might turn out like this:

In this paper I will support the thesis that interschool football should be discontinued at Consolidated High School because (1) the cost of interschool football is prohibitive, (2) scholarship is forced to take second place to football, and (3) the effect of interschool football on the student body is harmful.

Look again at the student paper "The Case Against High School Football" (p. 30). Study its *introductory paragraph* and then write one to fit the information you've just mastered on the thesis "Interschool football should be discontinued at Consolidated High School." Should these two paragraphs be exactly alike? What governs the differences? Suppose a whole class of students wrote a paper based on the sentence outline given above for interschool football. Why would each paper still be unique?

This chapter has emphasized the following skills:

Prewriting thinking, planning, choosing
How to discover a single, limited subject
How to discover a specific controlling attitude
How to write a complete thesis statement, containing a limited subject area and a limited predicate area
How to discover supporting reasons for the thesis statement
How to classify supporting reasons into subject categories
How to write a complete purpose statement and plan a blueprint for the whole paper

exercises

A. The *sentence outline* on page 57 could easily be written as a *topic outline* if the key terms were taken from each sentence and simply listed. (Look at the controlling attitude in the predicate area of each sentence.)

A slight change in wording may simplify matters. For example, A, B, and C of part II of the sentence outline could appear in the topic outline as "lost class time," "diverted attention," and "lost study time." Practice spotting key terms by rewriting the sentence outline as a topic outline.

B. Use logical analysis to divide three of the following general subjects into limited subjects suitable for development in a short paper. For each general subject you choose devise a diagram similar to the one on page 41.
  1. Advertising
  2. Loving
  3. Congress
  4. Fires
  5. Drinking
  6. Smoking
  7. The newspaper
  8. Music
  9. Agriculture
  10. The city

If you have trouble with this exercise, check the discovery questions on page 46.

C. Choose three limited subjects from those you found in Exercise *B* and write a limited, specific thesis statement for each.

D. Finding ideas is a matter of *getting started*—"inside," as well as "outside" on paper. But all of us get stuck—often early in the discovery process. The following exercises should suggest many *ways* of getting your "inside" moving.
  1. Bring to class a full-page, color ad from a magazine. Study the ad closely and then answer the following questions (your instructor may want you to make notes):
    a. Disregarding the *words* of the ad, describe what is left. What are *all* the other things you see?
    b. Disregarding the "meaning," what can you still say about the *whole* ad?
    c. How many different *kinds* of information are you receiving from the ad? Are they equally important? Why?
    d. Do you *like* the ad? Can you say why (or why not)? Does it appeal to your thinking? To your emotions? Or to both? Explain.
    e. What does the ad want you to *assume* that is not actually stated? How can you tell?
    f. In what ways is this ad *similar* to other ads? (You could look at your neighbors' ads.) How is yours *different* from the others?
    g. Does the ad remind you of other things you've experienced or observed? For example?
    h. What are the main "parts" of the ad? How do these parts work together?
    i. To what line of thinking is the "statement" of the ad apparently a conclusion? Explain.
    j. Can the "statement" in the ad be proven? Is the "statement" supported? How?
    k. Is there a play on words in the ad? What is the purpose? Can you take the words literally?

    1. Disregarding the overall meaning, what *kinds* of objects and people are pictured? What are you supposed to assume about them? (Look closely.)

  2. Which of the questions asked above in part 1 of this exercise are included in the following *general* questions:

    a. Can you *define* the object and its parts?

    b. What kind of *structure* does it have?

    c. To what is it *similar?*

    d. How is it *different from* other objects like it?

    e. What *cause-effect relationships* does it suggest?

    f. What other *relationships* does it suggest?

    g. What does it suggest about the *possible?* the *impossible?*

    h. Who *needs* it? Who *uses* it? Who ought to use it?

    i. What can be affected by it? In what ways?

    j. Do you *react to it favorably? Unfavorably? Why?*

  3. Apply the general questions given in part 2 of this exercise to five of the following:

    a. An automobile

    b. A science teacher

    c. Love (or fear)

    d. Power (or law)

    e. Milk (or water)

    f. A television set (or stereo)

    g. Aspirin (or morphine)

    h. A paper clip (or an oak tree)

    i. Death (or sleep)

E. 1. On the basis of your experience in the first three parts of this exercise list five *basic* questions you think you can ask about *any* subject.

  2. Be prepared to discuss what you have learned about the discovery process.

F. Once you have discovered a subject and a thesis statement and have jotted down some details to use in support, you will find classification an effective way to sort and organize thoughts. Here are some exercises in classification.

  1. Examine the following foods carefully, then arrange them into groups so that the items within each group all have something in common (label each group clearly): ice cream sundaes, iced tea, green beans, beef stew, french fries, cakes, milk, pies, beef steak, coffee, peas, fried chicken, cokes, carrots, meat loaf, roast beef, hot chocolate, pudding, hamburger steak.

  2. Suppose you have been asked to write a simple expository paper titled "Major Causes of Automobile Accidents." Quickly jot down at least a dozen causes. Now examine this list of causes and arrange them into two or three major groups, each clearly labeled. When you have done this classification, you should be able to complete the following statement:

> The major causes of automobile accidents are
> (a) _____, (b) _____, and (c) _____.

G. Choose one of the five thesis statements you wrote for Exercise *C* (above) and quickly jot down all the supporting details you can think of. Now arrange these details into major groups (each labeled) that might serve as the main points presented by a paper on the chosen thesis statement. (If you have trouble with this exercise, recheck the exercises on page 55 and the outline on page 57.)

H. You may not have agreed with the paper about football in Chapter 2 (p. 30). Copy the following diagram and fill it in, taking the opposite view. Start with a thesis statement that says something like *Football is the best thing that ever happened to our high school,* and give your reasons. Make your reasons and your support for the reasons as strong as you possibly can. Don't forget to put your most persuasive reason last.

Thesis Statement: _____
                (The thesis statement is valid because. . . .)
    Reason 1: _____
          (Reason 1 is valid because. . . .)
      Reason A: _____
      Reason B: _____
      Reason C: _____
         (The thesis statement is valid because. . . .)
    Reason 2: _____
          (Reason 2 is valid because. . . .)
      Reason A: _____
      Reason B: _____
      Reason C: _____
         (The thesis statement is valid because. . . .)
    Reason 3: _____
          (Reason 3 is valid because. . . .)
      Reason A: _____
      Reason B: _____
      Reason C: _____
Concluding Statement: _____

I. Write a purpose statement from the outline you composed in Exercise *H.*

J. Write a five-hundred-word paper from the outline for **Exercise** *H.*

K. Rewrite the outline used in Exercise *H* so that it is (a) a topic outline, or (b) a good sentence outline.

REVIEW TERMS

The skills you have learned in this chapter are related to the terms listed below; test your understanding of them and you'll improve your mastery of fundamental steps in the writing process.

A. Prewriting, single subject, limited subject, thesis statement, controlling attitude, focus, direction, purpose statement, general subject, multiple subject, logical analysis, logical division, main division subdivision, subject class, subject category, unity, discovery questions, argumentative attitude, funnel effect, support, evidence, classification, sentence outline, topic outline, controlling categories

B. Independent clause, coordinating conjunction, dependent clause, phrase, limited subject area, limited predicate area, grammatical subject, complete sentence, verb, completer, modifier, active verb, passive verb

maintaining unity and coherence

his chapter will help you improve the focus and direction of your paper and of every paragraph you write. Inventing a single, limited subject and a specific controlling attitude for thesis statements and topic sentences is an important first step. And presenting clearly related supporting evidence or reasons also helps. But *writing to support a sharp argumentative focus or direction* requires additional skills.

Suppose someone asks you for directions to the nearest hospital. Telling him about several hospitals will only confuse him because you are giving unnecessary information. And even if you concentrate your directions on how to get to one hospital only, he could still miss his destination if your instructions aren't *orderly* or sufficiently illuminated with *signals* to guide him. Good communication uses both processes—concentrating on a *single*, limited subject (unity) and providing clear directional *signals* (coherence).

A short paper works toward clarifying a single point or idea (limited subject) by making every statement in the paper support the controlling attitude toward this single idea. The aim is to convince readers that this single idea is valid. To achieve this goal, the paper must have unity, singleness of purpose: *one* subject, *one* controlling attitude, *one* tone. At the same time, while every sentence and every paragraph contributes to this single aim, all of the paper's parts must hold together to guide readers and keep their attention as they move from part to part. Coherence devices hold sentence to sentence and paragraph to paragraph, guiding both writer and readers from thought to thought in support of the thesis statement. Unity can be called the "togetherness" of all the ideas in the paper's parts, the sense that all the ideas presented are logically related to one another. Coherence is the resulting overall effect provided through directional signals; it is the easy, natural movement of ideas from part to part, reenforcing and emphasizing the paper's unity. Trying to move through a paper with inadequate coherence signals can be as frustrating as trying to drive behind a car that gives no directional signals.

UNITY   In communication, unity means oneness. *One subject, one controlling attitude, one tone.* In all your writing—sentences, paragraphs, short and long papers—you will work for this oneness.

The key to unity is to keep focused on the argumentative controlling attitude toward your single, limited subject. This controlling attitude is a *pointer*; it provides the *focus* and logical *direction* for all the paper's ideas. Unity works much as a compass does. A compass gives direction. By following a specific compass direction, you can move steadily south or east or north or west—or any marked direction between these main points. But if you don't follow only *one* point on the compass, you will never reach your chosen destination. Exactly the same is true of writing: Move in a single logical direction (your specific controlling attitude) and stick to it. Unity in writing is consistently maintaining the *single*, specific logical direction you head for at the beginning of your paper (or paragraph). If you don't, your work is likely to project a split personality and seem to run in several directions at the same time.

Through its specific controlling attitude, the thesis statement provides the single logical direction to be followed throughout an *entire paper*, whether it is a short paper like the five-hundred-word theme or a long research paper. Similarly, through its specific controlling attitude, the topic sentence provides the single logical direction each developmental paragraph follows in support of the thesis. Look again at the sentence outline given on page 57. The diagram on page 67 shows how the specific, limited controlling attitudes of the thesis statement and the three topic sentences in the outline provide the single logical direction needed for unity of thought. Notice how the predicate area of the thesis statement serves as a pointer to provide a single logical direction for the supporting thought of each topic sentence:

should be discontinued (because) . . .
       I. the cost is prohibitive
      II. scholarship takes second place
      III. the effect on the student body is harmful

Similarly, the predicate area of the first topic sentence also serves as a pointer to provide single direction for the supporting thought of each sentence that follows:

(cost) is prohibitive (because) . . .
      A. money lost by school
      B. high stadium costs
      C. coach's salary

If you deviate from directly supporting the controlling attitude of the thesis statement or of a topic sentence clearly tied to the thesis statement, you violate the principle of unity. A good thesis statement or topic sentence, therefore, provides *two* fundamental keys to unity:

    1. A single, limited subject area
    2. A specific, limited predicate area (controlling attitude)

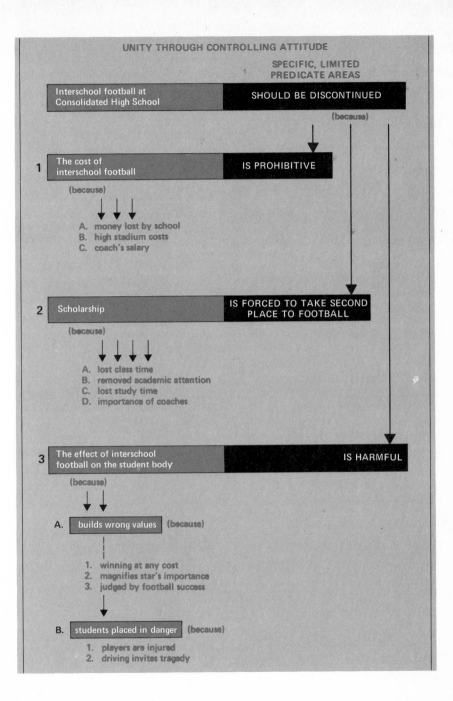

UNITY THROUGH CONTROLLING ATTITUDE

SPECIFIC, LIMITED
PREDICATE AREAS

Interschool football at
Consolidated High School   SHOULD BE DISCONTINUED

(because)

1 The cost of
   interschool football   IS PROHIBITIVE

   (because)

      A. money lost by school
      B. high stadium costs
      C. coach's salary

2 Scholarship   IS FORCED TO TAKE SECOND
                                 PLACE TO FOOTBALL

   (because)

      A. lost class time
      B. removed academic attention
      C. lost study time
      D. importance of coaches

3 The effect of interschool
   football on the student body   IS HARMFUL

   (because)

   A. builds wrong values   (because)

         1. winning at any cost
         2. magnifies star's importance
         3. judged by football success

   B. students placed in danger   (because)

         1. players are injured
         2. driving invites tragedy

Later, Chapter 9 discusses *tone* as a third key to unity (pp. 277–278); it isn't listed here because it is really part of controlling attitude. You can see why it is so important to think through your idea before you begin and to use great care in phrasing both the thesis statement and the topic sentences of your papers.

Remembering the two fundamental keys to unity, let's look at the following paragraph:

> European castles still standing prove that life in those great damp structures was far from comfortable. Cold, wet drafts blew through the long corridors, and heating such a barn was difficult and expensive. Although many bedrooms had fireplaces in them, the beds still had to be heavily curtained in winter before the occupants could keep from freezing to death. Walls were draped with tapestries and curtains to keep the cold winds out of other rooms. Five hundred years ago, it might have been easy for a lord to retain a hundred carpenters to build enough heavy oak pieces to furnish his manor, but today such an undertaking would cost thousands of dollars. For instance, just installing wall-to-wall carpeting in one of the gigantic rooms would make a dent in a multimillionaire's bank roll. And think of the staff that would have to be maintained if a castle were to be lived in today. There would be the kitchen help, a whole battalion of housekeepers. several moat cleaners, and an army of grounds keepers.

At first reading, this paragraph may seem to be fairly good, since it does say a number of interesting things about old castles. But if you study it more closely, you'll see that it lacks unity: It does not move in a single logical direction even though it discusses only old European castles (a fairly good single, limited subject). The paragraph does not fulfill *both* requirements for unity: although it has a single, limited subject, it does not focus on only *one* specific, limited predicate (controlling attitude). Because it introduces three—perhaps four—unrelated controlling attitudes, the paragraph actually moves in three different logical directions. The writer points out that these old castles:

were *uncomfortable*
were *cold*
were *expensive to heat*
were *costly to furnish*
were *difficult to staff*

Clearly, the writer can't seem to decide whether to talk about the lack of *comfort,* the *cold,* the *cost* of heating and furnishing, or the problems of *staffing.* He hasn't decided what to say *about* the castles. He hasn't decided on a specific controlling attitude. Consequently, the paragraph fails to make *one* point only. It violates the principle of unity. A unified paragraph could be written on any one of the four ideas.

Though written tongue-in-cheek, the following paragraph concentrates on only one specific controlling attitude, the *cost* of castle-keeping:

> At today's prices, maintaining a castle in the way the feudal lords of the Middle Ages did would be impossible even for the Really Rich. Any castle worth mentioning needed a big enough staff of domestics to at least keep the chewed-on bones shoveled up off the mead hall floor while the fulltime silversmith hammered out the amulets for next week's dragon slayers. Then there would have to be thatch put on the gardener's hut while he replanted the rosemary and thyme, and scullery jacks and jills to turn the pig on the spit in the galley. Menservants stood by in platoons to weld the knights into their armor and to let down the drawbridge and grind it up again if the Danes tried sneaking through. Add knights and embroidered squires waiting permission to Crusade, and pink and pretty ladies-in-waiting standing by to deliver the next sonnet to Milady's courtly lover. Add the cost for all this to the expense of feeding the Poor Porters, the cellarful of emaciated unknowns, and the fishes in the moat. The monthly expense of the noble family's entourage would be enough to eat the heart out of any modern multimillionaire's paycheck.

This paragraph also has a single, specific subject—old medieval castles. But in addition, it focuses on only one controlling attitude—a multi-millionaire today *could not afford* the upkeep of a medieval castle—and it sticks to this specific focus from start to finish. It has unity of purpose: *one* subject, *one* controlling attitude, *one* tone. It has unity of tone throughout, established mainly by the use of exaggeration and some special effects: *chewed-on bones, dragon slayers, scullery jacks and jills, embroidered squires, pink and pretty ladies-in-waiting, Poor Porters, emaciated unknowns.* The writer's controlling attitude toward the subject remains consistent; he concentrates on cost and always maintains the tongue-in-cheek, humorous feeling he wants to communicate to his readers. Together, this oneness of subject and controlling attitude give the paragraph a strong sense of unity. In your writing, you too must strive for unity of purpose: one subject, one controlling attitude, one tone.

Here is another paragraph for analysis. Read through it carefully to see if it maintains complete unity:

> Egypt was civilized long before there was any written history of the country. Egypt has an area of 386,000 square miles. Ancient Egyptians knew so much about embalming that some of their mummies are preserved for us to view in museums. The people of the world are concerned about saving these treasures, and others, now that the course of the Nile River is to be altered in the next decade. The Egyptians carried on commerce with neighboring nations. They studied and were successful with military strategy. For a time they lived under a system of government—controlled production. There is a wide area of fertile farmland along the Nile River. The early Egyptians built great halls and temples whose ruins still stand. Without modern machinery, they built the great pyramids near Cairo. Tourists come in great numbers each year to visit them. Today Cairo is the country's hurried and noisy commercial capital. Long before the birth of Christ, Egyptians knew how to turn wastelands into arable fields. They encouraged the arts and held great meetings where learned men gathered. They were always a religious people, holding to their beliefs in many gods until about 1400 B.C. when Aton, the single god who represented the life—giving power of the sun, was established as the Egyptian deity. In 1945, Egypt gained charter membership in the United Nations.

You should see quickly that this paragraph does not maintain unity but races from idea to idea, each loosely associated with Egypt. To analyze this paragraph, look first at the opening sentence. According to the basic diagram for the five-hundred-word paper in Chapter 2, this sentence is the topic sentence for the paragraph. That is, it specifically announces the subject the paragraph is going to be concerned with. This sentence gives the paragraph its single direction.

The opening sentence of the paragraph is: *Egypt was civilized long before there was any written history of the country.* If the remainder of the paragraph is to support this topic sentence and to be concerned with no other subject, the sentence must contain a word or phrase that can be called the *pointer* (the controlling attitude). It points to the single direction the remainder of the paragraph must follow to be unified. The topic sentence about Egypt has such a pointer. The word *civilized* controls the direction the paragraph will follow. If any sentence does not prove that Egypt was civilized, it does not belong in the paragraph, and it must be deleted.

For purposes of analysis, here are the sentences of the paragraph listed and numbered.

1. Egypt has an area of 386,000 square miles.
2. Ancient Egyptians knew so much about embalming that some of their mummies are preserved for us to view in museums.
3. It is these treasures that the world is concerned about saving.
4. Early Egyptians carried on commerce with neighboring nations.
5. They studied and were successful with military strategy.
6. They lived under a system of government-controlled production.
7. A wide area of fertile farmland edges the Nile.
8. The Egyptians built great halls and temples whose ruins still stand.
9. Without modern machinery, they built the great pyramids near Cairo.
10. Tourists come in great numbers each year to view Egypt's ruins.
11. Long before the birth of Christ, Egyptians knew how to turn wastelands into arable fields.
12. They encouraged the arts and held great meetings where learned men gathered.
13. They were always a religious people.
14. In 1945, Egypt gained charter membership in the United Nations.

These sentences need to be analyzed one at a time to see if they give support to the pointer word, *civilized,* in the topic sentence. Sentence 1, since it tells about the land area of Egypt, has nothing to do with Egypt's being civilized. It does not support the topic sentence. Delete it. Sentence 2, which tells about the Egyptian's knowledge of embalming, does support the idea that Egypt was civilized, so it may remain a part of the paragraph. Sentence 3 says that the world is concerned about saving Egyptian treasures, but because it discusses the present world's concern and not Egypt's past, it must be eliminated if the paragraph is to follow a single direction. Sentence 4, about Egypt's commerce with neighboring nations, can be retained because it does explain Egypt's past civilization, as can 5 and 6, about the early Egyptian's knowledge of military strategy and control of production. Sentence 7 must be left out; the fact that there is fertile farmland in Egypt does not prove that Egypt was civilized. But that the Egyptians built great halls, temples, and pyramids— Sentences 8 and 9—does prove their civilization, so they stay. The number of tourists who visit Egypt does not prove that Egypt was civilized because tourists often visit places that have not been civilized. So Sentence 10 must go. Sentence 11, which tells about the Egyptians' farming abilities, does indicate that ancient Egyptians were civilized, and this sentence can be retained. Any nation that cultivates the arts and holds conferences of learned men would be said to have a fairly high level of civilization. Sentence 12, then, should stay in the paragraph. Sentence 13, about the Egyptians' religious feelings, does not necessarily establish their civilization, for uncivilized peoples also have deep religious inclinations, and the sentence must be deleted. That Egypt gained charter membership in the United Nations has nothing to do with Egypt's past civilization. It is concerned with the present only, and so Sentence 14 will have to be left out.

Eliminating those sentences not supporting the topic sentence with its pointer leaves these:

2. The ancient Egyptians knew so much about embalming that some of their mummies are preserved for us to view in museums.
4. Early Egyptians carried on commerce with neighboring nations.
5. They studied, and were successful with, military strategy.
6. They lived under a system of government-controlled production.
8. The Egyptians built great halls and temples whose ruins still stand.
9. Without modern machinery they built the great pyramids near Cairo.
11. Long before the birth of Christ, Egyptians knew how to turn wastelands into arable fields.
12. They encouraged the arts and held great meetings where learned men gathered.

The remaining sentences can be put together into a unified paragraph, but it is neither well-developed nor readable.

Egypt was civilized long before there was any written history of the country. These ancient people knew so much about embalming that some of their mummies are preserved for us to view in museums. These people carried on commerce with neighboring nations. They studied, and were successful with, military strategy. They lived under a system of government-controlled production. The Egyptians built great halls and temples whose ruins still stand. Without modern machinery, they built the great pyramids near Cairo. Long before the birth of Christ, Egyptians knew how to turn wastelands into arable fields. They encouraged the arts and held great meetings where learned men gathered.

Now, with all the material that does not directly support the topic sentence deleted, the paragraph is at least unified. All the remaining sentences support the idea that ancient Egypt was civilized.

Here is one more paragraph to analyze for unity.

The composition student, in one year alone, sees enough waste to permanently destroy his sense of well-being. He sacrifices fifty minutes a day, five days a week, thirty-six weeks of the otherwise useful year. If his scooter is missing or if Mary

Lou wasn't home when he called last night or if breakfast was burned, it's hard for him to keep his mind on paper writing. No matter how full of vitality he is when he marches into the classroom, the essay writer droops away, physically exhausted, when the final bell rings. One of those "dedicated" teachers can turn a potential writer into a nervous, quaking mouse with her constant shoulder-tapping, headshaking, and advice-giving. Even the most enthusiastic student is ready to give up when he has to be listening always to reprimands about spelling and where to put the semicolon. Writing is bad enough, but writing under such a dictator who denies the classroom citizen his basic freedoms is unbearable. Writing materials are wasted, too. High school students have to buy ball point pens for one class, cartridge pens for another, and compasses and drawing pencils for others. It's sometimes pretty difficult to figure out how the Public Education System can call itself "free." Some of the less expensive notebooks fall apart when one semester is about half through, which means probably the notebook was not a wise choice after all.

The topic sentence of this paragraph is, as expected, the first sentence in the paragraph: *The composition student, in one year alone, sees enough waste to permanently destroy his sense of well-being.* The pointer here is the word *waste.* Any sentence that does not show the waste a composition student sees does not belong in this paragraph. This paragraph can also be analyzed by considering each sentence separately to determine if it is following the direction the pointer indicates. This time the sentences that do not follow this logical direction, that is, that do not support the idea of waste in composition, are marked through.

1. He sacrifices fifty minutes a day, five days a week, thirty-six weeks of the otherwise useful year.
2. ~~If his scooter is missing, or if Mary Lou wasn't at home when he called last night, or if breakfast was burned, its hard for him to keep his mind on paper writing.~~
3. No matter how full of vitality he is when he marches into the classroom, the essay writer droops away, physically exhausted, when the final bell rings.
4. ~~One of these "dedicated" teachers can turn a potential writer into a nervous, quaking mouse with her constant shoulder tapping, headshaking, and advice-giving.~~
5. ~~Even the most enthusiastic student is ready to give up when he has to be listening always to reprimands about spelling and where to put semi colons.~~
6. ~~Writing is bad enough, but writing under such a dictator who denies the classroom citizen his basic freedoms is unbearable.~~
7. Writing materials are wasted, too.

8. ~~High school students have to buy ball-point pens for one class, cartridge pens for another, and compasses and drawing pencils for~~ others.
9. ~~It's sometimes pretty difficult to figure out how the Public Education System can call itself "free."~~

This analysis indicates that only three sentences out of the whole paragraph follow the direction indicated by the pointer.

1. He sacrifices fifty minutes a day, five days a week, thirty-six weeks of the otherwise useful year.
2. No matter how full of vitality he is when he marches into the classroom, the essay writer droops away, physically exhausted, when the final bell rings.
3. Writing materials are wasted, too.

Put in their simplest form, these three sentences say that the composition student who writes in class *wastes* his time, his vitality, and his materials.

At this point, you are no doubt concluding that a paragraph is simply a short paper, as indeed it is. The methods of development are the same for both. Both have a single, central thought that is to be explored and developed. For the paper, that central thought is contained in the thesis statement; in the paragraph, it is contained in the topic sentence. As in the thesis statement, the predicate area of the topic sentence contains the pointer word or phrase, the controlling attitude that is the key to the content of the paragraph, and consequently to the single direction of the paragraph.

Look again, for instance, at the paragraph about the composition student and waste. It leads off with a topic sentence: *The composition student, in one year alone, sees enough waste to permanently destroy his sense of well-being.* In its predicate area, the single word *waste* is the pointer. The rest of the paragraph answers the question, *Why does the student see waste?* It gives three reasons: The student sees waste because he wastes (1) his time, (2) his vitality, and (3) his writing materials. The paragraph will be unified as long as it sticks to developing these three reasons.

A unified paragraph can be illustrated by a diagram as shown on page 75.

exercises

A. Pick out the pointer in each of the following topic sentences.
   1. We are a frustrated generation.
   2. Vague words can be useful.
   3. History has indicated that these rulers were unduly optimistic.
   4. Reasoning from analogy is dangerous.

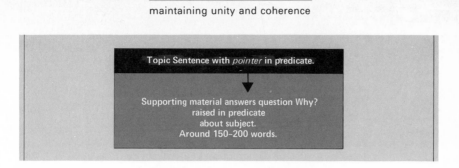

Topic Sentence with *pointer* in predicate.

Supporting material answers question Why?
raised in predicate
about subject.
Around 150–200 words.

5. The small car has suffered an astounding decline in popularity.
6. Reason is opposed to dogmatism.
7. Marriage demands cooperation between husband and wife.
8. Chaos reigned everywhere.
9. The good cook needs only a few simple rules.
10. The computer has changed management procedures.

B. For each of the following paragraphs, first write down the pointer in the topic sentence, and then list by number the sentences that support the pointer.

1.

(1) The family predicted that Jodie would some day make a fine veterinarian. (2) He had always shown a real tenderness toward animals. (3) Stray dogs and cats seemed to collect around the farm. (4) Once a beautiful trained Collie showed up and never left again, but that wasn't as surprising as the pair of sleek Siamese cats that moved in. (5) Those cats killed every rat in the barn inside of a week. (6) Animals all loved Jodie, too. (7) Folks used to drive out from town on Sundays to look at the whole families of painted buntings that ate with Jodie's chickens. (8) He kept Rhode Island Reds, mostly. (9) They say the bunting is rare in this part of the state. (10) Jodie was the quickest kid for learning things. (11) His teachers every one had nothing but praise for him. (12) He was never content to play until he had all of his homework done. (13) And he never missed a Sunday but once, going to church all through grammar school.

2.

(1) Elmer Dugan studied the coffee table. (2) There was something embarrassing about it, he realized. (3) The bowl of slightly melted Christmas candy should have been cleaned and refilled weeks ago. (4) Beside the candy jar sat an ashtray running over with bobby pins, bits of rickrack, and three spools of yellow thread. (5) Next to the ashtray was the current issue of Wild and Free magazine, the trashy literature his wife and her good friend next door read and traded constantly. (6) John Thompson was getting a little nervous. (7) Elmer hoped that John and his loud-mouthed wife would get bored enough to leave soon. (8)

But they didn't, and Elmer's gaze wandered to the second tier of the coffee table. (9) Adele Thompson was raving on about her eight-year-old's ballet accomplishments. (10) She could go on forever, and Mary kept encouraging the chatter. (11) Elmer counted eight magazines on the second shelf of the coffee table, and one darning egg. (12) He supposed the darning egg had its rights, but why couldn't Mary keep it on the thirty-nine-dollar, three-legged, Early American rock maple sewing stand she had insisted he buy for her last Christmas? (13) What he saw next, and couldn't believe, was a small, dead, and dried scorpion that Mary had reported killing three weeks ago. (14) The phone rang, a wrong number, and Adele Thompson started in on one of her favorite and most boring of all topics, the community and its telephone manners.

3.

(1) It was plain to the doctor that his day was going to be dreary. (2) Already twelve patients waited in the outer office. (3) The happy Tiller teenager giggled over a comic book as she rolled up her sleeve for her shot. (4) It was a joy to chat for a moment now and then with a happy, healthy, and well-adjusted kid. (5) It didn't improve the day, either, to be haunted by the difficult tonsillectomy facing him Monday morning. (6) By mid-afternoon poor old Mrs. Clark would come begging for another bottle of sugar pills to pull her through another half-dozen "heart attacks." (7) The Everson infant needed surgery, but there was no convincing his backward parents, and the telephone jangled constantly. (8) Both the Mumford twins were down with a dangerous relapse. (9) Not that he had really hoped to fish tomorrow, but already a cold mist was falling. (10) By morning his little world would be iced over. (11) At least Nurse Hearne wouldn't be around to annoy him. (12) Never again. (13) He had gladly let her go when she demanded a sizeable pay raise and an extra half-day off. (14) He meditated for the length of one cigarette, coughed, and studied the frayed edge of his office carpet. (15) Craig Adams' test had come back positive, of course, and young Mrs. Adams would go into hysterics. (16) It would take until closing time to calm her. (17) And the town drunk, in for another Cure, was at this moment passing out in the waiting room.

C. Read this paragraph by E. B. White.

It is a miracle that New York works at all. The whole thing is implausible. Every time the residents brush their teeth, millions of gallons of water must be drawn from the Catskills and the hills of Westchester. When a young man in Manhattan writes a letter to his girl in Brooklyn, the love message gets blown to her through pneumatic tube—pfft—just like that. The subterranean system of telephone cables, power lines, steam pipes, gas mains and sewer pipes is reason enough to abandon the island to the gods and the weevils. Every time an incision is made in the pavement, the noisy surgeons expose ganglia that are tangled beyond belief. By rights New York should have destroyed itself long ago, from panic or fire or rioting or failure of some vital supply line in its circulatory system or from some deep labyrinthine short circuit. Long ago the city should have experienced an insoluble traffic-snarl at some impossible bottleneck. It should have been wiped out by a plague starting in its slums or carried in by ships' rats. It should have been overwhelmed by the sea that licks at it on every side. The workers in its myriad cells should have succumbed to nerves, from the fearful pall of smoke-fog that drifts over every few days from Jersey, blotting out all light at noon, and leaving the high offices suspended, men groping and depressed, and the sense of world's end. It should have been touched in the head by the August heat and gone off its rocker.[1]

This paragraph maintains unity through its tight organization. To determine its organization, answer the following questions.

1. What is the topic sentence of the paragraph? State the limited subject area and the predicate area. What is the controlling attitude? What is the pointer?
2. Two principal reasons are given in support of the topic sentence and its pointer. What are they?
3. These two reasons also have supporting details to establish their validity. Write down the two principal reasons supporting the topic sentence, one at the head of one column and one at the head of another. Then, making two columns, list the supporting details for each of the two reasons.
4. a. List some of the words or phrases that seem to give the paragraph a relaxed, half-serious feeling.
   b. Does the writer maintain this feeling throughout the paragraph? How?
   c. On the basis of your answer to Question 2, what would you conclude about the author's attitude toward New York?
   d. On the basis of the pointer you found in the topic sentence and the feeling you examined in *a* and *b*, what else could you conclude
5. about the author's attitude toward New York?
   On the basis of your answers to Question 4, is unity of subject matter and support the only kind of unity in this paragraph? Be prepared to explain and support your answer. (If you have trouble with Questions 4 and 5, recheck the comments on page 69.)

COHERENCE   Unity is a matter of *logical direction*, coherence is a matter of *interlocking connection.* As you have seen, in any paragraph or paper unity is the logical thought relationship established between sentences and paragraphs, resulting from choosing one subject, one controlling attitude, one tone. Coherence is the effect of interlocking connection

[1]From pp. 24–25 in *Here is New York* by E. B. White. Copyright 1949 by E. B. White. Used by permission of Harper & Row, Publishers, and Hamish Hamilton, London.

provided by directional *signals* of many kinds, designed to guide the reader in the one direction established through unity. The key to coherence is the word *interlocking.* Through interlocking devices, the writer ties sentence to sentence and paragraph to paragraph. The result is coherence.

Consider, for instance, these two sentences taken out of context:

Mr. and Mrs. Vitek thought that under the circumstances there was only one course to take. The young man on my left saw several alternatives.

These two sentences are on the same subject, but the second sentence appears at first glance to be on another subject because of the mention of an unnamed *young man.* Readers must pause to get their bearings when they reach the second sentence because of this apparent change in subject. They are momentarily confused. Yet note that the addition of one word, *but,* before the first word in the second sentence avoids this confusion:

Mr. and Mrs. Vitek thought that under the circumstances there was only one course to take. But the young man on my left saw several alternatives.

Now, readers can go easily from the first sentence to the second with no pause, with no confusion. The two sentences are drawn together by the one word *but.* The use of such a transition word is one method of achieving coherence. But there are more. Some of these interlocking devices that serve as signals are grammatical, some are rhetorical, and some are mechanical. Let's look at the most important ones.

1. coherence through consistent point of view

Point of view is the position in time and place from which a writer views his or her subject. It is most often a grammatical problem, though it can also be a matter of physical perspective, as you will see shortly. Considered grammatically, point of view involves two basic elements:

1. The grammatical subject of each sentence (person)
2. The verb (tense as a time indicator)

A year spent teaching in the "shacks" adjacent to the city schools provides a unique education to any teacher. The classroom temperature gets awfully cold sometimes. You cannot imagine how hard it is to teach when it is forty—six degrees inside the build—

ing. Field mice race over the student lockers just as the teacher begins an important assignment. As summer approaches with its rising temperatures and increased noise level, the teacher has decided that she would gladly trade her unique experience for anyone's traditional classroom. The water fountain is so far away that it occupies a good part of the class time for teacher and students to get a drink.

This paragraph has unity. In the first sentence, *unique education* is the controlling attitude (pointer), and the remainder of the paragraph shows how the teacher gets this education from teaching in the shacks. But it is not coherent. The writer doesn't guide the reader smoothly from sentence to sentence. The reason should be obvious; the *grammatical signals* are at fault, causing point of view to shift from sentence to sentence. You can see the shift by picking out the subject of each sentence after the topic sentence. The subject of the second sentence is *temperature*. The subject of the third sentence is *you*. The fourth uses *field mice;* the fifth, *teacher;* and the sixth, *water fountain*. Therein lies the trouble with coherence in the paragraph. Because the paragraph obviously concerns a teacher and her experiences, each sentence should be about the teacher. A simple revision of this paragraph, using *teacher* (or its equivalent) as the subject of each sentence, greatly improves coherence.

A year spent teaching in the "shacks" adjacent to the city schools provides a unique education to any teacher. She learns to adjust to a temperature of forty-six degrees inside her classroom, a condition that persists although all the radiators are working at full capacity. She learns to cope with the problem of field mice racing over the student lockers just as she begins an important assignment. As summer approaches with its rising temperatures and increased noise level, the teacher has decided she would gladly trade her unique experience for anyone's traditional classroom. She learns to control her thirst and teaches this lesson to her students, since the water fountain is so far away it is almost impossible to get a drink.

Now the grammatical subject of all the sentences after the topic sentence is *teacher* (or its pronoun substitute, *she*), and as a result the point of view is consistent. Note that when you make the subject the same throughout, you also make other changes almost automatically, improving the whole paragraph.

But another kind of grammatical shift is possible. Suppose, for example, the writer became careless with verbs in the revised version and shifted the tenses unknowingly. The result could look something like this:

```
    A year spent teaching in the "shacks" adjacent to the city
schools provides a unique education to any teacher. She learns to
adjust to a temperature of forty-six degrees inside her class-
room, a condition that persisted although all the radiators were
working at full capacity. She learned to cope with the problem of
field mice racing over the student lockers just as she begins an
important assignment. As summer approached with its rising tem-
peratures and increased noise level, the teacher has decided she
would gladly trade her unique experience for anyone's traditional
classroom. She learns to control her thirst and teaches this
lesson to her students, since the water fountain was so far away
it is almost impossible to get a drink.
```

In this version, even though the grammatical subject remains consistent (in color), the time indicators (underscored verbs) shift from present to past for no logical reason. The result is again a lack of coherence because of a grammatical shift in point of view. The sentences don't interlock properly, do they?

2. coherence through pronoun reference

You should be able to see from the above discussion of the grammatical subjects in a paragraph that coherence through pronoun reference is closely related. Repeating the same noun too often in a paragraph, especially if repetition isn't needed for clarity, will usually bore the reader. With care, you can use a series of pronouns to do the job; the result is a series of interlocking, pointed grammatical signals clearly referring to an antecedent noun and providing logical continuity. The result is coherence through pronoun reference. Study the way in which the pronouns in the following paragraph create this interlocking effect of coherence.

> This doctrine of the relativity of morals, though it has recently received an impetus from the studies of anthropologists, was thus really implicit in the whole scientific mentality. It is disastrous for morals because it destroys their entire traditional foundation. That is why philosophers who see the danger signals, from the time at least of Kant, have been trying to give to morals a new foundation, that is, a secular or nonreligious foundation. This attempt may very well be intellectually

successful. Such a foundation, independent of the religious view of the world, might well be found. But the question is whether it can ever be a practical success, that is, whether apart from its logical validity and its influence with intellectuals, it can ever replace among the masses of men the lost religious foundation. On that question hangs perhaps the future of civilization.[2]

Note the number of times the pronoun *it* has been circled and tied to the *proper* antecedent noun. Any pronoun may be used to achieve this interlocking effect (*he, she, they, we, you,* or any other form). This method is a simple means of maintaining coherence. It is closely related to consistency in the point of view and to the next coherence technique, repetition of key words.

3. coherence through repetition of key words

Look again at the paragraph quoted in the previous section and notice the words now connected by lines.

This doctrine of the relatively of morals, though it has recently received an impetus from the studies of anthropologists, was thus really implicit in the whole scientific mentality. It is disastrous for morals because it destroys their entire traditional foundation. That is why philosophers who see the danger signal, from the time at least of Kant, have been trying to give to morals a new foundation, that is, a secular or nonreligious foundation. This attempt may very well be intellectually successful. Such a foundation, independent of the religious view of the world, might well be found. But the question is whether it can ever be a practical success, that is, whether apart from its logical validity and its influence with intellectuals, it can ever replace among the masses of men the lost religious foundation. On that question hangs perhaps the future of civilization.[3]

Note the obvious interlocking effect in this paragraph. The word *morals* appears in the first three sentences; *foundation,* the key word repeated most often, appears five times. *Question* appears twice, and *trying* and *attempt* are synonymous enough to be repetitions. This repetition of key words would probably not be noticed on a first reading, if the words were not marked as they are here, and that is the way it should be. But this method of achieving coherence, when the paragraph is analyzed, appears to be the chief means of holding the paragraph together.

[2]W. T. Stace, "Man Against Darkness," *The Atlantic Monthly.* Copyright 1948 by *The Atlantic Monthly.* Reprinted by permission.
[3]Stace, "Man Against Darkness."

The author of the above paragraph is an experienced and successful writer; he uses this method of achieving coherence well. The beginning writer, however, must use caution to prevent the method itself from becoming obvious and obtrusive. In this example, a student has attempted to use repetition of key words to achieve coherence.

> It is necessary for a student to receive a balanced education before he goes to college. This balanced education will help him decide what his goal is and how to achieve it. This balanced education will also help him if he fails in his endeavors by giving him the necessary background to start in another field of work. With this balanced education a student. . . .

In this example, the student has repeated *balanced education* four times in four sentences in an attempt at coherence. He has succeeded, however, only in annoying his reader by starting three of the four sentences with these same words. The student removed the annoying repetition and came up with this more successful version.

> A student entering college needs a balanced high school education. It will help him decide what his goal in college is and how he will achieve that goal. It will enable him to choose from more than one college curriculum, if he finds his first choice unsatisfactory or if he fails in that field. With it a student. . . .

4. coherence through spatial order of sentences

In using a spatial order to achieve coherence, a writer explains or describes objects as they are *arranged in space*. What this means is that the physical perspective or position from which the writer views these objects moves in an orderly, logical manner, giving the reader clear directional signals to follow from place to place. It is the nongrammatical aspect of point of view. (See Section 1, above.) The trick is to choose a specific position as your starting point and then direct the reader to follow your eye as it moves in an orderly pattern from the chosen point. For example, to describe a room, you might choose a position in a doorway as your starting point. You would begin by guiding the reader to the wall to your right as you describe it, then direct attention to the wall opposite you as you describe it, then describe the wall on your left, and finally take the reader into the center of the room as you describe what it contains. You could just as easily reverse this order, of course. The result is that you will impose an *order* on your descriptions, creating an interlocking effect and giving your descriptive paragraph greater coherence. Try following the description in this paragraph.

> The main characteristic of the little farm we had walked over was disorder. The winding, narrow road was bumpy and rough, and weeds grew rank and tall on each side of it. Near the barn stood a battered, unpainted tractor, plow, and rake. On the other side of the road, weeds sapping lifegiving substances from the soil were also growing among the small, withered cotton plants. The house needed paint and repairs. The steps and porch were rickety, and several of their boards were broken. The fence around the pasture was badly in need of repairs. The broken window panes in the house had pieces of tin and boards over them. On one side of the road lay bundles of grain decaying from long exposure to wind, rain, and sunshine. The wire was broken in many places, and the wooden posts, rotten at the ground, were supported by the rusty wire. The yard was littered with rubbish—tin cans, broken bottles, and paper. The barn lacked paint; its roof sagged and some shingles needed to be replaced. In the pasture, diseased with weeds and underbrush, grazed thin, bony cattle, revealing their need for more and better food and shelter.

This paragraph has unity. The pointer in the topic sentence is *disorder*. All the details in the paragraph indicate the disorder on the little farm. But it lacks coherence because the description of the disorder is presented to the reader at random; the writer has not taken a position from which to describe the disorder. The result is that the paragraph itself is disordered, as an analysis will quickly disclose. The second sentence, following the topic sentence, tells of the road and the weeds on each side of it. The third sentence talks about the barn. The fourth goes back to the road again. The fifth jumps to the house, and the sixth, to the pasture. The seventh returns to the house, and the eighth the road. The ninth describes the fence around the pasture; the tenth, the yard around the house; the eleventh, the barn; and the twelfth the pasture and cattle. But if the writer rearranges the sentences so that they present the objects on the farm as one would see them from a position of walking up the farm road to the house, the paragraph will be more coherent.

> The main characteristic of the little farm we had walked over
> was disorder. The winding, narrow road was bumpy and rough, and
> weeds grew rank and tall on each side of it. On one side of the road
> lay bundles of grain decaying from long exposure to wind, rain,
> and sunshine. On the other side, among the small, withered cotton
> plants, weeds sapped the soil. The fence around the pasture was
> badly in need of repair. The wire was broken in many places, and
> the wooden posts, rotted at the ground, were supported by the
> rusty wire. In the pasture, diseased with weeds and underbrush,
> grazed thin, bony cattle, revealing their need for more and bet-
> ter food and shelter. Near the barn stood a battered, unpainted
> tractor, plow, and rake. The barn itself lacked paint; its roof
> sagged and some of the shingles needed to be replaced. The house,
> too, needed paint and repairs. The steps and porch were rickety,
> and several of their boards were broken. A screen hung on one hinge.
> The broken window panes were mended with tin and boards. The yard was
> littered with rubbish—-tin cans, broken bottles, and paper.

The paragraph now has a logical spatial order; it takes the reader
from the road to either side of the road, to the pasture, and to the
barn and house. Having decided on the spatial order, the writer gives
the reader clear directional *signals: each side, on one side, on the
other side, around the pasture, in the pasture, near the barn, the
barn itself.* These signals are similar to those given by the transition
words discussed in Section 7.

5. *coherence through chronological order of sentences*

Chronological order means simply the order in which events happen.
This order is seen most often in narrative—writing that tells a
story—and narrative is often a part of expository writing, particularly
in illustrating a point. Narrative is not necessary, however, to the
use of chronological order. For instance, a chronological order may
be superimposed on the *revised* paragraph about the teacher, and
the coherence of the paragraph becomes even stronger. Look at this
further revision.

> A year spent teaching in the "shacks" adjacent to the city
> schools provides a unique education to any teacher. In the fall,
> the teacher learns to cope with the problem of field mice racing
> over the student lockers just as she begins an important assign-
> ment. In the winter, she learns to adjust to a temperature of

forty-six degrees, a condition that persists inside the classroom although all the radiators are working at full capacity. In the spring, she learns self-control of thirst and teaches this lesson to her students, since a trip to the water fountain occupies a good part of the class time. In summer, with its rising temperatures and increased noise level, she has decided that she would gladly trade the unique setting for anyone's traditional classroom.

This version, as indicated by the phrases shown in color, takes the teacher through the seasons in chronological order during the school year. Imposing the chronological order resulted in beneficial changes. Note here that there is not just one coherence device used in a paragraph but that methods are combined within any one paragraph.

6. coherence through related sentence patterns

Holding a paragraph together by repetition of sentence patterns within the paragraph is a relatively difficult means of achieving coherence because it requires more care in designing sentences, but it is an effective means. Look at this paragraph.

(1) To be genuinely civilized means to be able to walk straight and to live honorably without the props and crutches of one or another of the childish dreams which have so far supported men. (2) That such a life is likely to be ecstatically happy I will not claim. (3) But that it can be lived in quiet content, accepting resignedly what cannot be helped, not expecting the impossible, and thankful for small mercies, this I would maintain. (4) That it will be difficult for men in general to learn this lesson I do not deny. (5) But that it will be impossible I will not admit since so many have learned it already. [4]

Note that after the first sentence, the four remaining sentences are cast in the same form and are arranged in pairs, the second and third sentences constituting one pair, and the fourth and fifth sentences another. Look at the second sentence in the paragraph. It starts with a dependent clause *That such a life is likely to be ecstatically happy* and then finishes with a short independent clause *I will not claim.* The third sentence starts with a *but*, which ties it to the second sentence, and continues with exactly the same structure as that of the second sentence: *That it can be lived in quiet content . . . this I would maintain.* The first pair of sentences, joined together with *but*, is complete. The fourth sentence starts out exactly as the others,

[4]Stace, "Man Against Darkness."

85

That it will be difficult for men in general to learn this lesson, and finishes with the identical short independent structure as the others, *I do not deny.* The fifth sentence begins with a *but,* which ties it to the fourth. Then comes the same type of dependent clause that has started the last three sentences, *that it will be impossible* followed by the independent clause, *I will not admit.*

Such related sentence patterns are called *balance,* which can consist of *parallel structure, contrasting ideas* (antithesis), or both. Parallel structure is a matter of grammar and arrangement of words, so that successive words, phrases, clauses, or sentences form very nearly the same patterns; contrast results when ideas logically oppose one another. Here are some simple illustrations:

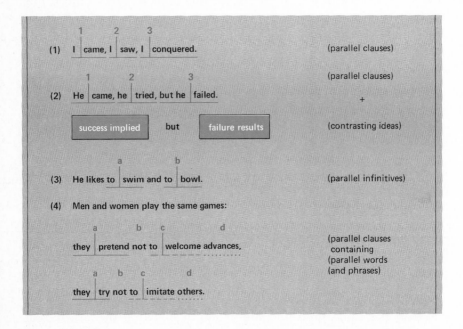

Balance is only one of many sentence patterns that can be used to add coherence. The author of the sample paragraph uses both types of balance to gain coherence, as illustrated in the following diagram.

To be genuinely civilized means to be able to walk straight and to live honorably without the props and crutches of one or another of the childish dreams which have so far supported men.

(2)   That such a life is likely to be
                       ecstatically happy
                                    ⌐ I will not claim.

        But

(3)   that it can be lived in quiet
                    content . . .
                            —this I would maintain.

(4)   That it will be difficult for men in
               general to learn this lesson
                            —I do not deny.

    But

(5)   that it will be impossible
                            —I will not admit
               since so many have learned it already.

Both the four dependent clauses and the four independent clauses following them are examples of parallel structure. The *but* which begins the third and fifth sentences introduces contrasting ideas that force the reader to weigh them against the ideas of the preceding sentences. These balanced patterns force the ideas into a closer relationship; they give the paragraph coherence by creating an interlocking effect.

7. coherence through transition words

Probably the easiest, and most abused, method of pulling together the thought in a passage is through the use of transition words. Transition words or phrases serve as signals to interlock sentences. They direct the reader from the thought of one sentence to that of another and indicate the relationship between the two sentences. An example of the way transition words work appeared earlier.

John and Mary Vitek thought that under the circumstances there was only one course to take. *But* the young man on my left saw several alternatives.

The word that interlocks the two sentences is *but,* which serves as a signal to the reader. The reader immediately expects a *contrast* to the thought of the previous sentence and proceeds without a pause *to see what that contrast is.* This word provides a *transition* between the two sentences and shows their relationship—contrast.

The English language furnishes a sufficient supply of transition words to express any relationship between two sentences. The diagram below illustrates some uses of transition words.

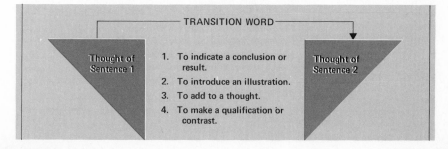

TRANSITION WORD

Thought of
Sentence 1

1. To indicate a conclusion or result.
2. To introduce an illustration.
3. To add to a thought.
4. To make a qualification or contrast.

Thought of
Sentence 2

TO INDICATE A CONCLUSION OR RESULT	EXAMPLES
therefore as a result consequently accordingly in other words to sum up thus then hence	1. *Therefore,* his action can be justified by valid explanation. 2. *As a result,* hollow, vain aristocracies have been established on American campuses. 3. *Consequently,* the number of qualified voters remains small.

TO INTRODUCE AN ILLUSTRATION	EXAMPLES
thus for example for instance to illustrate namely	1. *For example,* suppose I ask myself, "Will socialization ever come about?" 2. *For instance,* sophisticates can easily ridicule popular notions of government. 3. *Namely,* those who complain the loudest are often themselves the most guilty.

TO ADD A THOUGHT	EXAMPLES
second in the second place next likewise moreover again in addition finally similarly further in fact and	1. *Similarly,* the German university can profit by adopting the American practice of letting the student do most of the talking. 2. *Second,* human happiness feeds itself on a multitude of minor illusions. 3. Then *again* we work *and* strive because of the illusions connected with fame. 4. *Moreover,* the child assumes an attitude that he knows is false. 5. Effective leaders are effective communicators. *And* leadership positions demand higher salaries.

TO MAKE A QUALIFICATION OR CONTRAST	EXAMPLES
on the other hand nevertheless still on the contrary by contrast however but or nor	1. He was not, *however,* completely qualified for the task he had undertaken. 2. The Dobu, *by contrast,* are portrayed as virtually a society of paranoids. 3. *Nevertheless,* these theories do contain real insights into the nature of value judgments. 4. *On the contrary,* one should not blindly assume that our birthrate will continue to climb.

To use these transition words effectively, the beginning writer will have to consider each situation carefully, keeping in mind three general guide-lines.

1. Use transition words sparingly. The overuse of these words weakens writing style. Look at these sentences, for example:

James went to the resort planning to stay three weeks, but he became disgusted after the first day. *Consequently,* he packed and went home.

The weakness in this example is indicated by the string of three independent clauses joined together in thought by transition words. It is much better to delete at least one transition word and change one of the independent clauses to dependent.

James planned to stay three weeks at the resort, but after one day he became so disgusted that he packed and went home.

Here, the *consequently* has been dropped from the last sentence and the whole has been made into a dependent clause, *that he packed and went home.* This revision is an acceptable sentence; but why not add some meaningful details, and make a good sentence out of it:

Although James had planned a leisurely three weeks' stay at the resort, doing what he pleased when he pleased, he found himself caught up in so many planned activities—all arranged by a loud-mouthed, back-slapping "entertainment" leader—that he packed his bags and left in disgust after one day.

2. Use transition words to indicate logical relationships. Consider this example:

The College of Veterinary Medicine at Glory University is the only one in the state. Therefore, it is an excellent school.

In this example, the transition word *therefore* is not followed by a logical conclusion drawn from the evidence presented in the first sentence. Just because Glory University has the only College of Veterinary Medicine in the state, it does not necessarily follow that the college is excellent. This revision is much better:

Glory University's College of Veterinary Medicine, the only one in the state, is an excellent school.

Or consider this sentence:

Mary was healthy and robust, and she was born in Cincinnati in 1916.

The two parts of this sentence, *Mary was healthy and robust,* and *she was born in Cincinnati in 1916,* are not sufficiently related to be joined by a transition word. Apparently, the intent of this sentence is to comment on Mary's health for her age because her birth year is given. The place of her birth has nothing to do with any idea expressed in the sentence. The thought can be conveyed much better with a sentence such as this one:

At fifty-eight, Mary was healthy and robust.

Although the means of achieving coherence are considered separately in this chapter, it is not intended that only one of these means should be used in, say, one paragraph. The experienced writer may use several, even all, of them in any one paragraph to achieve the coherence he wants in his writing.

3. *Use relative and demonstrative words accurately.* Remember that certain adjectives and pronouns, when used accurately, create the interlocking effect of coherence. *These* important transition words include the following:

> *Relative pronouns:* who, which, what, that
> *Personal pronouns:* he, she, it, they, them, you
> *Demonstrative pronouns / adjectives:* this, that, these, those

These aren't the only ones, of course, *that* tie sentence parts and sentences together, but *they* probably are the most important. Use *them* with care, making certain *their* ties are unmistakably clear. Check the italicized words in *these* sentences; can *you* readily follow *their* ties? You will find additional information about pronouns and their antecedents on page 217.

exercises

A. Examine this paragraph to see if its coherence can be improved.
1 One of the fastest-growing fields of study is wildlife ecology. The growth
2 is reflected in the increasing college enrollment in agriculture and
3 forestry. Student interest in conservation is the dominant force behind
4 the new popularity of these and such related fields as range science,

5 oceanography, and marine sciences. In the last decade college-bound
6 students have become increasingly aware of the great need for profes-
7 sionals trained in the management and conservation of natural resources.
8 Reports from the Carnegie Commission on Higher Education suggest
9 that the job market for ecology-minded graduates will continue to grow
10 into the next decade.

ANALYSIS

1. Examine first the subjects of the sentences. The subject of the first
   sentence (line 1) is *one*. In the second it is *growth* (line 1), in the
   third it is *interest* (line 3), in the fourth, *students* (line 6), and in the
   fifth, *reports* (line 8). This examination shows that the student should
   maintain a more consistent point of view to give the paragraph coherence.
2. Examine the paragraph for evidence of other methods of maintaining
   coherence. There is some repetition of key words: *Growth* (line 1) and
   grow (line 9) echo *growing* (line 1), *fields* (line 4) repeats *fields* (line
   1), *students* (line 6) repeats *student* (line 3), *conservation* appears in
   lines 3 and 7, *increasingly* (line 6) echoes *increasing* (line 2), and *ecology*
   appears in lines 1 and 9. Despite these echoes, the paragraph lacks
   coherence because the ideas have no clear *direction*, there are no
   transition words, there is no pronoun reference, and there are no related
   sentence patterns. Obviously, the coherence of this paragraph can be
   improved. Consider this revision.

1 The marked increase in the number of students enrolled in the field
2 of wildlife ecology has caused it to become one of the fastest-growing
3 professions. This increase also reflects the growing need for professionals
4 trained in the management and conservation of natural resources.
5 Moreover, in the last decade college-bound students have become in-
6 creasingly aware of this need. Thus, the resulting student interest in
7 conservation has also become the dominant force behind the new
8 popularity of such related fields as range science, oceanography, and
9 marine sciences. Furthermore, reports from the Carnegie Commission
10 on Higher Education suggest that the job market for ecology-minded
11 professionals will continue to grow into the next decade.

Note the number of methods used to achieve coherence in this
version. The most important change is in *direction:* There is a more
logical movement from sentence to sentence, partly because the ideas
have been rearranged and partly because sentence subjects are repeated.
The subject of the first two sentences, for example, is *increase* (lines
1 and 3), while the subject of sentence four, *student interest* (line 6),
echoes the subject of the third sentence, *college-bound students* (line
5). Moreover, the paragraph contains a number of transition words—*also*
(line 3), *moreover* (line 5), *thus* (line 6), *also* (line 7), and *furthermore*
(line 9). Two modifiers (*this* in lines 3 and 6) and a pronoun reference
(*it* in line 2) also add to the coherence. The paragraph repeats all the
key words in the original version, but this time they appear in an
order that improves the coherence. Note particularly the following
sequence: *students* (line 1), *professions* (line 3), *professionals* (line 3),

students (line 5), *student interest* (line 6), and *professionals* (line 11). A similar repetition is seen in the use of *increase* and *growing,* and *ecology, need,* and *conservation.* Of 113 words in the paragraph, 30, or 26.5 percent, are key words repeated to maintain coherence. This is not an unusually high percentage. Explain why this version of the paragraph would (or would not) work as a developmental paragraph in a paper. How could you improve it?

B. In the following paragraphs, find the coherence devices and be able to point them out. Lines of the paragraphs are numbered for your convenience.

1.

1 I have given the impression that the Farm was remote, but this is
2 not strictly true. Not half a mile on each side of us was another farmhouse,
3 and clustering near the one to the east were three or four cottages.
4 We formed, therefore, a little community, remote as such; in Doomsday
5 Book, we had been described as a hamlet. The nearest village was
6 two or three miles away, but to the south, so that it did not count
7 for much until we began to go to school, which was not until toward
8 the end of the period of which I write. Northward our farm road ran
9 through two fields and then joined the highroad running east and west;
10 but eastward this road soon turned into a road running north and
11 south, down which we turned northward again, to the Church five
12 miles away, and to Kirby, our real metropolis, six miles away.[5]

2.

1 The farmhouse was a square stone box with a roof of vivid red tiles;
2 its front was to the south, and warm enough to shelter some apricot
3 trees against the wall. But there was no traffic that way: All our exits
4 and entrances were made on the north side, through the kitchen, and
5 I think even our grandest visitors did not disdain that approach. Why
6 should they? On the left as they entered direct into the kitchen was
7 an old ash dresser; on the right a large open fireplace, with a great
8 iron kettle hanging from the reckan, and an oven to the near side
9 of it. A long deal table, glistening with a honey gold sheen from much
10 scrubbing, filled the far side of the room; long benches ran down each
11 side of it. The floor was flagged with stone neatly outlined with a
12 border of some softer yellow stone, rubbed on after every washing.
13 Sides of bacon and plum dusky hams hung from the beams of the
wooden ceiling.[6]

3.

1 By day it was the scene of intense bustle. The kitchenmaid was down
2 by five o'clock to light the fire; the laborers crept down in stockinged

[5]From *The Innocent Eye* by Herbert Read. Copyright © 1947 by Herbert Read. Reprinted by permission of Harold Ober Associates, Incorporated.
[6]Read, *The Innocent Eye.*

3 feet and drew on their heavy boots; they lit candles in their horn lanthorns
4 and went out to the cattle. Breakfast was at seven, dinner at twelve,
5 tea at five. Each morning of the week had its appropriate activity:
6 Monday was washing day, Tuesday ironing, Wednesday and Saturday
7 baking, Thursday "turning out" upstairs and churning, Friday "turning
8 out" downstairs. Every day there was the milk to skim in the dairy—the
9 dairy was to the left of the kitchen and as big as any room in the
10 house.[7]

4.

1 At dinner, according to the time of the year, there would be from
2 five to seven farm laborers, the two servant girls, and the family,
3 with whom, for most of the time, there was a governess—a total of
4 from ten to fifteen mouths to feed every day. The bustle reached its
5 height about midday; the men would come in and sit on the dresser,
6 swinging their legs impatiently; when the food was served, they sprang
7 to the benches and ate in solid gusto, like animals. They disappeared
8 as soon as the pudding had been served, some to smoke a pipe in
9 the saddle room, others to do work which could not wait. Then all
10 the clatter of washing up rose and subsided. More peaceful occupations
11 filled the afternoon. The crickets began to sing in the hearth. The
12 kettle boiled for tea. At nightfall a candle was lit, the foreman or
13 the shepherd sat smoking in the armchair at the fireside end of the
14 table. The latch clicked as the others came in one by one and went
15 early up to bed.[8]

5.

1 Many critics of our society have said that we lack standards. This
2 has been said so often by preachers and by the makers of commencement
3 addresses that we have almost stopped asking what, if anything, it
4 means to say that our society "lacks standards." But that we do lack
5 standards for welfare and standards for education is obvious. Welfare
6 turns into vulgar materialism because we have no standard by which
7 to measure it. Education fails because it also refuses to face the
8 responsibility of saying in what education consists. Both tend to become
9 merely what people seem to want.[9]

6.

1 Duration is not the only political virtue, but it is a virtue. Constitutions,
2 by their name and function, can be deemed successes only if they last
3 long enough to give stability to the political life of the society they
4 are supposed to serve. The American Constitution passes that test.
5 But a constitution can survive in a form that makes it less and less
6 adequate for the needs of the society it purports to serve, and either

---

[7] *Ibid.*

[8] *Ibid*

[9] Joseph Wood Krutch, "Life, Liberty, and the Pursuit of Welfare," *Saturday Evening Post,* July 15, 1961. Copyright 1961 by The Curtis Publishing Company.

7 that society is cribbed, cabined and confined, held within an armor
8 that forbids adaptation or growth, or the constitution is disregarded
9 and the true political forces grow up beside it, paying only lip service
10 to the antique and obsolete forms, as Prussia grew up in the carapace
11 of the constitution of the Holy Roman Empire of the German People.
12 That has not happened in the United States. The Constitution is still
13 at the center of American government and politics. It must be reckoned
14 with every day by the President, by the Congress, by the courts, by
15 labor, by business. It has proved sufficiently adaptable to permit the
16 expansion of the thin line of newly emancipated colonies along the
17 Atlantic seaboard to the Pacific, the multiplication of the population
18 fifty-fold, and the extension of the armed power of the United States
19 almost around the globe. It has permitted the growth of these remote
20 and, in 1789, impoverished colonies to an economic power and a material
21 wealth unprecedented in human history. And it has done all this without
22 distorting its fundamental character or denying the political theories
23 and system of values on which it was based. [10]

7.

1 Studies serve for delight, for ornament, and for ability. Their chief
2 use for delight, is in privateness and retiring; for ornament, is in
3 discourse; and for ability, is in the judgement and disposition of business.
4 For expert men can execute, and perhaps judge of particulars, one
5 by one; but the general counsels, and the plots and marshalling of
6 affairs, come best from those that are learned. To spend too much
7 time in studies is sloth; to use them too much for ornament is affection;
8 to make judgement wholly by their rules, is the humour of a scholar.
9 They perfect nature, and are perfected by experience: for natural abilities
10 are like natural plants, that need pruning by study; and studies
11 themselves do give forth directions too much at large, except they be
12 bounded in by experience. Crafty men contemn studies, simple men
13 admire them, and wise men use them; for they teach not their own
14 use; but that is a wisdom without them, and above them, won by
15 observation. Read not to contradict and confute; nor to believe and
16 take for granted; not to find talk and discourse; but to weigh and
17 consider. Some books are to be tasted, others to be swallowed, and
18 some few to be chewed, and digested; that is, some books are to be
19 read only in parts; others to be read, but not curiously; and some few
20 to be read wholly, and with diligence and attention. . . . [11]

REVIEW TERMS

The skills you have learned in this chapter are reflected in the terms
listed below; test your understanding of them to improve your mastery
of unity and coherence.

[10] From D. W. Brogan, *Politics in America.* Copyright 1954 by D. W. Brogan. Used by permission of Harper & Row, Publishers, and Hamish Hamilton, Ltd.
[11] Francis Bacon, "Of Studies." Many editions.

A. Unity, coherence, directional signals, pointer, logical direction, interlocking connection, interlocking devices, tone, rhetorical signals, grammatical signals, point of view, key words, transition words, synonyms, spatial order, chronological order, balance, parallelism, contrast

B. Grammatical subject, limited subject, pronoun, antecedent, pronoun reference, relative pronoun, personal pronoun, demonstrative pronoun, phrase, clause, adjective, demonstrative adjective, dependent clause, independent clause, infinitive

writing
paragraphs

d iscovery, organization, style. These are the three main subjects of this book—if style is understood to include mechanics as well as rhetorical techniques. In Chapter 1 you learned the value of communicating without misunderstanding. In the Chapter 2 you learned about the organization of the whole paper—its basic structure, its main parts, the relationship of the parts to the whole. In Chapter 3 you learned about discovering and limiting a general subject, and about writing a complete thesis statement. You learned how to get started. The chapter you just finished showed you how to give your paper unity and coherence through the techniques of single logical direction and interlocking connection. The next step is to learn how to write the developmental paragraphs that make up the paper.

IN SEARCH OF THE PARAGRAPH   The chapter on organization showed the paragraph to be the basic building block in writing. One way to define the paragraph is to describe it as a series of carefully connected sentences presenting relevant ideas on a single subject. This is what thesis statements, topic sentences, unity, and coherence are all about. This definition, however, although it fits most writing, doesn't explain the paragraph variations professional writers often use. It is the definition of what many books call a "standard paragraph"; it is an accepted convention.

But good writers also see the paragraph as a convenience—for the writer as well as the reader. The experienced writer knows, for example, that a long paragraph will probably drive away the average reader. No one likes to read a page with no paragraph breaks. And so writers often break paragraphs that normally would function as standard building blocks. But doesn't this destroy continuity and fragment unity? Not necessarily.

In writing, the techniques of single direction and interlocking connection (unity and coherence) suggest a fundamental thought process that usually functions whether or not the boundaries of a standard paragraph are observed. Any good sentence—and especially a thesis sentence or a topic sentence—presents to the reader a promise or commitment to be kept. Consider, for example, these two sentences.

Pollution is a serious problem we all face.
Violence provides no answer to personal problems.

Most readers would not normally *expect* to find these two sentences next to each other in a paragraph, since the second can't be readily associated with the first. Most readers would expect the first sentence

97

to be followed by one commenting on how we all face the problem of serious pollution. The *expectation* created by the second sentence is that it will be followed by some comment on the uselessness of violence.

Meaningful, rational thought processes *naturally* include this continuity or chain of meaning, no matter where the writer puts paragraph breaks. Here, for example, is how a five-sentence paragraph on "Subject A" might be represented.

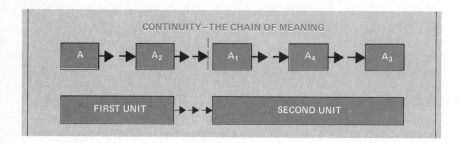

What the diagram tries to show is that if **A** is the sentence about pollution, then the first thoughts following it are *likely* to be about pollution, though perhaps not in the best order. Break this series anywhere you wish, and the resulting two units (paragraphs of convenience) still say something about "Subject A." This process of natural association lets a writer use paragraph breaks for convenience—to keep the reader's eye interested, to emphasize the main ideas in one unit of an argument, to create a pleasing effect on the page, and so on. Check any newspaper and you'll find that paragraph units of this kind will contain a number of related statements, even though they may not fit the definition of a standard paragraph given above.

In the carefully organized papers you are asked to write, however, avoid breaking paragraphs merely for the sake of convenience. Build each paragraph so that it sticks to a single, limited subject presented in a series of sentences with a logical, coherent sequence. Save the paragraph of convenience for other kinds of writing.

You have already studied several kinds of paragraphs—introductory, developmental, concluding. In this chapter you will learn more about the uses of introductory paragraphs, many ways of presenting the information of developmental paragraphs, and some additional tips about concluding paragraphs. You will practice the basic, direct introductory paragraph first; then you'll be introduced to some other techniques. And you will learn to develop paragraphs by use of *detail,* by use of *definition,* by use of *illustration* and *example,* by use of *comparison* and *contrast,* and by use of *reasons.*

INTRODUCTORY PARAGRAPHS Have you ever thought about how much information you've received by the time you've read through the first sentences of a writer's introductory pitch? Do you hear someone talking? Someone who seems aware of you as an audience? What is the writer's attitude toward his audience and subject—bold or hesitant, quiet or loud, formal or informal, serious or playful, expository or argumentative? Do you get a sense of order and direction? How specifically does the writer state the subject? Although you will concentrate on only two major purposes of the introductory paragraph of the five-hundred-word paper, you should be aware of some of the other problems and possibilities.

A paper's opening paragraph is supposed to *introduce:* Quite independently of the paper's title, the introductory paragraph leads the reader into the subject and points him in a specific direction. Although both the leading and the pointing can be done in many ways, in all of the first papers you write, concentrate on two purposes:

1. In a general statement introduce the subject of the paper.
2. In the last sentence of the paragraph specifically introduce the thesis statement to be supported in the developmental paragraphs that follow.

The introductory paragraph need be only about fifty to seventy-five words, long enough to establish the subject of the paper. A paper longer than five hundred words might require a longer introduction reviewing the background of the subject to be discussed. In short papers, however, there is no space for lengthy exploration of the subject; state your subject as efficiently as possible. Then, you can use the allotted space to best advantage in developing and supporting your thesis.

An introductory paragraph starts with a broad, general statement introducing the subject of the paper, and then qualifies this subject statement by narrowing it to the specific thesis statement of the paper. This construction can best be seen in the diagram on the next page, a simplified version of the diagram showing the "funnel effect" (page 18).

Then, look at an example of a student's introductory paragraph that follows this pattern.

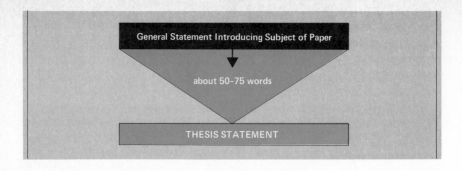

Women find various reasons for marrying: because it is convenient, or desirable, or highly acceptable to society, or sometimes even because it is necessary. But whatever her reasons, I
contend that a woman should not marry a college student.

Note that this paragraph starts with a general statement about the reasons women marry and in thirty-nine words reduces this statement to a specific thesis statement to be established in the remainder of the paper. It wastes no time in getting to the main business of the paper supporting the thesis statement in the developmental paragraphs.

Here is another example that does the same thing in seventy-eight words.

High school students, usually not avid readers of comic
books, sometimes resort to substituting "classic" comic books for
required reading. Basically honest, many of these students, under
pressure of heavy assignments and extracurricular activities,
think of the classic comic as merely a shortcut in completing an
assignment. Although these students may be able to write a plot
summary from their reading of the classic comic, they are cheating themselves when they take this easy way out.

Although this is the basic pattern you will follow at first, you will eventually want to try other kinds of introductory paragraphs and to practice ways of making your reader receptive to your ideas. You will remember that the diagram on the "funnel effect" suggests that the introductory paragraph should try to gain reader interest and acceptance before stating the thesis. Chapter 2 also reminds you that the end position for the thesis statement of the introductory paragraph is quite arbitrary. You could put it at the beginning of the paragraph or omit it entirely, letting readers determine for themselves the logical point supported by the evidence presented in the paper. The opening paragraph does more than merely introduce the subject in a thesis statement; it should establish tone and common ground with the reader, and it provides a "blueprint" for the ideas to follow.

Here, then, is a more complete summary of the basic purposes of introductory paragraphs:

1. To introduce the subject (general statement)
2. To present a thesis statement with an argumentative bias (logical appeal)
3. To give a "blueprint" suggesting the order of ideas
4. To get the reader's interest (emotional appeal)
5. To get the reader to accept the writer and the writer's views (ethical appeal)[1]

For the most part, you will concentrate on making your paragraph reflect the first two of these. The third reminds you that the order of the "because statements" in the thesis paragraph is usually the order they will follow in the developmental paragraphs. The result is a greater sense of direction for the reader. The last two purposes take care and practice, but they also give you a chance to be convincingly creative. First let's look at ethical appeal.

using ethical appeal

Your papers will be more successful if you always keep your audience in mind. Often, clear and well-supported logic is not enough to get the reader to say both "I understand" and "I agree." You can give your ideas an added push if you try to project a definite, positive image of yourself and your character. Here are a number of well-known ways to get your reader to accept and to believe you:

1. Use unemotional, calm, unprejudiced language.
2. Try to establish a common ground of understanding with your reader.
3. Praise your opposition (with restraint).
4. Give up part of your argument, admit that your position is weak (only in a minor way).

[1]Derived from the word *ethos,* the term *ethical appeal* is used to describe the appeal used in writing (and speech) that comes from the apparent, projected *character* of the writer himself. To get his audience to trust him and to believe what he says, the writer (or speaker) tries to create in his work the *impression* that he is fair, or good, or intelligent, or sympathetic, or honest. He may not actually possess these qualities, but if his work *appears* to have them he could still convince his audience to accept him and believe what he says. Ethical appeal works best when the writer really possesses the qualities he tries to project in his work, when he really believes what he is saying.

5. Tell the reader of your qualifications, preferably indirectly.

The words you use reveal your prejudices more than you think. Suppose, for example, you want to convince an audience of teenage readers that smoking marijuana is dangerous. Consider the effects of these two opening paragraphs.

A.

> Young people are sadly mistaken if they think smoking marijuana is a funride to freedom. A person is stupid to think that the only payment is the cost of the weed. Anyone who thinks at all knows that marijuana is dangerous because the stuff is illegal, it creates in the addicted user a sense of psychological dependence, and it turns users into bums who become dropouts from society.

Now compare Paragraph *A* with *B:*

B.

> Smoking marijuana is not an easy way to freedom. The user always pays more than just the cost of the drug. Repeated use of marijuana is dangerous because it is illegal, it creates in the user a sense of psychological dependence, and it may turn users away from active participation in the community.

Paragraph *B* tries to tone down the prejudiced judgments of the first version by removing such negative words as *sadly mistaken, fun-ride, stupid, weed, thinks at all, stuff, addicted,* and *bums.* On the other hand, the first version might very well catch the favorable attention of a group of mothers who have seen their children arrested, dropped from school, and sent to jail. A calm tone is best if you want to appear *objective.*

Suppose Paragraph *B* started this way:

C.

> I'm told it is fun to smoke marijuana, and I'm sure that is true. I'm told that legalizing the use of alcohol is not the cause of its abuse, that the same argument holds for marijuana, and I'm sure that is true. I'm told, also, that scientists have not proved that smoking marijuana harms the body, and I'm sure that, also, is true. But just because there is truth and sincerity in all these statements does not mean that smoking marijuana is not dangerous. [Now, continue with Paragraph B.]

The writer of Paragraph *C* is trying to be personal, trying to establish a common ground of understanding with readers; he says he agrees with a number of opposing arguments. By saying that these arguments are "true" and "sincere," he is praising the opposition and giving up part of his own argument (using marijuana is *dangerous*). Even with the toned-down language of Paragraph *B* following it, Paragraph *C* would probably not convince too many readers. Try to decide why.

The writer of these three paragraphs could add still one more ingredient to try to convince readers that he and his views are acceptable. He could mention or "project" his qualifications—personal experience, research, special skill. Study the following illustrations and try to decide what you would probably assume about the writer of each. Be prepared to support your opinion.

1. In the last issues of *Science* and *Science News* I read that medical authorities dispute the harmful effects of *Nicotiana glauca.* And the most recent issue of my *Christian Science Monitor* described corroborating research information.

2. Yesterday, both *Business Week* and *U.S. News and World Report* contained articles predicting that the inflation rate will increase to more than nine percent next year. A recent issue of *The Wall Street Journal* echoes this view.

3. The last issues of *Time* and *Newsweek* both contained real good articles about pot smoking. The articles point out that experts disagree about the harmful effects of pot. Recently I saw a newspaper article that said the same thing.

4. Many people disagree about the harmful effects of using marijuana. All the students I've talked to also disagree, and so do some of the so-called authorities.

With which writers are you more likely to agree? Why? Is the credibility of writers simply a matter of the kind of authority they use to support their views? What effect is produced by the kind of language used by each writer? What we assume, accurately or not, about each writer is based on what they seem to reveal about themselves; it is tied to the *ethical appeal* they seem to project.

Now, take another look at Paragraph *C*, above, and try to add two or three sentences to the beginning to improve the writer's credibility, his ethical appeal. To get additional ideas, study the following four introductory paragraphs from "In Favor of Capital Punishment," written by a professional writer.

IN FAVOR OF CAPITAL PUNISHMENT

A passing remark of mine in the *Mid-Century* magazine has brought me a number of letters and a sheaf of pamphlets against capital punishment. The letters, sad and reproachful, offer me the choice of pleading ignorance or being proved insensitive. I am asked whether I know that there exists a worldwide movement for the abolition of capital punishment which has everywhere enlisted able men of every profession, including the law. I am told that the death penalty is not only inhuman but also unscientific, for rapists and murderers are really sick people who should be cured, not killed. I am invited to use my imagination and acknowledge the unbearable horror of every form of execution.

I am indeed aware that the movement for abolition is widespread and articulate, especially in England. It is headed there by my old friend and publisher, Mr. Victor Gollancz, and it numbers such well-known writers as Arthur Koestler, C. H. Rolph, James Avery Joyce and Sir John Barry. Abroad as at home the profession of psychiatry tends to support the cure principle, and many liberal newspapers, such as the *Observer,* are committed to abolition. In the United States there are at least twenty-five state leagues working to the same end, plus a national league and several church councils, notably the Quaker and the Episcopal.

The assemblage of so much talent and enlightened goodwill behind a single proposal must give pause to anyone who supports the other side, and in the attempt to make clear my views, which are now close to unpopular, I start out by granting that my conclusion is arguable; that is, I am still open to conviction, *provided* some fallacies and frivolities in the abolitionist argument are first disposed of and the difficulties not ignored but overcome. I should be glad to see this happen, not only because there is pleasure in the spectacle of an airtight case, but also because I am not more sanguinary than my neighbor and I should welcome the discovery of safeguards—for society *and* the criminal—other than killing. But I say it again, these safeguards must really meet, not evade or postpone, the difficulties I am about to describe. Let me add before I begin that I shall probably not answer any more letters on this arousing subject. If this printed exposition does not do justice to my cause, it is not likely that I can do better in the hurry of private correspondence.

I readily concede at the outset that present ways of dealing out capital punishment are as revolting as Mr. Koestler says in his harrowing volume, *Hanged by the Neck.* Like many of our prisons, our modes of execution should change. But this objection to barbarity does not mean that capital punishment—or rather, judicial homicide—should not go on. The illicit jump we find here, on the threshold of the inquiry, is characteristic of the abolitionist and must be disallowed at every point. Let us bear in mind the possibility of devising a painless, sudden and dignified death, and see whether its administration is justifiable.[2]

These four paragraphs comprise only the *introduction* to a much longer essay which maintains the same ethical appeal throughout. In what ways does the writer reveal himself? His age, education, knowledge?

[2]Jacques Barzun, "In Favor of Capital Punishment." Reprinted from *The American Scholar,* Vol. 31, No. 2, Spring 1962. Copyright 1962 by the United Chapter of Phi Beta Kappa. By permission of the publishers.

Is he well known? Make a list of the words the writer uses that you probably wouldn't because they aren't in your active vocabulary. What kind of "voice" do these words convey? Point out at least three specific ways in which the writer tries to get on common ground with the readers who oppose his views.

Clearly, an introduction as long as this one would be out of place in a short paper. But the methods it uses to project the right ethical appeal could be applied to a one- or two-paragraph introduction to a much shorter paper. And there is no reason why you can't use some of its techniques in the one-paragraph introduction diagrammed for the five-hundred-word theme.

Remember, good writing demands *honesty* as well as supporting facts. If you assume that "anything goes" in order to convince your readers, you are likely to lose them when they spot insincerity because you overwork ethical appeal. Ethical appeal works best when writers really possess the qualities they try to project in their work (intelligence, fairness, objectivity, for example), when they really believe what they are saying.

creating reader interest

A final point: Introductory paragraphs should also try to get the reader's interest. Usually this means trying to get the reader involved psychologically or emotionally. If you compare the following opening paragraphs with the diagram for the introductory paragraph, you will discover changes in the pattern as well as other techniques of creating reader interest.

D.

Strictness or permissiveness? This looms as a big question for many new parents. A great majority of them find the right answer in a little while. For a few parents it remains a worrisome question, no matter how much experience they've had.

I may as well let the cat out of the bag right away as far as my opinion goes and say that strictness or permissiveness is not the real issue. Goodhearted parents who aren't afraid to be firm when it is necessary can get good results with either moderate strictness or moderate permissiveness. On the other hand, a strictness that comes from harsh feelings or a permissiveness that is timid or vacillating can each lead to poor results. The real issue is what spirit the parent puts into managing the child and what attitude is engendered in the child as a result.[3]

[3]From "Strictness or Permissiveness?" from *Baby and Child Care* by Dr. Benjamin Spock. Copyright 1945, 1946, 1957 by Benjamin Spock, M.D. Reprinted by permission of Pocket Books/A Division of Simon & Schuster, Inc.

Many writers use a provocative question to get started and to arouse the curiosity and interest of the reader. Here the author sets up a contrast to lead his reader into the work, withholding the thesis statement until the end of the second paragraph. But using a question or a series of questions to arouse interest and isolate a problem should be handled with restraint to keep the introduction from sounding insincere and overdone. Did you notice the series of questions used to introduce the "Introductory Paragraph" section at the beginning of this chapter?

If your subject is important and current, sometimes you can state it strongly in the first sentence of the introductory paragraph and get your reader involved immediately. Look at this opening to the first chapter of a highly successful book.

E.

Time talks. It speaks more plainly than words. The message it conveys comes through loud and clear. Because it is manipulated less consciously, it is subject to less distortion than the spoken language. It can shout the truth where words lie.[4]

The author boldly asserts the thesis of his chapter in a two-word sentence stating that time is one of the silent languages. Perhaps a weakness in this beginning is that the reader gets well into the chapter before he understands the significance of the chapter title, "The Voices of Time."

There are, of course, many other ways of introducing the subject and pointing the way for the reader. You can begin by logically dividing the subject into its parts and then telling your reader which you will emphasize. You let the reader follow your thinking process: *Flight? Flight of birds, flight of planes, flight of animals, flight of men, flight from freedom, flight to avoid punishment, flight from responsibility.* Or you can present an explanation or justification of your paper, particularly if it is one based on personal observation. Some writers lead up to a thesis statement by beginning the introductory paragraph with a relevant quotation or incident, a striking illustration, or an anecdote. Others begin by stating a view which they will oppose, creating interest through contrast. Here are two final illustrations.

F.

The philosopher Diogenes lived in a tub in the market place. He owned the clothes on his back and a wooden cup; one morning, when he saw

---

[4]Edward T. Hall, "The Voices of Time," from *The Silent Language.* Copyright 1959 by Edward T. Hall. Reprinted by permission of Doubleday & Company, Inc.

a man drinking out of his hands, he threw away the cup. Alexander the Great came to Athens, and went down to the market place to see Diogenes; as he was about to leave he asked, "Is there anything I can do for you?" "Yes," said Diogenes, "you can get out of my light."

At different times, and in different places, this story has meant different things. . . .[5]

G.

Childhood used to end with the discovery that there is no Santa Claus. Nowadays, it too often ends when the child gets his first adult, the way Hemingway got his first rhino, with the difference that the rhino was charging Hemingway, whereas the adult is usually running from the child. This has brought about a change in the folklore and mythology of the American home, and of the homes of other offspring-beleaguered countries. The dark at the top of the stairs once shrouded imaginary bears that lay in wait for tiny tots, but now parents, grandparents, and other grown relatives are afraid there may be a little darling lurking in the shadows, with blackjack, golf club, or .32-caliber automatic.

The worried psychologists, sociologists, anthropologists, and other ologists, who jump at the sound of every backfire or slammed door, have called our present jeopardy a "child-centered culture." Every seven seconds a baby is born in the United States, which means that we produce, every two hours, approximately five companies of infantry. I would say this amounts to a child-overwhelmed culture, but I am one of those who do not intend to surrender meekly and unconditionally. There must be a bright side to this menacing state of civilization, and if somebody will snap on his flashlight, we'll take a look around for it.[6]

Paragraph *F* uses an interesting anecdote to catch the reader. Illustration *G* gives the first two paragraphs of a serious article on children. Despite its serious subject, it is imaginative and humorous. It wins readers over with its informal tone, teases them with a "fake" thesis statement at the end of the first paragraph, and then provides a genuine, contrasting thesis statement at the end of the second paragraph. The first *two* paragraphs provided the "introduction" to the article. The main aim of the first one is to create reader interest by overstatement and emotional appeal, with such statements as "gets his first adult," "running from the child," "offspring-beleaguered countries," "darling lurking," and "blackjack." The second paragraph uses less exaggeration and adds ethical appeal: The writer uses "I"

---

[5]From *A Sad Heart at the Supermarket* by Randall Jarrell. Copyright 1955 by Street & Smith Publications; copyright 1962 by Randall Jarrell. Reprinted with the permission of Atheneum Publishers.

[6]Copyright © 1960 by James Thurber. From "The Darlings at the Top of the Stairs," in *Lanterns and Lances,* published by Harper & Row, New York, and Hamish Hamilton, London. Originally published in *Queen,* England.

and "we" to seem closer to the reader, adding that he will not "surrender meekly" and that "there must be a bright side" which *we* should look for (*together,* presumably).

Introductions that take more than one paragraph give the writer a chance to make both an emotional and an ethical appeal; they can be fun and they are always a challenge. However, a careless writer runs the risk of using appeals that fall flat: They can sound insincere and exaggerated rather than humorously honest, especially if the writer's main method of catching readers is to entertain them. Before experimenting with emotional and ethical appeals, therefore, you should master the method of straightforward logical appeal (in *one* paragraph), as diagrammed at the beginning of this discussion. You must conceive and state your thesis clearly if your additional efforts are to succeed. Turn back to page 32 and check the student theme on "Law and Order" for emotional and ethical appeals. Do you think the appeals succeed? Or, you can study the examples of introductory paragraphs given on pages 279–82 in the section on tone; these also go beyond simple logical appeal.

exercises

A. By now you have probably written introductory paragraphs for several themes (see pages 40 or 55). Rewrite two of your introductory paragraphs, paying special attention to reader interest and reader acceptance, assuming that the reader is
  1. Your school's principal or president
  2. Your best friend
B. Make a list of the kinds of changes you made in Exercise *A,* listing some examples (words, sentences, information, and so on). Be prepared to comment on the changes you needed to make most in order to alter the tone of your original paragraphs.

DEVELOPMENTAL PARAGRAPHS   The developmental paragraphs are the meat of your paper because they present the evidence you have to support your thesis statement. They are the "standard paragraph" discussed earlier in this chapter. Again, a diagram explains the developmental paragraph. (See page 109.)

In this diagram, the space representing the first sentence in the paragraph is divided. The first part, labeled Transition, indicates that a word, phrase, clause, or sentence should ordinarily be used in this position to provide the interlocking connection between this paragraph and the preceding one. The second part is the topic sentence,

```
┌─────────────────────────────────────────────────────────┐
│              THE DEVELOPMENTAL PARAGRAPH                  │
│  ┌──────────────────────┬──────────────────────────┐    │
│  │     Transition       │      Topic Sentence       │    │
│  └──────────────────────┴──────────────────────────┘    │
│                                                          │
│           Detail, definition, illustration, com-         │
│           parison, contrast, reasons or any              │
│           combination of methods establish-              │
│           ing the topic sentence as valid.               │
│                                                          │
│              (About 150 to 200 words)                    │
│                                                          │
│      MAINTAIN UNITY:      Stay on the single sub-        │
│                           ject given in the topic        │
│                           sentence.                      │
│                                                          │
│      MAINTAIN COHERENCE:  Use transitional               │
│                           devices to relate              │
│                           sentences.                     │
└─────────────────────────────────────────────────────────┘
```

which leads into the paragraph. For example, look at this opening sentence:

I am arguing, *then,* that there are *two readers* distinguishable in every literary experience. . . .

Then is a transition word that suggests a summing up and a continuation of the thought of the preceding paragraph. The *two readers* in the last part of the sentence are to be explained in the remainder of the paragraph.

> *I have given the impression that the Farm was remote,* but *this is not strictly true.*

The first part of this beginning sentence points back to the preceding paragraph. The last points forward to the remainder of the paragraph by announcing its topic.

Closely associated with *this distinction* between author and speaker, *there is another and less familiar distinction* to be made. . . .

This distinction in the first of the sentence is *obviously* the subject of the preceding paragraph. *Another and less familiar distinction* is the subject of this paragraph.

Although fraternity *expenses* are less hindrance to affluent members, the society *interferes* indiscriminately *with the studies* of its members. . . .

Here *expenses* refers to the subject of the preceding paragraph;

interferes with the studies is the subject of the paragraph the sentence introduces.

These sentences all demonstrate transitional techniques needed for the reader's easy progress from the main point of one paragraph to the main point of the next. They provide the interlocking connection or coherence you studied in Chapter 4. Use these techniques to give your whole paper coherence and apply them *within* each developmental paragraph as well, regardless of the method of development—whether you use specific detail, illustrations or examples, comparison or contrast, reasons or causes, definition, or a combination of methods.

Equally important, you may already have discovered that most developmental methods are effective only if the information presented is factual or, if not, when it is acceptable for other reasons. For example, your reader will probably respect your supporting evidence *if you are careful to distinguish between personal opinion and fact,* and *if your statements are specific rather than general.* Before examining specific methods of paragraph development, let's look at these two related problems so often found in supporting evidence.

supporting evidence: fact, judgment, opinion, inference

If you are to get your reader to say, "I understand," "I agree," you will need to learn not to use opinion, judgment, or inference as fact. Your *evidence,* the specific details presented to support your thesis statement (or a topic sentence in a paragraph), must consist of *facts* or clearly qualified *opinions, judgments,* or *inferences.*

Facts.   A *fact* is a verifiable statement, an accurate *report* of happenings, or accurate comments about persons, objects, or ideas. It is something everyone will *agree* to. For instance, the following sentences are all facts. All are verifiable.

1. Yesterday a car wreck occurred on Highway 6 about three miles south of the city limits. (This statement is easily verifiable by the police or the newspapers. Anyone will accept the validity of either source.)
2. The Weather Bureau reported that 3.00 inches of rain fell on the city yesterday. (Here the question of fact is not whether 3.00 inches of rain fell but whether the Weather Bureau reported it. Again, this fact is easily checked in the newspaper or at the Bureau.)
3. There are sidewalks on each side of the street. (Anyone who questions this statement can check it simply by looking at the street. Probably, no one would want to question it.)
4. In 1974, Texas had a population of 12,017,000. (Easily verified by the government census reports in official documents.)

5. John Jones told me that he saw a leopard change its spots. (Here again the question is not whether John Jones *saw* a leopard change its spots but whether he *told* me that he saw it. As long as John Jones will admit that he told it, the statement is verifiable. If he will not, the question must be resolved by the reliability and reputation of the two people involved.

Opinions. An *opinion* is a conclusion or conviction formed about any matter. An opinion is stronger than a mere impression but less strong than positive knowledge. It is usually based on evidence of some kind, as are most conclusions and personal convictions. Though an opinion is thought out, it is open to dispute because the evidence can be logically sound or logically fallacious. An opinion is not a clearly proved matter. To be convincing, opinion should be based on factual evidence, and a person expressing an opinion should be able to support it with fact and sound logic. Or the person should have such a reputation for experience with the subject and knowledge of it that he is recognized as an authority. He would then try to project credibility by using ethical appeal. But without either fact or authority, an opinion isn't very convincing in any discussion.

Judgments. Many writers use the word *judgment* to mean *opinion.* As used in this book, however, a judgment is a statement expressing a person's *approval* or *disapproval* of objects, happenings, persons, or ideas. It is a form of opinion, also usually based on evidence of some kind, and also open to dispute because the evidence can be logically sound or logically fallacious. Or the evidence for the opinion can be simply inadequate, resulting in a hasty generalization.

For instance, suppose your family bought a house from a real estate agent named John Jones and that before you made the down payment he promised to put a new roof on the house. When no workmen appeared to start work on the roof and you asked Jones when he was going to order the roof put on, he denied making any such promise. Your first reaction would probably be "John Jones is a crook," and you might make this statement to your friends. But wait. Even though Jones has wronged you, to call him a crook is to say that he has been a crook and always will be a crook in business dealings. On the basis of this one example only, such a judgment is hardly justified. About all you can say is that in this situation you think Jones dealt with you unethically.

Or suppose you bought a Waumpum car two years ago and have now driven it for 75,000 miles with only a few minor repairs. You might well say, "The Waumpum is an excellent car." Yet the fact may be that yours is the only Waumpum to go over 50,000 miles without a major overhaul. Again, on the basis of experience with one car of one model, such a judgment is not justified. It is clearly a hasty generalization.

Inferences. An *inference* is a conclusion, a guess about the unknown based on the known, a statement based on evidence. Again, this evidence can be logically sound or logically fallacious, it may be adequate or inadequate and, therefore, it isn't necessarily valid.

Imagine yourself in a situation such as this one: You observe a woman you have seen many times before, and you turn to your friend and say, "There goes that wealthy woman I see all over town." Your friend says, "Really? How do you know she is wealthy?" "Well," you reply, "she wears obviously expensive clothes, she drives a large, late model car, and she lives in a house that anyone would call a mansion." "That doesn't prove anything," says the friend. "She may just be deep in debt." Your friend would be right; you have not proved your point. You did, however, draw an *inference* about the woman: To *infer* is to *conclude.*

But an inference is not necessarily a valid conclusion because there are usually *other* conclusions you could just as logically derive from the evidence. For instance, suppose in the middle of a classroom lecture the student sitting next to you suddenly bangs his book closed, grimaces, rises, and stomps out of the room, slamming the door behind him. You might say to yourself, "Something the professor said made him angry." But again you might be wrong. The student may have had a sudden and uncontrollable stomach cramp from something he ate for lunch and had to leave the room at once. What other possible inferences could you draw on the basis of this evidence only? To be accurate and factual, how could you describe *and* comment on the episode?

Even when you have more than one piece of evidence on which to base a conclusion, the inference you draw can be hasty and faulty. The diagram on the next page provides a good example.

What this diagram shows is that on the basis of four rather limited experiences the student has made a general, hasty inference: "Today's teachers are dull and boring." Then, on the basis of this questionable conclusion and the same evidence he generalizes further: "They don't care" and "they certainly don't know how to teach." Supposing that the four experiences were fresh in the student's mind, he might *feel* quite justified in reaching his conclusions. But the evidence, clearly, does not support him. Did he consider *all* the lectures he has heard? Are the four teachers representative of *all* teachers? The student's final inference would be more valid if he said, simply, "The four lectures I heard today were dull and boring." Then he

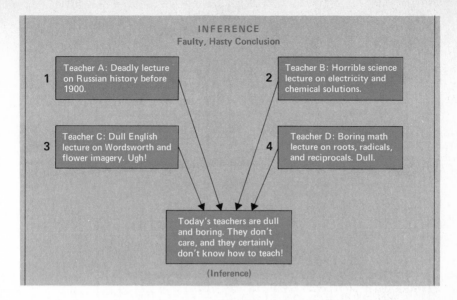

INFERENCE
Faulty, Hasty Conclusion

1 Teacher A: Deadly lecture on Russian history before 1900.

2 Teacher B: Horrible science lecture on electricity and chemical solutions.

3 Teacher C: Dull English lecture on Wordsworth and flower imagery. Ugh!

4 Teacher D: Boring math lecture on roots, radicals, and reciprocals. Dull.

Today's teachers are dull and boring. They don't care, and they certainly don't know how to teach!

(Inference)

might add, "*Some* teachers don't *seem* to care, and they don't *seem* to know how to teach effectively." At least these inferences don't suffer from a fault most of us have—making hasty generalizations. We jump to conclusions because we have a tendency to emphasize *similarities* and ignore *differences* in the experiences we've had.

Opinions, judgments, and inferences cannot be stated *positively as if* they were valid conclusions or absolute truth. With care, you'll learn to avoid them and stick to specific, factual details when presenting supporting evidence. Or, if you decide to use opinions, judgments, or inferences as evidence, you'll learn to qualify the conclusions you reach. You will be accurate and specific. "John Jones is a crook" will become "John Jones behaved unethically." And "The Waumpum is an excellent car" will become "*My* Waumpum is an excellent car." Similarly, the inference "There goes that wealthy woman" will become "There goes the woman with the expensive clothes and the late model car." These revised statements are now more accurate and more specific. And they are also more convincing. Your reader is now more likely to say, "I understand," "I agree." As you can see, being specific and factual requires careful thinking and precise writing. Test your understanding of the material in this unit by doing the following exercises.

exercises

A. Identify the following statements as fact, opinion, judgment, or inference.
   1. My history teacher has asked me a question in class every day for the past two weeks.

2. Don't take that history course—it's tough.
3. The referee penalized our team seventy-five yards in that game with Primitive U.
4. We lost that game to the referee.
5. We would have won that game with Primitive U if we had not been penalized so much.
6. That referee was no good.
7. Since Congressman Stayaway missed several more House roll calls than Congressman Faithful, clearly Faithful has a better record in Congress.
8. Termites have damaged the floor joists in that house.
9. I studied everything and went to class every time, but I still didn't pass because the teacher doesn't like me.
10. That's the worst teacher I ever had.

B. The first statement in this group is fact and the others are based on it. Identify them as judgment or inference.
1. There is a six-foot fence around their house.
2. They don't want people to visit them.
3. Their house looks like a prison.
4. They want privacy in their home.
5. There must be something wrong with those people.
6. Those people are crazy.
7. They must have something to hide.
8. I don't like that house with its high fence.

C. List the inferences that might be drawn from these sets of circumstances.
1. He was weaving as he walked along. He staggered several times. He suddenly sat down on the curb and held his head in his hands.
2. The man ran from the store in great haste. He jumped in his car and sped away. The store's owner ran out on the curb and shouted something after him.
3. After dinner she went straight to her room, took out paper and pen and spent busy hours writing her English paper. She received a failing grade on it.
4. Everyone must be convinced by now that cigarette smoking does contribute to the high incidence of lung cancer. Yet the rate of cigarette consumption in the United States increases each year.
5. While the population of the United States has been increasing, church attendance has been decreasing.

D. Select from each of the lists you have written for Exercise C the inference you think is likely to be the most valid, and indicate your reasons for thinking so.

E. Be prepared to discuss both the evidence and the conclusions in each of the following examples.
1. *Larry:* It's safer taking a long trip than driving into Houston to shop.
Hazel: What? You've gotta be kidding.
Larry: No, I'm right. You know that half of all auto accidents occur within five miles of home.

2. A recent article in *The New York Times* presented verified statistics showing that test scores on the Scholastic Aptitude Test are going down in the United States. The article concludes that students are not as well educated as they used to be.
3. Figures from the American Medical Society on Alcoholism show that more than 80 percent of alcoholics studied had a blood relative who also was an alcoholic. The AMSA concludes that an inherited biochemical deficiency could be the reason why some people become alcoholics while others do not.

distinguishing between the specific and the general

In the section you've just finished you were asked to learn three basic skills.

1. Use detailed FACTS to support ideas.
2. Use detailed FACTS to support opinions or judgments.
3. Qualify all inferences accurately to make them valid.

To these you will add a fourth skill before going on to the material on developmental paragraphs.

4. Use *specific* rather than *general* ideas to develop your supporting evidence.

Although the most obvious use of this fourth skill is in developing paragraphs by using specific detail, you'll also need to use the *specific* rather than the *general* in most of the other kinds of developmental paragraphs. And of course you'll use specific rather than general statements in supporting opinions, judgments, or inferences.

The *general* includes *all* of a class, type, or group. For example, *people, men, women, toys, students, athletes* mean ALL people, men, women, toys, students, and athletes. To mean anything else they must be qualified by a modifier or an explanation (*some men, most students, track stars at our school*). The general is so common in speech and writing that most of us often must add, "What I meant was. . . . " Learning to be specific will help get rid of all those "What I meant" qualifiers.

To change a general statement to a more specific one requires thought and some awareness of levels of generalization. For example, consider the following statements.

Young people don't dress right.

Students are careless about their clothes.

College students are too casual in dress.

Freshman girls wear jeans to class.

Hazel came to class barefooted, wearing jeans.

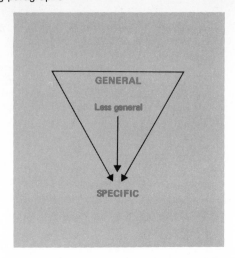

You have already seen this process at work in limiting both the subject and predicate areas of thesis statements. Here you can see it at work in making all supporting statements specific. The subject area of the original statement, *young people*, has become increasingly specific, until *Hazel* represents the specific illustration to be used. Similarly, *don't dress right* has been transformed into *barefooted, wearing jeans*, which isn't necessarily judgmental.

To make your supporting statements specific, you need to examine all the individual words carefully, choosing the exact, specific word that applies. For example, *structure* is a general word because there are many types of structures. The *specific*, on the other hand, refers to a *particular* in a class, type, or group. A building, a bridge, a television transmitting antenna, or a radar tower are each a particular of the general class, *structure*. Therefore, *building* is more specific than *structure*, because it is only one member of the whole class. In the same way, *box* is more specific than *container*, because a box is only one type of container. *Horse* is more specific than *vertebrate; boat*, more specific than *vehicle; meat*, more specific than *food;* and *furniture*, more specific than *household goods.*

But all these terms can be made yet more specific. *Building*, even though it is a type of structure, is still a general term that can be divided into types. A house, a service station, a garage, or a greenhouse can all be called buildings and are, therefore, more specific than *building*. Again, a filly is a type of a horse, a wooden crate is a type of box, a chair is a type of furniture, beef is a type of meat, and a kayak is a type of boat. These terms can be made still more specific by reference to building material, color, location, shape, or size. For instance, *brick house* is more specific than *house,* and *red brick house* is still more specific. *The red brick house on Lincoln Street* will specify even further by pointing to a particular house.

Similarly, beef is a type of meat, steak is a type of beef, sirloin steak is a type of steak, and grill sirloin steak is one type of sirloin steak. And the sirloin can be made more specific by describing its appearance: *grilled sirloin steak, charred on the outside, raw within.*

To be convincing, your supporting information should project this type of specific detail. Your reader isn't likely to misunderstand an illustration like *grilled sirloin steak, charred on the outside, raw within.* Test your understanding of the general and the specific by doing the following exercises.

exercises

A. Select from the following groups the most specific in each group.
  1. (a) dog (b) mammal (c) large bird dog (d) setter (e) canine
  2. (a) a great boy (b) a witty and charming boy (c) a boy with a top-notch personality (d) a wonderful boy to know.
  3. (a) John and Mary served a large quantity of food. (b) Their table literally groaned with an abundance of viands. (c) They served a quantity of foods suitable for the Thanksgiving season and tempting to the most jaded palate. (d) In the center of their table was a large baked turkey surrounded by dishes of cranberry sauce, sweet potatoes, giblet gravy, rolls, and pumpkin pie. (e) Their cuisine was liberally illustrated by the delicious and nourishing products of culinary art distributed on the table in great number.
Answers: In Group 1, *setter* is the most specific term, because it names the type of dog involved. In this group, *mammal* is the most general term, followed by *canine, dog,* and *large bird dog.* If you picked *witty and charming boy* in Group 2, you were correct. In fact, of the choices here, this is the only one that gives any specific information about the boy. Group 3 is easy. Answer (d) is the only one in this group that tells specifically what food was on the table.

B. Select the most specific from each of these groups.
  1. (a) mosquito (b) blood-sucking insect (c) creature (d) invertebrate insect with two wings
  2. (a) man (b) person (c) individual (d) student (e) one
  3. (a) a building with an established place in the history of one of our largest states (b) a historical shrine revered by Texans (c) an old stone mission where, in 1836, Santa Anna's 4,000 Mexican troops, after a thirteen-day siege, defeated and slaughtered Colonel Travis' Texas garrison of 180 men (d) a rambling structure, once a church, where Texas history was made (e) an old mission where the Mexican forces massacred the defending Texans.
  4. (a) He wore a battered brown derby, a new light-orange sport jacket, red slacks, frayed white spats, and black shoes. (b) He was extremely

oddly dressed. (c) His hat and his spats were certainly from another era, but his coat and slacks were modern, although their colors were so loud they hurt the eyes of the onlooker. (d) No piece of his clothing matched any other piece. (e) He wore an old derby, a coat that clashed sharply with the color of his slacks, spats, and shoes.

5. (a) The book ends with a scene of mounting interest and excitement that leaves readers sitting on the edge of their chairs. (b) The ending of the book is simply magnificient in the gripping realism of its final scene. (c) At the end of the book, after Jack's followers, now complete savages, have set fire to the island and have hunted Ralph down to kill him, the reader understands with almost unbearable clarity the cruelty inherent in all mankind. (d) At the end of the book, after a series of highly interesting scenes, the reader is brought face to face with certain facts about modern life.

summary

1. Start an introductory paragraph with a general statement and narrow it to the thesis statement.

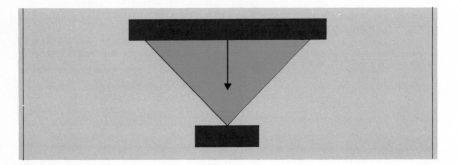

2. Learn to distinguish:

Fact:	a statement that is verifiable.
Inference:	a guess based on known fact. (May be valid but may not be)
Opinion:	a conclusion, or conviction, established about a matter. (May be based on no fact)
Judgment:	statement made of approval or disapproval. (May be based on no fact or insufficient fact)

3. In supporting inferences, opinions, or judgments (generalizations), use *specific facts*.

General: a broad term covering many particulars (the whole).

Specific: a narrow term specifying a particular (a small part of the whole).

Thesis statements and *topic sentences* are supported by related, factual, specific statements.

PARAGRAPH DEVELOPMENT BY USE OF DETAIL   Have a look at two students' paragraphs and the discussion of them that follows. Here is the first one.

> People who buy foreign economy cars are not getting what they think they are paying for. Foreign cars are not really any more economical to operate than are American cars. Those who talk about how good foreign cars are simply do not know what they are talking about. They should spend more time studying the durability record of American cars than just thinking about gas mileage. Many small foreign cars are worn out after 50,000 miles and have to be replaced. American cars will run much longer than this. So foreign cars are not good buys.

This paragraph was written by a student who had been assigned a paper to write in class at the beginning of the semester. After completing this paragraph and making several attempts to continue writing the paper, the student appealed to his instructor for help. What, he wanted to know, could he say next? The instructor explained that the general ideas in the paragraph were undeveloped and that the student needed to use detail to support his ideas and to convince his reader. Consider, for instance, the general statement that foreign cars are not any more economical to operate than are American cars. What detailed facts could the student present to make this statement more than just an assertion? Without the facts, thousands of foreign car drivers may not agree with him.

Here is the second one.

> The adoption of Medicare can cause serious damage to our system of free enterprise and private medicine. It would ruin many medicinal-producing corporations and cause unemployment for thousands of workers. The control of medicine would pass from the doctors to the government. Our system of medicine has worked for over 180 years. Why destroy it now with Medicare? Why take from the skilled hands of our doctors and give to untrained "butchers" of socialized medicine? This can not be allowed in the United States. Medicare must not be allowed to destoy our democratic system.

This student apparently feels quite strongly about the subject, so strongly, in fact, that he has let the discussion get out of hand. Personal belief in a subject is not enough to convince others. And no matter how readers personally feel about Medicare, they certainly must recognize this paragraph as ranting and fanatic opinion unsupported by evidence. Logically, the paragraph is impossible. It equates free enterprise, private medicine, and democracy. These are not interdependent, as can be easily shown, and one does not necessarily collapse when one of the others does. How, for instance, can Medicare ruin *medicinal-producing corporations* and cause unemployment? Why are the practitioners of socialized medicine called *butchers?* Are Medicare and socialized medicine the same thing, as this paragraph asserts? How can Medicare *destroy our democratic system?* How will it damage *free enterprise?* All these questions are unanswered, and we must conclude that this student needs to support opinions with detailed, specific evidence.

To make these two paragraphs acceptable, their writers must apply the four basic skills discussed in the two sections immediately preceding this one. Here they are again:

> Use detailed facts to support ideas.
> Use detailed facts to support opinions or judgments.
> Qualify all inferences accurately to make them valid.
> Use specific rather than general ideas to develop supporting evidence.

The next section shows these skills at work.

using specific, factual details in paragraph development

In diagram form, here is the paragraph developed through use of detail.

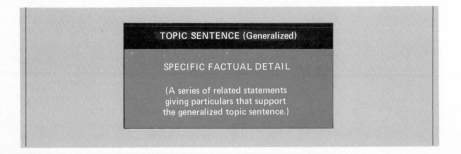

TOPIC SENTENCE (Generalized)

SPECIFIC FACTUAL DETAIL

(A series of related statements giving particulars that support the generalized topic sentence.)

Here is an example of a paragraph developed through use of details taken from the work of a successful writer.

> Freeman Halverson is tall, fast on his feet, and works hard. On his slender shoulders are laid many of the responsibilities of the little community. He is postmaster, storekeeper, driver of the school bus. He is chairman of the community study group, head of the newly organized conservation unit, president of the state alfalfa seed growers' association, editor of the Hub News. He is on the citizens' advisory board of the state agricultural college. He leads the Lonepine band. At times he trains the girls' chorus. And then toward the evening he plays the clarinet at home in the family ensemble.[7]

This paragraph establishes the pointer in the topic sentence, *responsibilities*, by detailing the duties Freeman Halverson carries in the community. When readers finish the paragraph, they can only agree with the author that Halverson does, indeed, carry many of the responsibilities of the community.

Read this paragraph. You can recognize it as coming from the same work.

> Freeman Halverson is the downtown population of Lonepine, he and perhaps Ted Van der Ende, the cheesemaker. Freeman Halverson is postmaster and the owner and operator of the general store. His place is the rendezvous. *The post office is on one side of the room.* For a time the public library also was housed here. Below are freeze lockers. The butcher shop with its big refrigerator is at the back. In *this* building with its somewhat informal front porch may be bought a *wide variety of goods. Sales* are announced in the weekly *news sheet,* and the prices paid for local produce are revised to suit the season.[8]

You have already seen how effectively this author uses detail to support his ideas; therefore, you might be immediately suspicious of this paragraph, particularly if you examined the italicized parts. These parts indicate where detail might be used to good effect. In fact, the author didn't write this paragraph in quite this way. He supplied the needed details. Look at the way he actually wrote it. The details he used are italicized.

> Freeman Halverson is the downtown population of Lonepine, he and perhaps Ted Van der Ende, the cheesemaker. Freeman Halverson is postmaster and the owner and operator of the general store. His place is the rendezvous. The *tiny* post office, *not much larger than a telephone*

[7]From Baker Brownell, *The Human Community* (Harper & Row, 1950). Reprinted by permission of Harper & Row, Publishers, Inc.

[8]Brownell, *The Human Community.*

booth, is on *the drygoods side* of the *big* room. For a time the public library also was housed here. Below are freeze lockers. The butcher shop with its big refrigerator is at the back. In this *rambling frame* building with its somewhat informal front porch may be bought a *modern cream separator or a pair of overalls, a pound of cheese or a tube of lipstick, a silken, western neckerchief, a saddle or a pound of old fashioned chocolate creams.* Brisk bargains are announced in the weekly *mimeographed* sheet of *news* and *market items,* and the prices paid for local eggs and *poultry, vegetables, seeds, potatoes,* and *fruit* are revised to suit the season.[9]

Now the paragraph is specific in its detail, and the reader has a much better idea of the effect the author intended to create.

Here are some students' paragraphs developed through the use of detail. Examine them carefully, for they will serve as models for your writing:

> The catcher is the "quarterback" of baseball. In effect, he runs the team. He is the only man who sees every player on the field and observes every move that takes place. He calls the pitches by giving signals to the pitcher. Sometimes he directs much of the defensive play by stationing the players in key spots and by directing the moves against the opposition. He is the one player on the team who can never for a moment relax, whether his team is in the field or at bat. He must know wind directions in every ball park, and he must study the opposing batteries, the mental condition of his own pitcher, and the spacing of his field-ers. And he must watch runners on base, keeping track of the tac-tical situation and seeing that the rest of the team knows it also.

This paragraph uses the details of the catcher's job to establish the point that the catcher "runs" the baseball team. The writer includes enough detail to make the point of the topic sentence quite clear. Here is another example paragraph.

> We could not use the table he showed us. The wood was rough and saw-marked, and the finish was dull and spotty. The top was marked with several cigarette burns, although a label on the bot-tom promised that it was fireproof. Stains and scuffs also marred the top. The construction was poor; the joints were ill-fitted, and one leg was held on by a wire. The metal cap on one of the legs, provided originally to protect the carpet, was missing, and the drawer, which had no handle, could not be opened more than three inches. Furthermore, the table was too long for practical use and too wide to be easily moved through the door.

[9]*Ibid.*

In this paragraph the writer uses abundant detail to support the point of the topic sentence: The table was beyond use.

Here is a paragraph written by a student in business administration with previous business experience, which provides the specific details.

> Few people know the significant criteria that a financial manager must consider in devising a company's financial plan. He must keep abreast of the general level of business activity to determine the company's needs for assets and funds. To operate efficiently he must interpret and use money and capital markets to the fullest extent. He must know the effects of tax rates and whether an increase or decrease in the tax rates will raise or lower the desirability of indebtedness. He must cope with seasonal and cyclical variations in business activity. To as great a degree as possible, he must know the nature and effects of competitors. He must use regulations and customs to the best practical extent. He must know the credit standing of his company and strive to keep it as high as possible.

Written by an expert bowler, a student who gave bowling lessons at the student union lanes, the next paragraph provides convincing, specific details.

> Although the experts all claim that proper form is the most important aspect of good bowling, consistency is the real secret for a bowler. The bowler may push the ball away too fast, but if he does it the same way every time, his game will not suffer. He may backswing too high or too low, but if the ball reaches the identical spot in the backswing arc in each delivery, the high score compiled for each game will not reveal the weakness. He may take more or fewer steps than the recommended four, as long as he takes the same number in each approach. The bowler may even commit the unpardonable sin of releasing the ball while on the wrong foot, provided he can do it exactly the same way every time. In other words, the bowler can do everything "wrong" and still be an expert bowler, if he will do it "wrong" consistently.

This paragraph makes its point about consistency being the secret of good bowling by detailing the things a bowler may consistently do wrong but still bowl well.

This paragraph, written by a young high school teacher who had returned to college after teaching for a year on a temporary certificate, persuades through the use of details.

Although many people think the work of a public school teacher is easy, the school teacher actually has the responsibility of many jobs. Before school opens in the fall, the teacher must attend meetings every day, sometimes for as long as a week, in preparation for the fall semester. During the semester, the teacher has official meetings, such as those for the faculty and the PTA, that he must attend. He is expected to sponsor clubs, coach athletics, and help promote such fund-raising activities as carnivals. He has monitorial duties to perform when he is not in class. But, of course, his primary job is teaching. He must teach about five classes a day and sometimes conduct an additional study hall. In preparation for instructing his classes, the teacher spends about five to six hours a week preparing materials and reading to supplement textbooks. Still he must spend some of his "off" hours at school helping individual students having personal problems or difficulty learning the material. Furthermore, he must grade papers, evaluate the students' progress, make reports of various kinds, and even interview the parents of his students. But this is not all. To keep up with new teaching methods and programs the teacher himself must often go to school in the summer and attend conventions. And occasionally, he must take part in such community affairs as luncheons and civic organizations.

After reading this paragraph with its detailing of teachers' duties, aren't you ready to agree with the point stated in the topic sentence?

exercises

If you have trouble finding details for this assignment, you should check the "discovery exercises" on pages 60–62.

A. List the details that might be used to support five of the statements below.
1. The college student's life is full of (opportunity) (demands) (roles).
2. Cats are clever hunters.
3. A young man can't get along without a car.
4. Car manufacturers are (are not) meeting human needs in automobile safety.
5. Television programs can be highly (instructive) (frustrating) (boring).
6. The dating game can be a (nuisance) (disaster) (threat) (joy).
7. Fixing a big breakfast is (fun) (messy) (challenging).
8. I didn't know where to start cleaning my room.
9. The clock I brought home from the discount house was incredible.
10. Horror movies create humor at the drive-in.
B. Rewrite these paragraphs and supply appropriate, specific detail at the italicized points. Freely add and change material that is here.
1. He stared at the carnival booth as if hypnotized. From it issued

highly amplified sounds that almost overcame him with their intensity. Its *many* shelves were stacked with a *variety of flashy goods.* *Some men stood* at the booth's counter intently concentrating on looping hoops over a *stick some feet away.* A *few boys* chased each other through the *people* standing at the booth.

2. They entertained the *group of visitors* as best they could with such short notice. First, there was a *lunch outdoors,* followed by a long walk through *interesting gardens* of the city. After resting, the visitors were taken to a *local museum* where they were shown *relics of bygone days,* and in the evening they saw a *stage show of their choice.* At the end of the planned activities, the host took the entire group to his home, where they were joined by *friends of the hosts* for a *party to climax the delightful visit.*

3. A *manufacturing firm nearby* went all out to advertise their products and to establish goodwill in the community at the same time. They ran a contest in the spring that offered a *costly grand prize* for the best slogan in praise of their products. In the winter, they offered an all-expense-paid trip *to the South* for the merchant who arranged the Ideal Display of the firm's products. For the consumer who could think up original ideas for putting the firm's merchandise to use, *there was a reward.* The community showed its appreciation *in many ways.*

4. The bride-to-be found it difficult to display all her lovely gifts in her parents' *small* home. Relatives from out of town had sent *lightweight but expensive knicknacks.* All these had arrived early and seemed to get choice spots in the living room. *Gifts of bedding and kitchenware* from nearby kinfolk covered the dining table and took all the space *on other furniture* in the dining room. Chums in her own age group had sent the bride more *"mod" gifts,* and these took over the TV room and what shelf space *there was in the house. Her gift from the groom's parents,* the one she treasured most highly of all, because of its resale value, the bride kept in her purse and brought it out for frequent praise from *interested parties.*

C. Using three of the lists you made in Exercise *A* write three paragraphs developed through the use of detail. If you have trouble getting started, check again the exercises beginning on page 60.

PARAGRAPH DEVELOPMENT BY USE OF DEFINITION Before studying the means of using definition in paragraph development, read through this paragraph, a definition of *democracy,* written by the well-known historian Carl Becker. It will give you a good idea of the use of definition to develop specific supporting evidence.

In this antithesis there are, however, certain implications, always tacitly understood, which give a more precise meaning to the term democracy. Peisistratus, for example, was supported by a majority of the people, but his government was never regarded as a democracy for all that.

Caesar's power derived from a popular mandate, conveyed through established republican forms, but this did not make his government any less a dictatorship. Napoleon called his government a democratic empire, but no one, least of all Napoleon himself, doubted that he had destroyed the last vestiges of the democratic republic. Since the Greeks first used the term, the essential test of democratic government has always been this: the source of political authority must be and remain in the people and not in the ruler. A democratic government has always meant one in which the citizens, or a sufficient number of them to represent more or less effectively the common will, freely act from time to time, and according to established forms, to appoint or recall the magistrates and to enact or revoke the laws by which the community is governed. This I take to be the meaning which history has impressed upon the term democracy as a form of government.[10]

This paragraph starts with a conventional topic sentence using *implications* as the pointer to give the paragraph unity. It explores these implications chronologically by use of examples starting with the Greeks (Peisistratus) and ending with France's Napoleonic Empire. When the paragraph comes to a statement of the principal implication, which is Becker's one-sentence definition of democracy, it maintains coherence by reference to the Greeks, mentioned early in the paragraph. After the one-sentence definition, . . . *the source of political authority must be and remain in the people and not in the ruler,* the paragraph explains in more detail what this definition means. In the final sentence, the paragraph declares that this is the meaning of democracy that Mr. Becker is to use throughout his book, and the reader need have no misunderstanding of what he means when he uses the word.

As Becker has done in his paragraph, you must also often define the terms you use in writing, if there is any chance that your reader may use a different meaning from the one you intend. Many a verbal argument has ended with some such statement as "It has become obvious that we are not defining our terms in the same way, and I won't accept your definitions." This usually ends the argument, because without acceptable definitions there is no real communication. One group talks about one thing and the other group is arguing another, although they seem to be talking about the same subject. Throughout one presidential campaign, for instance, there was a running argument over whether the United States is a republic or a democracy, but nowhere in the campaign were these two terms satisfactorily defined, nor was the distinction between the two made clear. Consequently, the argument carried little weight with the voting

[10]Carl Becker, *Modern Democracy.* Copyright 1954 by Yale University Press. Used by permission.

public. So make the meaning of the terms you use in writing clear to the reader. Defining terms will not necessarily make the reader agree with you, but without adequate definitions, you run the risk of being misunderstood.

When you decide a term needs defining, you will not want to copy verbatim the dictionary definition and use it in your paper with a phrase like "Webster defines socialism as. . . ." Such a practice defeats your purpose, which is to make clear the exact meaning *you* are attaching to a word. You can devise your own definitions, using one or more of the following five basic methods. And remember, to define is to explain.

1. Classification
2. Synonym
3. Example or Illustration
4. Enumeration
5. Function

Consider these methods one at a time.

definition by classification

Sometimes called the Aristotelian method, definition by classification is the one most often found in dictionaries. The method is quite simple and involves only two steps:

1. Place the word to be defined in its family (genus).
2. Differentiate the word from all others in its family.

For instance, if you wanted to define the relatively simple word *bridge* (to indicate that you do not mean the card game or a part of the nose or of a pair of spectacles or an arch to raise the strings of a musical instrument or a raised platform on a ship or a transition in music), you would first place the word in its family:

A bridge is a structure.

You have already seen that *structure* is a general term including many specific structures, a bridge being one of them. The second step, then, is to differentiate *bridge* from all other structures—buildings, houses, towers, and so forth. This can be done by naming its function:

A bridge is a structure carrying a roadway over a depression or obstacle.

Examine these definitions by classification:

WORD	FAMILY	DIFFERENTIATION
Bird	vertebrate	covered with feathers and having wings.
Insect	invertebrate	having head, thorax, and abdomen, three pairs of legs, and one or two pair of wings.
Chair	seat	having four legs and a back, for one person.
House	building	serving as living quarters for one or more families.

In defining by classification, there are three missteps to guard against.

1. Look at this definition of *net* from Samuel Johnson's dictionary:

A net is any reticulated fabric, decussated at regular intervals, with interstices at the intersections.

Since you know what a net is, you can probably make out what this definition says. But suppose you do not know what a net is. Could you possibly make sense from this definition without looking up several words in the dictionary? Probably not. So when you see the necessity of defining a word, follow this rule:

Do not use words that might not be clear to the reader (that is, obscure, ambiguous, or figurative).

Suppose you read this definition: *A democracy is a government in which the citizens are sovereign.* This is a perfectly good definition as long as you know what the word *sovereign* means. The writer could have avoided the use of this word by spelling out its meaning. For instance, he might have written this clearer definition: *A democracy is a government is which the citizens hold supreme power by periodically electing, either directly or indirectly, their representation in the government.*

2. Consider this definition: *A democracy has a democratic form of government.* Here no defining has taken place, because the definition offered leaves readers at the same place they started. The writer has used a form of the defined word in the definition itself. This definition has the same trouble: *A good man is one who performs good deeds.* The word that is being defined here is *good,* but this word has also been used in the definition of it, so nothing has been clearly defined. Stick to this rule, also:

Do not use any form of the defined word in the definition of the word.

3. Look at this definition: *Democracy is when the citizens are sovereign.* You have probably been told throughout your scholastic career that you cannot define by saying that something "is when. . . ." Logically, you cannot make the adverbial construction (showing condition), *when the citizens are sovereign,* equal to the noun, *democracy;* but the use of the verb *is* says that they are. In defining, then, you must also remember this rule:

The word defined must always be equal to the definition.

That is, wherever the defined word is used, you should be able to substitute your definition in its place. You can say, for instance, *The government of the United States is a democracy,* but when you try to substitute for the word the definition of democracy just considered, complete nonsense results: *The government of the United States is when the citizens are sovereign.* So a good definition of democracy is needed, one that can be substituted wherever the word itself is used. Here is a definition that will work: *Democracy is a form of government in which the citizens are sovereign.* Now we can substitute this definition for the word *democracy* in the sentence, *The government of the United States is a democracy: The government of the United States is* a form of government in which the citizens are sovereign. Note that placing the word in its family and then applying differentiation corrects this misstep.

definition by synonyms

Using other words that mean the same thing as the defined word but that are likely to be more easily understood is one of the easiest ways to define. For instance, if you are not certain your readers will know what *prevaricating* means, you can define it by saying that it means *lying* or *fibbing.* Or you can say that to *limit* is to *restrict* or to *define.* Or you might define *bad* as meaning *bath* in German, but as meaning *evil, wicked,* or *naughty* in English. In using synonyms to define, you should understand three limitations.

1. Synonyms are useful in definition only when they are closer to the reader's experience than is the word defined.
2. Usually synonyms are not definitions but only approximations. They may best be used to clarify other kinds of definitions.
3. Even fairly close synonyms can have unlike connotations, affecting both tone and meaning.

The third of these limitations needs explanation. You can understand the problem if you examine the following groups of words, assuming that the first word in each group is the definition target for the synonyms which follow. Consider the problem in terms of *sender* and *receiver,* pointing out some of the misunderstanding in tone and meaning that the chosen synonyms could create.

1. *Friendly:* sociable, jovial, genial, approachable, chummy, companionable, affectionate, harmonious
2. *House:* home, dwelling, abode, residence, pad, domicile, address, living quarters, place
3. *Corpulent:* plump, heavy-set, fat, chubby, overweight, bulky, obese, stocky, paunchy
4. *Disapprove:* condemn, denounce, criticize, blame, dislike, censure, hate, resent, oppose
5. *Saving* (modifier): sparing, thrifty, tight, frugal, economical, careful, penny-pinching, scrimping, parsimonious, budget-minded

You should see at once that a *friendly* person isn't necessarily *chummy,* and someone who is merely *approachable* isn't very friendly. The *place* you live in may not be your *home,* which could be an apartment rather than a *house.* The *heavy-set* person probably doesn't mind being called *overweight,* but would probably resent being called *fat.* And a *saving* person who is *thrifty* and *sparing* isn't necessarily *tight* and *penny-pinching.* Clearly, then, you must choose synonyms with great care if they are to illuminate your meaning and prevent misunderstanding.

definition by example or illustration

Sometimes it's possible to make an unknown term clear to the reader by pointing out an example of something that is known and is the same thing. For instance, you can define the color green by pointing to a plot of live grass and saying, "Green is the color of that grass." Or if you happen to have anything at hand of the color you want to define, you can simply hold it out and say, "Magenta is this color." Or if you do not have any of the color at hand you can say, "Magenta is red with some blue in it—a purplish red." To define by illustration you can give a brief narrative (a story) that explains what is being defined. Here is an example of how you might define *spoiled child.*

When Roger is asked to do something he doesn't want to do, he sticks out his tongue or simply turns away with no response at all. He demands what he wants and gets it, or else he lies on the floor and screams until it is forthcoming. Roger is a spoiled child.

As you will see shortly, examples and illustrations needn't be restricted to the definition of terms *within* a paragraph. They can also be used as a basic method of developing a whole paragraph, or even a whole paper.

definition by enumeration

In defining words that are the names of general classes of objects, you can sometimes define the word by simply listing the members of the class represented by that word. For example, you can define *decathlon* by listing the athletic events included.

> The decathlon is an athletic event in which each contestant competes in the 100-meter, 400-meter, and 1500-meter runs, the 110-meter high hurdles, the javelin and discus throws, shot put, pole vault, high jump, and broad jump.

Or you can define the Pentateuch by listing the books of the Bible that compose it.

> The Pentateuch is Genesis, Exodus, Leviticus, Numbers, and Deuteronomy.

Some classes are too large to enumerate, but most frequently you can list enough of the members of the class so that the definition is made understandable. For instance, to list all the seasonings would take up more space than the definition is worth and would make tedious reading. But some of the seasonings can be listed and the effect is the same as if they were all listed.

> Salt, pepper, thyme, oregano, marjoram, are *common* seasonings. Fruits *such as* lemons, oranges and grapefruit are citrus fruits.

Note that the definition admits the listing is not complete. And, again, you must be sure that the reader will be more familiar with the members of the class than with the name of the class itself.

definition by function—operational definition

The operational definition concentrates on *function* by describing *how* something operates or how something is done. To define an effect, for example, you could define how it "works."

Acceleration: When you step on the gas pedal of your car, the effect you feel is acceleration.

Frictional electricity: When you walk on a rug, the rubbing of the shoes on the rug builds up a negative charge in you so that when you touch a metalic object a small spark is discharged and you feel a shock.

Seen in this way, the operational definition describes the effect being defined; it describes *how* the effect "works" or functions.

This same explanation of a process can also be applied to concepts.

Prejudice: A prejudice is a judgment or opinion about a person, race, religion, nation, or any particular group or object without careful consideration of facts. To feel antagonism at first meeting toward students from a rival college without actually knowing the students is to be prejudiced toward them.

A dictionary definition of *prejudice* (following the Aristotelian method described above under Definition by Classification) might read as follows: *Prejudice is a judgment or opinion that is preconceived and usually unfavorable.* What the operational definition above does is to show how prejudice operates. The same method can be applied to a word like *claustrophobia,* which a dictionary might define as *morbid fear of enclosed or confined places.* To this you could *add* an operational definition, which could read as follows:

Persons who, when confined in a small, enclosed space such as an elevator, experience a rapid quickening of heart beat, acute agitation, and a desperate desire to leave the enclosed space are suffering from a mental disturbance known as claustrophobia.

Again, the operational definition shows how claustrophobia operates (or functions). The result is a brief explanation of a *process,* suitable for inclusion in a developmental paragraph.

process explanation

This technique for explaining or describing a process also applies to longer papers (especially technical reports) in which the writer's main purpose is to define function. If you look for it, you'll find the method at work in a surprising number of explanations. For example, consider the following subjects.

Drilling an oil well. (→ How to drill an oil well.)
Operating a dishwasher. (→ How to operate a dishwasher.)
Cell division. (→ How living cells divide.)

Riding a bicycle. (→ How to ride a bicycle.)
Changing a car tire. (→ How to change a car tire.)
The piston gas engine. (→ How the piston gas engine works.)
Assembling a model airplane. (→ How to assemble a model airplane.)

As stated, all these subjects require a process explanation—how something functions or how something is performed or operated. The term *process explanation* is used here to describe two types of processes: (1) describing how to do something (i.e., giving a set of directions), and (2) describing how something works (as in *cell division* and *piston gas engine*). Though related, each type requires its own writing approach. Can you see why?

A little thought should tell you that all these longer *process explanations* require a far more systematic, step-by-step approach than the simple operational definition. All require:

1. A systematic description of *all* components and parts involved
2. A step-by-step description of how *all* these parts operate in relation to one another.

In the theme "Do the Hustle," the student effectively uses process explanation, systematically providing a step-by-step description of how to *do* something. You should be able to outline the major stages in the operation (the paragraphs) as well as the individual steps within each stage (details within each paragraph).

Do The Hustle

The vibrating beat of a Led Zepplin tape rolls over the parking lot as you deposit your car and boogie up the sidewalk to Sports Club's front door. After flashing your brand new, full-front driver's license picture at the bouncer guarding the entrance, you proceed as calmly and maturely as you possibly can while trying to ignore your racing heart and quickening pulse.

Upon successful entry into the Club, you are now prepared to begin the challenging "girl entices boy" hustling procedure. The first step involves looking nonchalantly for a table toward the center of the room near the dance floor. (This is where all the action supposedly occurs.) As you walk slowly and deliberately toward the table you just selected, suck in your stomach and think sexy. Be extremely careful threading your way through the crowd and try to avoid tripping over chair legs. It ruins your sophisticated, "I've been here before" image.

Once you get to the table, sit down gracefully and take several deep breaths. You deserve them. When the barmaid comes to take your drink order, play it safe and order a coke. This way, when you are approached, you'll be able to talk coherently and,

hopefully, half-way intelligently. Besides, a coke is cheaper.
After ordering your drink, survey the entire situation. Select
one or two men that appear interesting and in full command of
themselves and their surroundings. (Note: Be sure to select someone who doesn't have a girl hanging on his arm.) Now that you've
found someone to hustle, you're ready to establish eye contact.
Let your eyes wander slowly around the room several times before
allowing them to linger on him. Count to five and look away.
Repeat this procedure several times. If he's the right one, he'll
notice you flirting and return the look. If he doesn't, forget him
and proceed to your second choice.

   The next step in the hustling process is up to him. At this
stage in the game, you've done everything possible without making
the initial move yourself. When you notice him headed in your
direction, smile captivatingly, try looking mysterious (guys
love to figure girls out) and hope that you've made the guy
believe it was his own idea to approach you. If everything goes
according to plan, he will ask to sit down at your table or ask you
to dance. Don't giggle, appear overeager, or look bored because
he may turn away. Let him ask the first question when he is seated
and be prepared to answer him honestly. Avoid boring him with the
typical rundown of your life story because chances are he isn't
curious and he won't listen. As a successful hustler, you should
be able to probe him without seeming like Dick Tracy incognito. If
he asks you to dance, don't worry about making conversation; he
can't hear you over the Led Zepplin tape anyway.

   If you've followed the above procedure carefully, you'll
have absolutely no trouble finding someone to spend a few pleasant hours with in the Sports Club or anywhere else. However, just
in case you lack confidence in your capabilities, take a girl
friend along. She can always keep you company, and you can use her
to discourage any unplanned advances. From here on, you're on
your own. Good luck, and happy hustling.

Although explaining how to "do the hustle" is much simpler than
explaining how the piston gas engine works, it uses the same basic
approach. A paper on the piston gas engine, however, would be much
longer, would require several schematic diagrams, would necessarily
use some technical language to describe all the parts, and would
likely number and explain each step in the piston's operation. If you've
ever tried to assemble from a set of instructions even the simplest
garbage cart or household appliance, you know how important a clearly
written process explanation can be.

   Because the *process explanation* is so common and is so closely
related to the operational definition, your instructor may ask you
to practice writing a few. This practice will help you master the
operational definition and learn how to develop paragraphs and papers
in which a description of *function* is the main purpose. Some possible
subjects are suggested in the exercises which follow.

exercises

A. If any of these statements is not acceptable as a definition, indicate specifically what is wrong with it. If any is acceptable, mark it *C*.
1. Lapidation is when you hurl stones at someone.
2. A lanyard is a rope used in firing certain types of cannon.
3. A proletarian is a member of the proletariat.
4. Syneresis is closely associated with dieresis and synizesis because all of them concern the coalescence of two vowels or syllables.
5. English is where expository writing is learned.
6. Gamosepalous is the same as synsepalous.
7. Tabasco is the trade name of a sauce made from red pepper.
8. Tetrameter is a line of verse consisting of four metrical feet.
9. Second childhood means senility or dotage.
10. Debate is an element basic to any democracy.

B. Write your own definitions of the following words, using two methods of defining for each. Do not consult your dictionary.
1. Magazine
2. House
3. Free speech
4. Enemy
5. Chair
6. Money
7. Laws
8. A vehicle, machine, or gadget

C. Write short operational definitions of each of the following; begin (or conclude) each with an Aristotelian definition.
1. Panic
2. Love
3. Politician
4. Jargon (or slang)
5. Sneezing
6. Water skiing

D. Choose one subject from Exercise *B* or *C*, above, and *plan* a *process explanation* related to a brief operational definition you've written for the term. Make a list of "components" or "parts" involved and the most important steps in the process. Come to class prepared to discuss your discoveries and your detailed plan.

the extended definition

Now that you've learned some basic methods of defining, you are ready to write an extended definition. An extended definition is ordinarily a paragraph, but it can be much longer, using a combination of definition methods to explain the term to be defined, and starting with a definition by classification. A diagram of the paragraph developed by an extended definition, shown on the next page, will help clarify.

To see how this diagram works, apply it to the following student

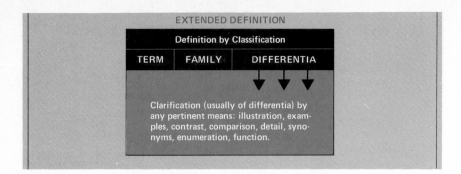

paragraph on jargon. The first sentence of the paragraph gives the term, *jargon,* names the family or class to which the term belongs, *a special vocabulary,* and presents the differentia, *understandable only to the users.* The student then extends the definition by presenting a series of short examples to explain why jargon is usually *understandable only to the users.*

> Jargon is a special vocabulary understandable only to the users. In Elmstown, one has only to pay a visit to Joe's Wagon Diner, at Tenth and Canal, to hear examples of its use. Table orders are taken by the waiters and given to the kitchen in such a manner that one hears expressions like, "One-eyed jacks up, no hog," meaning an order of two eggs fried on one side and no bacon; or "One brown with dogs, add straight," meaning an order of hash brown potatoes with sausage, and coffee without cream or sugar; or "Cream it with hens," meaning creamed eggs on toast; or "Dunk one all the way," meaning doughnut and coffee with cream and sugar.

Here are three more example paragraphs of extended definitions. Notice that the topic sentence (in color in each paragraph) is a definition by classification.

> A "turista" is any human being who finds himself in strange surroundings that he is not able to appreciate. The word is usually employed to describe middle-aged persons who have just started traveling. It is a fit description for a woman who upon arriving at the Grand Canyon rushes to the gift shop to buy postcards before she has had a look at the sight she has traveled to see. The word, although it has a feminine ending, is applied to the male traveler who goes to the Louvre and stares at female forms in the flesh and not at the Venus de Milo. The "turista" is constantly comparing his present surroundings with the heaven-

on-earth where he lives, making all listeners wonder why he had
not remained in that choice place. He is a steak-and-potato man
and is constantly griping about the food. He refuses to eat rein-
deer meat in Norway, but longs for it as he is eating lasagna in
Italy, proving to the uninterested listeners that he has been to
Norway. The word is never applied to anyone except Americans,
meaning anyone from the United States, and is used by persons in
foreign countries to show their dislike for individuals who spend
their money ostentatiously while traveling.

Elephant jokes, popular some time ago, are humorous devices
consisting of two lines--a question and an answer--in which an elephant is pointlessly involved. An example of this joke would be
"What was the elephant doing on the expressway?" and the answer,
"About three miles an hour." Or, with a side flavor, "What do you
call the black stuff between an elephant's toes?" Answer, "Slow
natives." Or, with a risque twist, "How do you make an elephant
fly?" Answer, "First, you get an eight-foot zipper." Often these
jokes are presented in a series, each joke related to the last. A
short example would be, "How do you tell an elephant from a blue-
bird?" Answer, "Elephants live in trees." Question, "How did the
elephant get flat feet?" Answer, "From jumping out of trees."
Question, "Why do elephants jump out of trees?" Answer, "How else
could they get down?"

A thunderstorm is a weather disturbance having lightning and,
consequently, thunder within it. There need not be rain falling,
but without lightning it is merely a rain shower and not a thunderstorm. Thundershowers come in three types--air mass thunderstorms, frontal thunderstorms, and thunderstorms caused by
unstable air over mountains. Air mass thunderstorms are common
along the Gulf Coast in the afternoon during the summer. Frontal
thunderstorms occur in the fall, winter, and spring along and ahead
of cold fronts. Since there are no mountains in this area, the third
type of thunderstorm never occurs here. Sometimes towering to
heights of 50,000 or 60,000 feet, thunderstorms can be quite
severe, bringing rain and hail and sometimes spawning tornadoes.

exercises

Select three of these topics and write a paragraph of extended definition
for each.

Rock music	Adequate diet
Beauty of soul	Vivacity of youth
Courtesy in everyday affairs	The home remedy
"Decency" at the beach	Jokes
Unethical behavior	Slang
Worthwhile fishing trips	Free enterprise
Any new slang word	Political liberals
Well-dressed man	Classical music
Good teacher	Promiscuity

Soul brother	Happiness
Obscene picture	Dirty politics
Integrity	Practical jokes
Sportsmanship	Excellent teachers
Trial marriage	Social fraternities

PARAGRAPH DEVELOPMENT BY USE OF ILLUSTRATION

Illustration, as used to support a topic sentence in the developmental paragraph, is narrative, that is, it tells a story. It usually gives a chronological account of what happened in a certain situation that would give validity to the topic sentence. Illustrations can be either real or hypothetical. You can use an account of some event you actually know about, or you can, in effect, "make up" one, provided the reader understands that the illustration is hypothetical. Usually the hypothetical illustration starts with something like "Suppose such-and-such a thing happened. What would be the result?" Then the writer goes on to supply a narrative of what would happen in the hypothetical situation.

Paragraphs may be developed by two kinds of illustrations—short and extended. A collection of short illustrations, all supporting the topic sentence, may be used as a paragraph. Usually, the narrative in a short illustration is quite brief. Or an extended illustration, a single, relatively long narrative, may constitute the paragraph. Of course, any combination of extended and short illustrations may be used to support the topic sentence.

The paragraph developed by the use of illustration can be represented by this diagram.

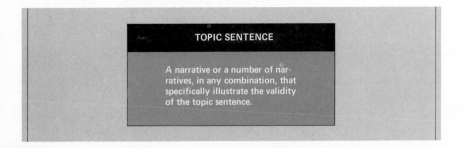

TOPIC SENTENCE

A narrative or a number of narratives, in any combination, that specifically illustrate the validity of the topic sentence.

Now, look at some examples of students' paragraphs using illustration. The first paragraph uses a series of short illustrations in support of the topic sentence.

American history is a record of courage. During the Revolution, Paul Revere, a Boston silversmith, rode his horse through the night to warn the Massachusetts colonists that the British were coming. Daniel Boone, Kentucky trailblazer and Indian fighter; Davy Crockett, hero of the Battle of the Alamo; and Lewis and Clark, leaders of the trail expedition to Oregon, all did their share in shaping the growth of a young country struggling against unknown obstacles. In more recent times, Charles Lindbergh, who by making the first nonstop flight from New York to Paris established the importance of air power to our country; General Douglas MacArthur, victorious against the Japanese after early defeat; and John F. Kennedy, who nearly lost his life as a PT boat commander in World War II but lived to become president of the United States, all displayed the personal bravery so apparent in American history.

That paragraph used seven short illustrations, arranged chronologically in American history, to support its topic sentence. The next paragraph is an example of the extended illustration.

Poor communication between the administration and staff results in misunderstandings among the employees of the Chemist's Laboratory. Recently, for instance, the department head told a graduate student employee, a good worker who had been carefully trained by another administrator in the same department, to go home and change out of Bermuda shorts or to consider himself fired. The incident, which occurred while several women employees were present, embarrassed the student so deeply that he determined not to work for such a man. The student resigned, and the department lost a well-trained and efficient worker because neither administrator had taken the responsiblity of telling the employee what dress was acceptable for work.

Here is another example of the use of a series of short illustrations.

Many people in show business have become famous because of a "gimmick." In the thirties, for example, such entertainers as Helen Kane with her "boo-boop-a-doop," and Joe Penner with "Wanna buy a duck?" rose to national prominence. In the fifties, Elvis Presley achieved adulation and stardom as a rock-and-roll singer by wiggling his hips and charming the teenage world by his wild gyrations. Frank Fontaine became popular because of a humorously stupid laugh. And more recently, the Beatles, an English singing group, were an immediate sensation, not so much for their singing as primarily for their clothes and long hair.

Here is another use of extended illustration, a hypothetical one.

> Despite the general opinion that it is recreation, an all-night fishing excursion is more work than pleasure. Suppose, for example, a typical fisherman decides to fish in his favorite lake, an afternoon's drive from his home. Since he plans to spend the night, he will spend all morning packing his gear—boat, fish lines, bait, food, cooking utensils, tent, bedding, and clothing. Then, after driving all afternoon to reach the lake, he will begin the tiring job of establishing camp. This task completed, he must back his boat trailer to the edge of the lake and laboriously ease his boat into the water. He then must find what he considers the perfect spot for setting out and baiting his lines. On his return to camp, he will perspire over an open fire while preparing his supper. After supper and again at two o'clock in the morning, he must run his lines, rebaiting where necessary. If he is lucky, he may net a fish or two before returning to camp for a few minutes of rest. As the sun appears on the horizon, he will cook and eat breakfast and begin to repack his gear for the long journey home. Four hours later, after an exhausting drive, he will walk into the house and collapse on the bed for a well-earned rest.

You will note that this paragraph does not contain an actual illustration, that is, the experience recounted in the paragraph did not happen to a specific person, necessarily, but it simply indicates what would likely happen to anyone on an overnight fishing trip.

The next sample is similar to the preceding one in that it involves a hypothetical individual and situation. But this example was written by a respected, published writer.

> The tribes we have described have all of them their nonparticipating "abnormal" individuals. The individual in Dobu who was thoroughly disoriented was the man who was naturally friendly and found activity an end in itself. He was a pleasant fellow who did not seek to overthrow his fellows or to punish them. He worked for anyone who asked him, and he was not filled by a terror of the dark like his fellows, and he did not, as they did, utterly inhibit simple public responses of friendliness toward women closely related, like a wife or sister. He often patted them playfully in public. In any other Dobuan this was scandalous behavior, but in him it was regarded as merely silly. The village treated him in a kindly enough fashion, not taking advantage of him or making a sport of ridiculing him, but he was definitely regarded as one who was outside the game. [11]

[11] From Ruth Benedict, *Patterns of Culture*. Copyright 1934 by Ruth Benedict. Reprinted by permission of Houghton Miffin Company.

The next two paragraphs from the same book indicate how the author uses an extended illustration about a real individual as he has been observed in the Zuñi society. Note that the illustration extends over two paragraphs but that each paragraph makes its own point with its own topic sentence.

The dilemma of such an individual is often most successfully solved by doing violence to his strongest natural impulses and accepting the role the culture honors. In case he is a person to whom social recognition is necessary, it is ordinarily his only possible course. One of the most striking individuals in Zuñi had accepted this necessity. In a society that thoroughly distrusts authority of any sort, he had a native personal magnetism that singled him out in any group. In a society that exalts moderation and the easiest way, he was turbulent and could act violently upon occasion. In a society that praises a pliant personality that "talks lots"—that is, that chatters in a friendly fashion—he was scornful and aloof. Zuñi's only reaction to such personalities is to brand them as witches. He was said to have been seen peering through a window from outside, and this is a sure mark of a witch. At any rate, he got drunk one day and boasted that they could not kill him. He was taken before the war priest who hung him by his thumbs from the rafters till he should confess to his witchcraft. This is the usual procedure in a charge of witchcraft. However, he dispatched a messenger to the government troops. When they came, his shoulders were already crippled for life, and the officer of the law was left with no recourse but to imprison the war priests who had been responsible for the enormity. One of these war priests was probably the most respected and important person in recent Zuñi history, and when he returned after imprisonment in the state penitentiary he never resumed his priestly offices. He regarded his power as broken. It was a revenge that is probably unique in Zuñi history. It involved, of course, a challenge to the priesthood, against whom the witch by his act openly aligned himself.

The course of his life in the forty years that followed this defiance was not, however, what we might easily predict. A witch is not barred from his membership in cult groups because he has been condemned, and the way to recognition lay through such activity. He possessed a remarkable verbal memory and a sweet singing voice. He learned unbelievable stories of mythology, of esoteric ritual, of cult songs. Many hundreds of pages of stories and ritual poetry were taken down from his dictation before he died, and he regarded his songs as much more extensive. He became indispensable in ceremonial life and before he died was the governor of Zuñi. The congenial bent of his personality threw him into irreconcilable conflict with his society, and he solved his dilemma by turning an incidental talent to account. As we might well expect, he was not a happy man. As governor of Zuñi, and high in his cult groups, a marked man in his community, he was obsessed by death. He was a cheated man in the midst of a mildly happy populace. [12]

[12]*Ibid.*

exercises

A. Select two of these topic sentences and write two separate paragraphs. In one, use a series of short illustrations to support the topic sentence. In the other, use an extended illustration.
  1. College (high school) freshmen have a rough time.
  2. The principal did not always act so wisely.
  3. The clean-up drive produced noteworthy results.
  4. Students are uncomfortable in the new high school.
  5. Cheating is (is not) widespread in _____ High School.
  6. Today's hair styles are ridiculous.
  7. Seventeen is a frustrating age.
  8. Country music has distinctive qualities.
B. This exercise reviews some of the material already covered.
  1. Look again at the paragraph about American history on page 139, and answer the following questions.
    a. What is the pointer in the topic sentence?
    b. Are there any sentences that do not help to establish this pointer as valid?
    c. What is the purpose of the phrases *During the Revolution* and *In more recent times?*
    d. What is there in the last sentence that ties it to the first sentence?
    e. Would you say, then, that this paragraph is coherent? Why or why not?
  2. Answer these questions on the paragraph about fishing on page 140.
    a. What is the pointer in the topic sentence?
    b. Examine the subjects of the sentences. Is a consistent point of view maintained?
    c. In what other ways is coherence achieved?
    d. About two-thirds of the way through the paragraph the word *perspire* is used. Would you prefer another word here? Why or why not?
  3. These questions concern the two paragraphs about the Zuñi society on page 141.
    a. What is the pointer in the topic sentence of the first paragraph? Of the second paragraph?
    b. In the first paragraph, what coherence device is employed in the sentence that starts *In a society that thoroughly distrusts. . . .* and in the next few sentences?
    c. What is the purpose of the phrase *At any rate* about half-way through the first paragraph? Has the principle of unity been violated just before the use of this phrase?
    d. Look at this sentence a little more than halfway through the first paragraph: *This is the usual procedure in a charge of witchcraft.* As you read through the paragraph (try it aloud), this sentence seems to be out of the tone of the rest of the paragraph. What makes it seem so? Try to rewrite it to make it fit in better. You might try including it in the preceding sentence.
    e. What is the purpose of *however* in the first sentence of the second paragraph?

f. What purpose is served by *As we might well expect* in the third sentence from the end of the second paragraph?

g. Is the second paragraph coherent? What means of achieving coherence are used?

PARAGRAPH DEVELOPMENT BY COMPARISON OR CONTRAST — Comparison and contrast, as developmental methods, are so much alike that they can be considered together. First, the two terms must be defined.

Comparison: indicates similarities between two objects, people, places, or ideas for the purpose of clarifying or explaining one or the other.

Contrast: indicates differences between two objects, people, places, or ideas for the purpose of clarifying or explaining one or the other.

Comparison shows similarities, contrast shows difference. Developing a paragraph by comparison or by contrast is not difficult, but it is better to compare or contrast point-by-point than to take the whole of the first object of comparison and then the whole of the other object. For instance, if you were comparing two cars it would be better to compare, say, the performance of one to the performance of the other, next their economy, and finally their appearance, than to describe these three points for one car and then describe them for the other.

Here is a diagram of the paragraph developed by comparison or contrast.

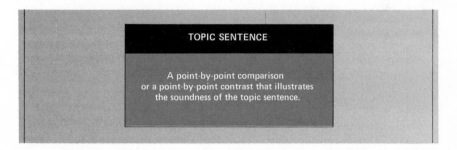

TOPIC SENTENCE

A point-by-point comparison or a point-by-point contrast that illustrates the soundness of the topic sentence.

Note how the following student paragraph makes this point-by-point comparison between a school and a game of basketball.

School is like a game of basketball. In both, the time is short, and the student uses all his resources in the class as the player does in the game. The student has a background of knowledge that enables him to meet the challenges in class; the player relies on ability he has acquired previously. The student begins on registration day a period in which he matches wits with his opponent, the professor. The first whistle of the basketball game starts the player matching his wits with the opposing team. The student relaxes over the weekends, taking this time to catch his breath; time out in the basketball game allows the player to catch his breath. The student can slow down the class, if he is tired, by turning it into a bull session. The basketball player can also slow down the game. Each is aware that he runs the risk of being punished, as the professor can give a pop quiz, or the referee can call a foul. Each participant is striving for a measure of his ability, a grade for the student and a score for the player. At the end of the term, the student looks anxiously at the bulletin board just outside the classroom for the final verdict. The player's eyes scan the scoreboard for the outcome of his efforts. The result is the same. If the student makes a good grade or the player has the high score, both are pleased with their efforts. If either loses––but that is too horrible to think about.

And here is a paragraph written by a student who was very fond of her new foreign car. She planned her paragraph around the same point-by-point comparison.

The proud owners of big American automobiles look with scorn at my little foreign car and with contempt call it a beetle. Well, I suppose it is almost a beetle. Nature carefully designed oval-shaped, low bodies for beetles to decrease air resistance, and my tiny horseless carriage is as smooth, oval, and low as any real beetle. Most beetles are actually poor flyers and indeed, some, like my car, never fly. A true member of the beetle family is pow-erful but slow; my small auto cannot go over sixty miles per hour, but it can climb steep curving roads well in spite of ice, rain, or standing water. Bugs take in energy-giving food anteriorly, and my bug-car has its gasoline tank near its nose also. Real beetles have posterior air intake tubes just like my little foreign car, although the real beetles have more of them. Normally I dislike bugs, but I am so fond of my beetle-like Volkswagen that I may grow to like all beetles.

This paragraph compares first the appearance of the two objects, next the performance of the two, and finally the position of fuel and air intake openings.

This next paragraph is developed by use of contrast. Note that again the point-by-point plan is used, but here in contrasting rather than in comparing.

> The modern kitchen is different from the old-style type. It even looks different. The charm of the old kitchen lay in its design, from the wallpaper to the curtains to the tablecloth; but the modern kitchen has no designs, only shiny chrome and brilliant color. There's a different atmosphere, too. Grandma's kitchen was a place to talk things over, to have a hot drink and relax while savoring the odor of bread baking in the oven, to leisurely plan and put loving thought into every meal prepared there. But the modern kitchen is constructed for speed, for the fastest and easiest way to get the food on the table and the dishes washed so that the cook can go on to other activities. The modern kitchen seems to have a different role to play in our lives. Instead of being a center of family life, it has become a laundry, dining room, and office for the increasingly complicated job of the homemaker.

This paragraph compares the old and the new kitchen on three points: their appearance, their atmosphere, and their roles in family life.

The next paragraph, a comparison, was written by a disgruntled married student.

> Special words have been used to sympathize with the "golfer's widow," but no terms directly apply to the amateur mechanic's wife, who is no better off. Both are often left stranded for hours with no cars while the laundry waits to be washed and the pantry to be filled. The golfer cannot stand the thought of his friends putting on the green without him, and the auto maniac insists on being present after each exciting mechanical failure. Either situation may leave the wife floundering in a welter of broken social engagements. Although it is worse in some ways to break appointments for lack of transportation or an escort, the mechanic's wife and the golfer's wife are placed at further social disadvantages by knowing that, come spring, when afternoon picnics and cook-outs are enticing, the amateur mechanic wants to polish his car as well as those of his buddies, and the golfer wants to join his cronies on the golf course. Both leave their wives to wonder how the myth of "family companionship" persists.

As with most methods of paragraph development, an entire paper could be written using the methods of comparison and contrast, as in "A Pesty Roommate," the freshman paper given below. Read the paper carefully and check it for the following:

1. How does the introductory paragraph provide the general basis for comparison and contrast?

2. What kind of tone is set in the opening paragraph? How?
3. What two points about each roommate are being compared? What two are being contrasted?
4. Are the four developmental paragraphs adequately developed?
5. What important transitions are provided between paragraphs?
6. How could you improve the concluding paragraph?

A PESTY ROOMMATE

At the beginning of school, two hastily scrawled signs were left on my dorm door as a warning of things to come. One sign said, "Avoid objects that move hurriedly in the dark" and the other read, "Beware of Annoying Pests." Unfortunately, I wasn't aware that these signs were left by a far wiser and more experienced person than myself: the room's previous occupant. The meaning of these puzzling warnings became more apparent to me after meeting my two new, yet different, roommates, one of whom proved to be a strange creature.

I met my first roommate "A" when she arrived with her entire family in a station wagon crammed with all her personal possessions. She managed to step gracefully out of the car, after being sandwiched between her big brother and the door for hours, without a wrinkle in her beautifully coordinated pantsuit. In contrast, roommate "B" scurried in late one evening from a still unknown origin carrying everything she owned on her back and wearing a dirty brown coat. I soon noticed she did everything in that brown coat from eating dinner to sleeping.

As time progressed, I discovered roommate "A" differed greatly from roommate "B" not only in personal appearance, but in personal cleanliness as well. Roommate "A" often spent hours in the bathroom plucking her eyebrows, shaving her legs, and washing her hair. On the other hand, roommate "B" seemed to have a phobia concerning water because I rarely saw her go near it. One day, however, a little excitement did occur in the bathroom. I discovered roommate "A" sitting in the sink hollering, "Kill that bug, please kill that bug" while roommate "B" looking slightly offended stared at her with an open mouth. While attempting to kill the bug, I learned roommate "B" does not like the smell of Raid as I watched her crawl down the hall. She did not return to the room until the smell of bug spray had completely disappeared.

Although obvious distinctions did exist between my two roommates, several similarities were also evident. For example, both roommates regularly depleted my food supply. I was constantly finding one or the other nibbling at my homemade "goodies" and grinning mischievously. Once I became so angry at their chronic snitching, I hid my food. The minute I left the room, however, Roommate "B" flung up her food-detecting antennas and led roommate "A" right to it.

Furthermore, both roommate "A" and "B" frequently borrowed my clothes. Roommate "A" at least demonstrated some thought-

fulness and consideration by asking me if she could borrow my
favorite shirt, etc. before doing so. Roommate "B" never asked;
instead she repeatedly bugged me by running rampant through
everything I owned with her messy feet. An additional comparison
between the two was that both roommate "A" and "B" were free to
come and go as they pleased. Neither ever told me where she was
going, when she would return, or whom she was going out with.

 In spite of its annoyances, my first semester of dorm living
provided me with useful knowledge and insight. Armed with this
new enlightenment, I was able to decide that I preferred roommate
"A"'s company more than roommate "B"'s. Perhaps I enjoyed "A"
more because I discovered it is easier to speak intelligently
with a freshman biology major than with a filthy cockroach.

Were you surprised by the ending of this paper? If you were, recheck
it for the clues provided to guide you.

exercises

A. Select two of these topic sentences. Write one paragraph using comparison as a means of development and another paragraph using contrast.
1. The P.E. teacher insisted that the class would benefit far more
if they chose swimming rather than fencing (archery, golf, badmin-
ton, field hockey, handball) for the second semester's work.
2. Death is like sleep.
3. The prospective buyer has little choice among today's cars.
4. I didn't know whether to ask the tall blonde or the little, dark-eyed
brunette.
5. Mrs. Smith said that one conversation piece in the living room
was enough.
6. Fear is like fire (ice).
7. Youth has "rebelled" before.
8. Men and women are similar (opposites).
9. I have not found college so different from high school (or the opposite).
10. The feud between the Suffles and their neighbors included even
the landscaping of their lawns.
B. Your instructor may ask you to expand one of the paragraphs in Exercise
A into a short paper.
C. Make a list of the things you would have to do to develop a longer
paper (seven or eight paragraphs) from one of the two paragraphs you
wrote for Exercise *A*.
D. Devise a point-by-point outline to illustrate the structure of "A Pesty
Roommate."

PARAGRAPH DEVELOPMENT BY
REASONS
 The use of reasons in paragraph
development has already been dis-
cussed in the section about maintaining unity in the paragraph. Recall
that example paragraphs in the section gave two or more reasons

for the validity of the topic sentence and then supported those reasons. Also recall that this pattern of development is the one suggested in the chapter on the whole paper, except that in the paper the reasons (topic sentences) support the thesis statement of the paper. And because a paragraph is like a small paper, the same method of development can be used *within* the paragraph.

In one of the exercises of an earlier chapter, you were asked to analyze a paragraph by E. B. White. He developed this paragraph by using reasons. Have another look at it.

> It is a miracle that New York works at all. *The whole thing is implausible.* Every time the residents brush their teeth, millions of gallons of water must be drawn from the Catskills and the hills of Westchester. When a young man in Manhattan writes a letter to his girl in Brooklyn, the love message gets blown to her through a pneumatic tube—pfft—just like that. The subterranean system of telephone cables, power lines, steam pipes, gas mains and sewer pipes is reason enough to abandon the island to the gods and the weevils. Every time an incision is made in the pavement, the noisy surgeons expose ganglia that are tangled beyond belief. By rights *New York should have destroyed itself long ago,* from panic or fire or rioting or failure of some vital supply line in its circulatory system or from some deep labyrinthine short circut. Long ago the city should have experienced an insoluble traffic snarl at some impossible bottleneck. It should have perished of hunger when food lines failed for a few days. It should have been wiped out by a plague starting in its slums or carried in by ships' rats. It should have been overwhelmed by the sea that licks at it on every side. The workers in its myriad cells should have succumbed to nerves, from the fearful pall of smoke-fog that drifts over every few days from Jersey, blotting out all light at noon, and leaving the high offices suspended, men groping and depressed, and the sense of world's end. It should have been touched in the head by the August heat and gone off its rocker.[13]

The topic sentence of this paragraph is the first sentence. Its pointer is *miracle.* The two reasons that support this topic sentence are italicized in the paragraph. In its simplest outline form, the paragraph appears like this:

Topic Sentence: It is a miracle that New York works at all.
Main Reason 1:   The whole thing is implausible.
Main Reason 2:   New York should have destroyed itself long ago.

This outline as it stands could be assembled into a paragraph.

---

[13]From pp. 24–25 in *Here Is New York* by E. B. White. Copyright 1949 by E. B. White. Used by permission of Harper & Row, Publishers, and Hamish Hamilton, London.

It is a miracle that New York works at all. The whole thing is implausible for a number of reasons. There is so much congestion that New York should have destroyed itself long ago.

But you have learned that this is not a good paragraph because it does not supply details as supporting reasons. White did it like this:

> *Topic Sentence:* It is a miracle that New York works at all.
>   *Main Reason 1:* The whole thing is implausible.
>   *Supporting Reason 1:* Water must come from a distance.
>   *Supporting Reason 2:* Mail is carried through tubes.
>   *Supporting Reason 3:* Subterranean lines, cables, and pipes are hopelessly tangled.
>   *Main Reason 2:* New York should have destroyed itself,
>   *Supporting Reason 1:* From insoluble traffic snarls.
>   *Supporting Reason 2:* From hunger through failure of food lines.
>   *Supporting Reason 3:* From plague through slums or rats.
>   *Supporting Reason 4:* From the sea.
>   *Supporting Reason 5:* From workers' nerves.
>   *Supporting Reason 6:* From insanity.

A paragraph from the section on comparison and contrast may also be used to illustrate paragraph development through reasons. Look at it again.

```
        The modern kitchen is different from the old-style type. It
    even looks different. The charm of the old kitchen lay in its
    design, from the wallpaper to the curtains to the tablecloth; but
    the modern kitchen has no designs, only shiny chrome and
    brilliant color. There's a different atmosphere, too. Grandma's
    kitchen was a place to talk things over, to have a hot drink and
    relax while savoring the odor of bread baking in the oven, to lei-
    surely plan and put loving thought into every meal prepared
    there. But the modern kitchen is constructed for speed, for the
    fastest and easiest way to get the food on the table and the dishes
    washed so that the cook can go on to other activities. The modern
    kitchen seems to have a different role to play in our lives.
    Instead of being a center of family life, it has become a laundry,
    dining room, and office for the increasingly complicated job of
    the homemaker.
```

The topic sentence is the first sentence in the paragraph. The pointer is *different*. The paragraph lists three reasons for the difference. In diagram form, the paragraph looks like this:

Topic Sentence: The modern kitchen is different from the old-style type.
    Reason 1: It has a different appearance.
    Reason 2: It has a different atmosphere.
    Reason 3: It plays a different role in family life.

The development of each of the three reasons is accomplished by the use of contrast, that is, contrasting the old kitchen to the new on each of these three points. The paragraph, then, is developed by two methods—reasons and contrast.

exercises

A. Using two of these topic sentences, write two outlines for paragraphs to be developed by reasons. You may take the opposite point of view of any of these topic sentences.
1. We lost the game because of our star player's mistakes.
2. Dormitory life teaches the freshman self-reliance (caution) (tolerance).
3. Sally did not want to have a date with him.
4. Dress helps to make the man.
5. Her teaching methods were directed toward making the student think.
6. Downtown business centers in cities are certain to decrease in importance.
7. A universal metric system would allow freer world trade.
8. (Your school) was the proper choice for me.
9. Carolyn is a very pushy girl.
10. Bicycles are dangerous.

Follow this outline form:

Topic Sentence:
    Main Reason 1:
        Supporting Reason 1:
        Supporting Reason 2:
    Main Reason 2:
        Supporting Reason 1:
        Supporting Reason 2:
    Main Reason 3:
        Supporting Reason 1:
        Supporting Reason 2:

Your outlines must have at least two main reasons plus as many as you may need to develop the paragraph adequately. Each main reason must also have at least two supporting reasons.

B. Write paragraphs from the two outlines composed for Exercise *A*.

Writers don't ordinarily develop paragraphs or papers by using only one of the methods you have just studied. They combine methods, choosing those most suited to the subject and to the topic sentences. Although experienced writers don't usually decide deliberately to develop a paragraph or paper by any specific method, they do use methods. The method of development isn't an arbitrary pattern *imposed on* subject matter; rather, the subject matter almost automatically *demands* a certain method. For example, the topic sentences in Exercise *A* on page 150 seem to demand *reasons;* those in Exercise *A* on page 147 seem to demand *comparisons;* those in Exercise *A* on page 142 seem to demand *illustrations;* and, because of their modifiers or difficulty, the topics listed on page 137 seem to invite *definitions.* How a limited subject and controlling attitude are stated will usually point to one or more methods of development. For example, study the following subjects:

> Teacher.
> A teacher guides the students.
> A good teacher.
> A good teacher controls, informs, and inspires.
> All school systems probably contain both good and bad teachers.
> Good teachers and bad teachers are similar in some ways, but they are quite different in others.

Though these are all about teachers, clearly how they are conceived and phrased pretty well dictates the method of development. Get the *subject* and *controlling attitude* specific and clear in your mind, and the method of development should logically follow. For example, here are some paragraphs written by experienced writers. Note how each combines methods logically within a single paragraph.

1   Lasers—there are several varieties—are rather surprisingly sim-
2 ple devices which generate highly disciplined and coherent light rays.
3 To appreciate their impact one must first realize that until a few years
4 ago an important dividing line cut across the electromagnetic frequency
5 spectrum just above the upper limits of the microwave region. Below
6 this divide there were transistors and electron tubes which could generate
7 the coherent signals necessary for communications or computers or any
8 of the other tasks of modern electronics. Above it, in the infrared and
9 optical regions, there were only incoherent thermal sources—the sun,
10 light bulbs, arc lamps, flames. The electromagnetic radiation from these
11 sources is highly undisciplined, containing waves traveling in all possible
12 directions and made up of a scrambled mixture of all possible frequencies.
13   The development of the laser as a coherent light source means
14 that this division is now gone. Note that most lasers emit considerably

15 less total power than, say, a hundred-watt bulb. But the light bulb,
16 which is incoherent, emits its energy into so many frequencies and
17 directions that the amount emitted into any single specific frequency
18 and direction is minute. By contrast, the laser, which is coherent, emits
19 all of its energy at a single frequency and in a single direction and
20 in some cases does so in a single brief but extremely intense burst.
21 Within its single frequency and direction, therefore, the laser is incom-
22 parably brighter than, say, the sun or any other thermal light source.[14]

These two paragraphs are definition paragraphs. They attempt to define lasers in nonscientific terms so that an ordinary reader can understand. Several methods of development are used in the definition. Note that the first sentence is a simple definition by classification. From lines 3 through 8, the author uses explanation of background reinforced by reason. In lines 9 and 10, he defines *incoherent thermal sources* by enumeration. The last part of line 11 starts a definition by classification of the word *undisciplined* as applied to electromagnetic radiation. Lines 14 through 22 offer contrast as a method of development. Note that *incoherent* and *coherent light sources* are defined in this contrast. The last sentence is a conclusion, as shown by the transition word *therefore*.

Here is another paragraph by an experienced writer.

(1) An Indian coffeehouse, like an Indian Bazaar, has its own peculiar atmosphere. (2) It is a cheerful, unpretentious place in which to dawdle, encounter friends, talk, discuss, gossip. (3) Students make fiery speeches to each other; women meet for a break in the morning's shopping; idlers stop by for a rest, to watch the world go by, to pick up a chance colleague. (4) The actual drinking of coffee is the least important part of the whole affair. (5) Looking around at the tables, I couldn't help thinking that this particular sort of place doesn't exist in Moscow. (6) There, one can find restaurants (mostly rather expensive by any standard), or "Parks of Culture and Rest," or hotel dining rooms, and several varieties of bar ranging from the *pivnaya,* where as a rule you can't even sit down, where women are seldom seen, and where the customers walk to the bar, order a drink, down it and leave, all within the space of five minutes, to the stolovoye, which is considered more refined, more suitable for women, and where ordinary vodka is not served, though wines and brandy are brought to your table. (7) But India is not a drinking country—even in the states where there is no prohibition. (8) The sight of drunks being thrown out of restaurants with the offhand ruthlessness that Russians employ for such occasions is extremely rare in India.[15]

[14]Anthony E. Siegman, "The Laser: Astounding Beam of Light," *Stanford Today,* Autumn, 1964. Reprinted by permission of *Stanford Today,* Leland Stanford Junior University, Stanford, California.

[15]Santha Rama Rau, "Return to India," *The Reporter,* June, 1960. Published by the Reporter Magazine Company. Copyright 1960 by *The Reporter.* Reprinted by permission of William Morris Agency, Inc.

In this paragraph, Sentences 2, 3, and 4 use detail to explain the atmosphere of the Indian coffeehouse. Sentences 5, 6, 7, and 8 are concerned with a contrast between the drinking habits of Indians and of Russians. Note that Sentence 6 is filled with detail to describe the Russian bars.

exercises

A. Throughout this chapter you have written many paragraphs. Choose any three and rewrite them to change the tone to fit any of the following (use a different one for each paragraph): *formal, informal, personal, impersonal, critical, emotional, more argumentative, humorous, absurd.* You may want to discuss these tags before you begin this exercise.

B. Choose one of the six paragraphs involved in Exercise *A* and rewrite it to improve reader interest and reader acceptance (assume you are writing to a close personal friend). (If you have trouble with this assignment, reread pages 101–108.

C. 1. Think about each word in the following list and decide whether your feeling about the word is "favorable" or "unfavorable." Place a plus (+) beside those you respond favorably to, and a minus (−) beside those you respond unfavorably to. Those that don't fit either class or fit *both* label "neutral" (0).

crash	shout	eye	scold
rush	sit	fire	listen
cool	honest	foolish	cheer
talk	fair	hand	brag
walk	crush	careful	agree
quiet	say	clash	define
slap	frigid	stoop	jeer
wise	warm	silly	assure
run	stand	trip	beg

2. a. Be prepared to discuss your classification.
   b. What can you conclude about words and a person's feelings?
   c. Compare your list with others in the class. Why are there differences?
   d. Try to spot the "feeling" words in the paragraphs you wrote for *A* and *B*, above.

D. Now that you have worked Exercise *C*, turn back to page 20 to the theme, "Unleashed Danger." Make a list of all words that imply a "judgment" to you (for example, *restrain, fear, nuisance, damage, scare, affectionately*). After you have completed this list of "tone" words (you should be able to find several dozen), classify the words in the same way you did in Exercise *C*, above, but use only two classes, "favorable" (+) and "unfavorable" (−).
   1. Which "tone" words appear more frequently, (+) or (−)?
   2. Compare your list with others in the class. Why are there differences?

3. On the basis of your classification, what do you think the person "speaking" in the theme feels about dogs? Do you think the *writer* of the theme and this "speaker" are in agreement? Explain.

4. Your instructor may ask you to repeat this exercise using the theme on "Law and Order" (page 32).

REVIEW TERMS

Some of the following terms reflect information covered in previous chapters, but most point to information discussed in the present chapter on writing paragraphs. Be sure you understand them all before tackling the next chapter.

Thesis sentence, topic sentence, pointer, controlling attitude, standard paragraph, continuity, chain of meaning, natural association, paragraph of convenience, basic introductory paragraph, common ground, tone, blueprint, argumentative bias, logical appeal, emotional appeal, ethical appeal, writer's "voice," provocative question, relevant quotation, anecdote, transition, interlocking connection, fact, judgment, opinion, inference, fallacious, factual evidence, hasty generalization, to infer, hasty conclusion, faulty inference, the specific, the general, levels of generalization, specific details, definition term, classification, definition by classification, Aristotelian definition, family, general class, genus, differentia, synonym, definition by synonym, definition by example, definition by illustration, definition by function, operational definition, dictionary definition, process explanation, extended definition, illustration, short illustration, extended illustration, hypothetical illustration, comparison, contrast, reasons, combined methods of development

putting the parts together: the whole paper

ow that you have studied the parts of the five-hundred-word paper, it's time to put them all together. Remember, the writing techniques you have learned apply to *all* your writing—to individual paragraphs, to short papers, to long papers. The basic techniques remain the same:

Discovering a subject
Focusing through controlling attitude
Providing specific supporting evidence
Maintaining unity of subject and tone
Providing interlocking connections
Using suitable developmental patterns

As a reminder, look again at the five-hundred-word paper in a new basic diagram (page 157), a slightly different version because your knowledge of the writing process has greatly increased. This is the basic pattern you will use in writing your papers.

But you are better prepared now than you were when you wrote your first five-hundred-word theme at the end of Chapter 2. Your writing should reflect what you have learned in the meantime. Also, by now you should have a better idea of what your teacher looks for when reading your papers. Before writing any new themes, review the basic things he'll be checking. The grade assigned to your paper will be a composite evaluation of how successful you are in three or four main areas:

A. *Content.* Your teacher will decide whether you have a meaningful, limited subject and whether you develop it logically and support it adequately.

B. *Organization.* Your teacher will also determine whether you have a controlled thesis statement in the introduction; clear support in the topic sentences of each developmental paragraph; specific, detailed support for each topic sentence; and a conclusion that echoes the thesis statement without simply repeating it.

C. *Tone.* Your teacher may also bring to your attention problems concerning reader interest and reader acceptance, the way in which the writer's "voice" is coming across. Remember that the kind of "voice" readers hear as they go through your paper will influence their judgment of it.

D. *Mechanics.* Finally, your instructor will note any unacceptable spelling, punctuation, and grammar, faulty sentence structure (for instance, fragments that don't work), lack of unity and coherence, and faulty diction (that is, word choice, including worn out expressions, listless verbs, and the "who-which-that disease").

Keep in mind that a real weakness in any *one* of these major basic areas will influence your reader. You can, for example, have good

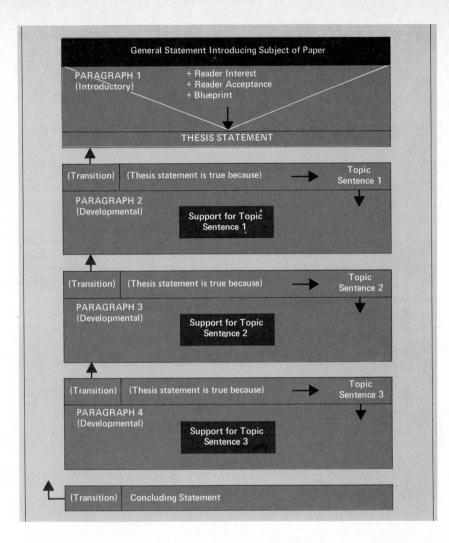

General Statement Introducing Subject of Paper

PARAGRAPH 1
(Introductory)
+ Reader Interest
+ Reader Acceptance
+ Blueprint

THESIS STATEMENT

(Transition) (Thesis statement is true because) → Topic Sentence 1

PARAGRAPH 2
(Developmental)
Support for Topic Sentence 1

(Transition) (Thesis statement is true because) → Topic Sentence 2

PARAGRAPH 3
(Developmental)
Support for Topic Sentence 2

(Transition) (Thesis statement is true because) → Topic Sentence 3

PARAGRAPH 4
(Developmental)
Support for Topic Sentence 3

(Transition) Concluding Statement

content and organization, but if the mechanics of your paper are poor, your grade could be disappointing. Similarly, your mechanics can be perfect and your organization good, but if your paper lacks ideas of consequence or is dull, the result may be the same. Usually the dull paper that is good in all other respects has a problem in *tone*; that is, it may have no reader interest, or it may lack ethical appeal (getting the reader to accept the writer and his views). Or it may have an informal tone where a more formal one is demanded by the subject; or it may sound insincere because the words are far too fancy for the subject. You will learn more about tone in Chapter 9 (see page 277). Meanwhile, if tone becomes a problem, study pages 101–4 on introductory paragraphs.

Here is a check sheet that summarizes the four basic areas your instructor will evaluate; note that it also lists some of the details within each of the four areas to help you revise your own work.

SIMPLIFIED CHECK SHEET FOR THE WHOLE PAPER	Excellent	Good	Acceptable	Weak	Poor
A. THOUGHT					
1. Does the paper have a meaningful subject?					
2. Is the subject limited?					
3. Is there a clear controlling attitude?					
4. Do developmental paragraphs give specific factual support?					
5. Is the support adequate?					
6. Does the whole paper have unity of thought?					
B. ORGANIZATION					
7. Is there a clear beginning, middle, and ending?					
8. Is the thesis statement adequate?					
9. Do all topic sentences support the thesis?					
10. Is there a "blueprint" to order the ideas?					
11. Does the whole paper have coherence?					
12. Does each paragraph have unity and coherence?					
C. TONE (The Writer's "Voice")					
13. Does the paper create reader interest?					
14. Does the paper try to get reader acceptance?					
15. Is there successful ethical appeal?					
16. Does the tone fit the subject and the reader?					
D. MECHANICS					
17. Good word choice: strong verbs, care with adverbs?					
18. Spelling, punctuation, grammar?					
19. Sentence structure?					

Use this check sheet before you turn in your papers to note those elements which need revision. Of course, if you don't reread your papers before turning them in, you won't be able to evaluate their success. The check sheet has several other uses: You can exchange papers with a classmate to spot each other's strengths and weaknesses; your instructor may want to use the check sheet for similar purposes, having the entire class evaluate its own papers; or to point out your problems quickly (especially if he does not have time to comment at length).

To further understand what your instructor will be looking for, consider the next three students' papers, which are analyzed as an instructor might do it. Examine them one paragraph at a time.

THE STUDENT AND CLASSIC COMICS

High school students, usually not avid readers of comic books, often resort to substituting classic comics for required reading books. Basically honest, many of these students, under pressure of heavy assignments and extracurricular activities, think of the classic comic merely as a short cut to an assignment. Although students may be able to write a plot summary, they are cheating themselves when they take the easy way out.

For the most part, this paragraph fulfills the requirements for a short introductory paragraph. It starts with a general statement (part of the thesis statement) and ends with a specific controlling attitude (the pointer): Students *cheat themselves* when they take the easy way out (by substituting classic comics for required reading). The remainder of the paper must show why students *cheat themselves* through this procedure. Note that the paragraph also tries to get reader acceptance by making a number of *positive* statements about students: They aren't usually "avid readers" of comic books, they're "basically honest," and they are under "pressure of heavy assignments and extracurricular activities." But there is no real attempt to create interest or to project ethical appeal. And there's no blueprint to order the ideas of the paper.

Here is the first developmental paragraph.

The student who depends on the comic book version of the world's great literature often deprives himself of an accurate presentation of the original story. For example, if he reads the comic version of Twain's A Connecticut Yankee, which eliminates any attempt at satire, he receives the impression that Twain was making an early effort at some type of science fiction. A student who relies on the comic classic of Huckleberry Finn misses many of Huck's adventures, such as the Grangerford episode, and finds the story ending in a manner that would startle the author. The unfortunate student who makes his book report from the comic classic The House of Seven Gables will overemphasize the Pyncheon ancestors and the family curse, saying little about Hepzibah, Clifford, and the other characters because mysterious deaths and family curses create better mystery stories than the effect of these circumstances on characters.

This developmental paragraph has a proper topic sentence, as the first sentence in the paragraph, indicating one reason that the thesis statement is valid: Students deprive themselves of an accurate presentation of the original story. To support this topic sentence, the writer uses three short illustrations from three famous works of fiction to show how each story is twisted in its comic book version. Because the pointer in the topic sentence is *deprives* and each illustration indicates how this deprivation comes about, the paragraph has unity. Each of the sentences in the paragraph uses *student*, or its substitute *he,* as the subject; therefore the paragraph maintains coherence through a consistent point of view. There are no mechanical errors.

Now, look at the second developmental paragraph.

(1) In addition to being deprived of accurate presentations of literature, each time the student resorts to the comic classic version of a novel he misses practice in critical reading and evaluation of literature. (2) The student has no concept of the underlying theme of a particular story or of persistent themes that recur in one author's works. (3) Since the comic classics present only what the characters say, the reader has no way of interpreting the author's purpose for writing a story. (4) Further, since symbolism and point of view cannot be adapted to comic book presentation, the reader misses these artistic devices. (5) Finally, the student fails to see the structure of the novel because the emphasis is always on plot and action. (6) Regardless of the importance of setting or characters in the original version, the student will see plot as the dominant factor.

Again, in this paragraph, the first sentence is the topic sentence. The pointer is *misses practice*; the remainder must show why this practice is missed. The paragraph is developed through reasons, and three reasons are given to indicate the validity of the topic sentence. The first is in the second sentence—the student misses the underlying theme or themes that recur in one author's work. The second reason is in the fourth sentence—the student misses symbolism and point of view. The third reason is in the fifth sentence—the student misses the structure of the novel because emphasis in classic comics is on plot and action only.

The paragraph maintains unity. The three reasons given directly support the topic sentence. The other sentences also contribute to the unity of the paragraph. The third sentence, for instance, explains the first reason given in the second sentence, and the sixth sentence explains the third reason given in the fifth sentence. The paragraph holds together well. The subject of each sentence is *student* or a pronoun or noun standing for student. To increase coherence, transition words are used twice. *Further*, in the fourth sentence, introduces the second reason, and *finally,* in the fifth sentence, introduces the third reason. Note also that the first part of the first sentence is used as transition to link this paragraph with the preceding one to improve the coherence of the whole paper.

Now consider the final paragraph.

---

(1) Of equal importance to the student who substitutes the comic classic version for the original novel, he does not enjoy the power and majesty of the English language as it has been used by our greatest authors. (2) He finds no new and interesting words to challenge him. (3) Because these books are intended primarily for a young, nonliterary audience, he encounters only simple, everyday words that he already knows. (4) Comparing the comic version with the author's, he finds the vocabulary confined to words with little, if any, connotative meaning. (5) The student will also find that most descriptive passages have been eliminated or reworded. (6) The author has described the actions and scenes in vivid, carefully chosen words, but the comic book reader sees only the crude and oversimplified drawings. (7) He discovers that he need not use his imagination to create a character because he has access to the stereotyped picture drawn by the comic strip artist. (8) Thus, he does not need the figurative language that enriches and encourages imagination. (9) Not only does the student miss the artistry of word choice and description, he cannot see the different combinations of words in sentences and sentences in paragraphs used by authors to create distinctive styles. (10) Since he is reading a condensed and altered version of the novel, he is not aware of the vividness of an author's use of dialect or his ability to make the most ordinary things seem out of the ordinary. (11) He misses the artistry of an author like Poe who chose words for sounds and then placed these words in sentences, almost rhythmic and poetic. (12) By reading this inaccurate presentation of the world's great literature, the student denies himself the opportunity of reading the literature of the past, the value of developing a critical attitude toward literature, and the pleasure of enjoying the power and beauty of his own language.

This paragraph, like the other developmental paragraphs, starts with the topic sentence. The point it develops is that the student who reads comic classics as substitutes for the real thing misses the full effect of the artistry used by our greatest authors. The developmental method is the use of detail—the piling up of reasons for what the student misses. The last sentence is the concluding statement. It contains the three reasons for the validity of the thesis statement that make up the topic sentences of the paragraphs.

Again, this paragraph is coherent and unified. All the sentences directly support the topic sentence. All the sentences use *student*, the pronoun *he*, or an equivalent subject. Notice, too, the use of the transition words *also*, in the fifth sentence, and *thus*, in the eighth sentence. Further, the beginning of the ninth sentence, *Not only does the student miss the artistry of word choice and description*, provides transition to the next group of ideas. The first part of the topic sentence, *Of equal importance . . .*, connects this paragraph with the preceding one.

An outline will demonstrate the overall organization of the whole paper.

Thesis statement:	Students cheat themselves when they choose the "easy way" of reading classic comics instead of required books.
Reason 1: (Topic Sentence)	They deny themselves an accurate presentation of the original story.
Reason 2: (Topic Sentence)	They miss the opportunity to practice critical reading and evaluation of literature.
Reason 3: (Topic Sentence)	They lose enjoyment of the power and majesty of the English language.

This paper could be marked good on organization, good on content, and good on mechanics, and it should earn a good grade. But the paper could be made even better. The writer could add interest to the paper by making the comment "vivid, carefully chosen words" even more specific, perhaps by quoting a phrase or two. He could also choose one of the "crude and oversimplified drawings" for comment, perhaps adding a touch of humor. While these changes are not absolutely necessary and could lengthen the paper, they could very well add the spark to make the result *excellent*.

When you write a five-hundred-word paper, it will need a title; so far, nothing has been said about titles. These eight guidelines will serve you well:

1. Use no more than five words, usually.
2. Use no period at the end of your title.
3. Make no *direct* reference to your title in the first lines of your paper.
4. Capitalize the first and last words of your title. Do not capitalize articles (*a, an, the*), conjunctions (*and, but, or,* and so forth), or prepositions.
5. Make your title honest, but try to be creative.
6. Summarize your paper in the title.

7. Do not make your title a sentence.
8. Never put quotation marks around your own title.

Take, for example, the title of the paper just analyzed, "The Student and Classic Comics." It requires only five words, has no final mark of punctuation, and has all words capitalized except the conjunction *and*. It is an honest title; it summarizes the paper; and it is not a sentence. Although it fulfills the requirements for a good title, it could be improved. Can you suggest a better version?

Now look at another paper.

THE LIBRARY, THE TEACHER, AND THE STUDENT

Students in the high school I attended have certainly lost the inquiring mind, if they ever had it, and they no longer even want to think for themselves. It seems, in fact, that our whole society has lost the zest for inquiry because of the loss of ideals and qualities. I cannot account for society's loss, but among students in my school I can see at least two reasons: inadequate libraries and prejudiced teachers.

This introductory paragraph is not bad. All the parts are there, but they are not organized. The first sentence is apparently the thesis statement. But this sentence is composed of two independent clauses: *Students in the high school I attended have certainly lost the inquiring mind* and *they no longer even want to think for themselves.* You have learned that this construction is questionable for a thesis statement because the clauses carry equal weight and there is no way for the reader to determine which is the subject of the paper. If you look at this sentence closely, however, you will realize that its author is saying the same thing in both parts. What he intends to be the thesis statement is that *students no longer want to think for themselves.* This idea should be given the important position in the sentence; it should be placed at the end of the first paragraph with the two reasons (the blueprint) given in the third sentence, because they are apparently going to be used as topic sentences in the paper. The second sentence in the introductory paragraph is a general statement about all people, not just students, and it needs to be recast and used as the first sentence of the paragraph. But take care in recasting to avoid such general words as *ideals* and *qualities*, because as they are used in the second sentence, they are not specific enough to be meaningful. Even so, this paragraph holds together. Note that *lost* in the first sentence is repeated in the second and that it appears as *loss* in the third. All three sentences are tied together by repetition of a key word. The whole paragraph, however, could use some reorganization.

The first developmental paragraph discusses the first reason students do not want to think for themselves.

In my high school, the library was pathetically inadequate. If we wanted to know about the latest scientific developments, we had no reference books to examine except a fifteen-year-old encyclopedia more suitable for the primary grades than for the high school. We could read no recent scientific magazines, because there were none, not even any fifteen years old. The most weighty current magazine in the library was The Reader's Digest, hardly the one in which to research a topic in, say, biology. If we were interested in literature, about the best we could do for modern fiction was Seventeen by Booth Tarkington or perhaps The Virginian. No teacher of any subject ever assigned us library work or outside reading. On the few occasions one of us did venture into the library on his own initiative, old Miss Spence, who had been librarian for twenty years, made it clear that she could not care less. If we came into the library, it only meant trouble for her. Under these conditions it is not surprising that the students did little inquiry into important human problems. They did not even know what these problems were; they had no way of knowing.

This paragraph appears to be a good one. It starts with a topic sentence that has a pointer, *pathetically inadequate*. Basically, it gives three reasons in support of the validity of this topic sentence: (1) resources for scientific research were nonexistent; (2) literary research, particularly modern, was equally difficult; and (3) the teachers and the librarian were uninterested in encouraging library work. Each reason is supported by illustration, and the paragraph ends with a summary sentence. The paragraph reads well as a unit. Note, for instance, the repetition of *fifteen* in the first part of the paragraph and of *library* and *librarian* in the last part to help coherence. Unity is maintained because all the evidence offered supports the topic sentence.

Here is the last paragraph.

---

(1) We have modified our society a great deal in the past few decades. (2) With the new advances in knowledge and in working and living conditions, we have come to expect more from other people than from ourselves. (3) Students revel in the new prosperity,

buying things, having fun, and joining clubs. (4) The sole aim of their lives has become to have pleasure, so much so that they simply do not have time for school or studies or satisfying their natural curiosity. (5) In fact, they do not even notice these things, because they do not contribute to what they consider their pleasure. (6) Teachers foster this pursuit of pleasure in their students by trying to make their students all conform to what they think students ought to be and to think. (7) Students are expected to parrot on quizzes the ideas the teacher has given out in class. (8) They do not want us to think for ourselves but to go to established authorities for even simple ideas and explanations. (9) These teachers, and other forces in society, who rebel against nonconformity (something may or may not be right, but they won't try to find out if it is or not) make certain that a teacher with other ideas is not allowed to exist in their little world. (10) This is well illustrated by the case of Mrs. Jane Doe, a former teacher of mine. (11) In her English classes, she discussed everything, always taking the view opposite that of the majority of her students. (12) She would rant in class in her attacks on the established order of society or politics or tradition, and actually spoke in favor of Communism just to get her students to argue with her. (13) Her attacks forced her students to think to support their views. (14) Forcing her students to think was the best thing she did for her students. (15) But Mrs. Doe was accused of being a Communist and fired because the other teachers, the school administrators, and the community did not appreciate her value. (16) With the lack of research facilities in the school library and with this sort of narrow-mindedness from our teachers, students at the high school I attended cannot think for themselves.

This paragraph is a jumble of ideas without unity, and what seemed to be a promising paper falls to pieces. The introductory paragraph announces that the paper will develop two reasons for the validity of the thesis statement: Students do not want to think for themselves because (1) the library is inadequate and (2) the teachers are prejudiced. This paragraph should be the one that develops the pointer *prejudiced*, but the word does not even appear in the paragraph.

What has happened to this student? He may have started writing the paper without thinking it through. Then when he reached this last paragraph, he was not sure what he would use to support his idea about the teachers being prejudiced. Rather than going back and reorganizing—not much change needed—he plunged ahead and ruined his paper. Or, he may have failed to see that his last paragraph discusses two subjects, not one. He changes direction in the middle of the paragraph. Through the fourth sentence, the paragraph has to do with the hectic life students lead and how it stops them from thinking. The remainder of the paragraph, however, is concerned with teachers' narrow-minded conformity and the way it restricts student thinking. Each of the two main ideas should have been developed in a separate paragraph. This paragraph is a good example of the use of hazy, undefined terms (*advances in knowledge and in working and living conditions, forces in society*) that allow the writer to wander off in all directions with no particular point being supported. It lacks a controlling attitude.

The third paragraph might be questioned at several points. The trouble is largely a matter of diction—the use of hazy, general words instead of specific ones that convey exact meaning. For instance, look at the beginning of the second sentence: *With the new advances in knowledge and in working and living conditions. . . .* What precisely does the general term *advances* mean to the writer? How can the reader know what he means? We can guess at the meaning, but we cannot be certain. In addition, how have these *advances* led us *to expect more from other people than from ourselves*? Because the writer doesn't answer this question and he doesn't define *advances*, the sentence seems meaningless. The instructor might mark this sentence simply with a question mark in the margin, or say it is "general" or "vague." These comments indicate that the reader can't determine what you mean and that you need to be more specific.

The ninth sentence will also have to be questioned. It begins *These teachers, and other forces in society, who rebel against nonconformity* (*something may or may not be right, but they won't try to find out if it is or not*) . . ., and stops readers cold. They cannot possibly continue into the sentence after this point without rereading this beginning carefully to determine precisely what is being said. The parenthetical material is confusing; something is being defined, but what? Further, the sentence introduces a new subject, *other forces in society*, that appears irrelevant to the discussion. The dependent clause following this phrase, *who rebel against nonconformity*, is twisted in such a way that the reader must stop to figure it out. Ordinarily, we speak of rebelling against conformity rather than against nonconformity. We rebel against what is established. Nonconformity could hardly be said to be the established way of life in our society. So the reader is confused by this clause. *Who support conformity* is a much better way of saying it here.

The illustration of the teacher who refused to conform is not a satisfactory one. It makes the reader wonder whether the school board was not perhaps justified in firing the teacher. She was apparently hired to teach English, but the illustration suggests that she taught everything but English. If she *ranted* in her classroom, it would make the school board's case more secure. But maybe this is another instance of the writer's difficulty in choosing precise words.

Read the next paper all the way through.

EXERCISE IN OUR DAILY LIVES

Exercise should play a very large role in daily life. Everyone, no matter what age, needs exercise every day. However, with modern life being what it is, few older people get the daily exercise they need. Probably television as well as other modern inventions plays a part in producing the physically unfit American.

There are many kinds of exercise that will help people keep physically fit, if they are done every day. First, there are setting-up exercises that anyone can perform for a few minutes every day. If more people would do setting-up exercises on a regular schedule, fewer people in America would be sick. Younger people need to play games to keep themselves physically fit. Football is one of the best games a young person can play for this purpose. But any game that requires running and bending and stretching will do the same thing. Of course, young people should take advantage of the athletic programs in their school and of the school gymnasium on every occasion. Body-building centers are springing up all over the United States. In these centers, anyone from the youngest person to the oldest can set up an exercise program under the supervision of an expert in body building. Or, of course, a family can always buy exercise equipment such as stationary bicycles, barbells, and slant boards on which to exercise daily. If more people would exercise daily, they would find they feel better all the time.

Television and other modern inventions could possibly be a factor that produces the physically unfit American. Television can be very educational. There are many educational programs for adults as well as for the young generation. "Face the Nation," for example, and news programs such as "Sixty Minutes" can help the people of the United States learn more about the advancing world. But mostly, television is just a waste of time, being concerned altogether with entertainment programs. Another modern invention that contributes to the physically unfit American is the automobile. People no longer walk any place. If they have to go only two blocks to the grocery store, they get in the car and ride there instead of walking. Even the young people don't walk, but expect their parents to give them a car at an early age. If people are going to sit for hours in front of their television sets and ride in their cars everywhere, they need to get exercise by doing setting-up exercises or working out on gym equipment.

In our progressing world, everyone seems to be looking for more and more entertainment and for easier ways of doing things. It is easier for a mother to have her children watch entertainment programs on television while she does her work around the house than it is to put her housework off while she takes her children outside for some healthy exercise or outdoor play. By doing this is the mother making things easier for herself or is she thinking about her children's welfare? A good mother will let her children play outdoors while she does her housework. Under the same conditions, adults will watch television rather than exercise as they should.

You should recognize at once that the paper is poor and should be able to point out its chief weaknesses. If an instructor attempts to mark everything unacceptable in this paper, the margins will not accommodate the marks and comments. Perhaps personal conferences with the instructor will guide this student writer.

One of the chief weaknesses of this paper is its content. The very title, "Exercise in Our Daily Lives," suggests emptiness and dullness. Almost any reader who sees the thesis statement, *Exercise should play a very large role in daily life,* knows the paper will not be vital. First, *very large* is not specific. How much exactly is a *very large role?* Second, who wants to read about so commonplace a subject, one that everyone knows about already?

Despite the confusion apparent in the introductory paragraph, the reader may discern three points the paper uses to support the thesis: (1) Everyone needs exercise every day; (2) few older people get the daily exercise they need; and (3) television and other modern inventions produce the unfit American. None of these supports the thesis statement *as given.* We need go no further into the paper than the brief introductory paragraph to predict the results—an unacceptable paper. The rest of the paper bears out such a prediction. The paragraphs are not unified. Each of them jumps from subject to subject, changing direction every sentence or so. Some second-paragraph material is discussed in the third, and some in the third is discussed again in the fourth. Therefore, the paragraphs cannot be coherent; no use of coherence devices will help these paragraphs, unless they are first rewritten for unity. Diction and sentence structure will have to be revised. Some sentences, possibly the result of too little thought or too hasty revision, come out unintentionally humorous. Look, for instance, at the last sentence. The writer has just explained that many mothers allow their children to waste time watching television because it speeds up housework. The last sentence says: *Under the same conditions, many adults will watch television in their spare time rather than exercise as they should.* The reader is tempted to counter, "Under what conditions? While their mother is taking care of them?"

writing assignments

A. 1. Select one of the following general topics (your instructor may add to this list).

Advertising	Movies
College	Parents
Commercials	Planes

Dating	Politics
Education	Sports
Flight	Television

If your instructor is going to ask you to do Writing Assignment *B or C*, you may want to read them before choosing your subject for paper *A*.

2. Restrict your selected general topic by dividing it into its parts and by choosing one of these restricted parts as suitable for development in a five-hundred-word paper.
3. Write a good thesis statement, with a specific controlling attitude.
4. Decide on at least three reasons for the validity of the thesis statement. (Your instructor may want to check what you have done before you go on.)
5. In one paragraph, use reasons as the basic method of development; in another, use either comparison or contrast; and in another, use illustration, either a series of short illustrations or one extended illustration. (Your instructor may substitute other methods for these.)
6. Underline your thesis statement and all topic sentences.
7. Write in the margin, beside each developmental paragraph, the principal method (or methods) of development used in that paragraph.
8. Before you turn in your paper, use the check sheet given on page 158 to evaluate what you have written.

B. After you get back the paper for *A*, read it again and then try to answer the following questions:
1. Does the paper still sound convincing?
2. Does it seem to have a definite reader in mind?
3. Does it try to create interest? How?
4. Check the exercises on page 153, then try to list the "feeling" words in your paper.

Now rewrite Paper *A*, or its first two paragraphs only, trying to improve reader interest and reader acceptance, but this time assume that you are writing to one of the following:
a. Your best friend (same sex)
b. A group of traditional old men
c. Junior high school students
d. Your mayor or congressman

Keep your ideas, thesis, organization, and illustrations basically the same as they were in Paper *A*. Concentrate on changing the interest and tone to fit the readers. In parentheses immmediately below your title, give your reader, like this: (Reader: My best friend, Agnes).

C. Here's another way to learn about creating a specific tone in a paper. First read these three student paragraphs (all by one student) and try to determine what three "voices" are used.
1. I took the ball on the handoff from the quarterback. I hid the ball behind my outside thigh as one does on a bootleg. The ball was hidden so well it fooled the end and the linebacker. Then I simply outran the rest of the clods to the goal.
2. Charlie's fake on that play was great—he was the fullback who took the first fake and dived into the line. The end and linebacker tackled him, thinking he had the ball. This enabled Fred to turn the end and cut up the field for the score.

3. The Slip Yeomen slid by the Elm Lions by a score of 7–0. The only score came late in the last half, when the right halfback took the ball from the quarterback and cut up field for 70 yards. But the play was a team effort: all the blocks and fakes were perfectly executed because the team had worked the play for the past two weeks.

What other things have changed in these paragraphs with the change in "voice"? (Consider such things as choice of words, pronouns, and general "feelings.")

Now try to do something similar with the first two paragraphs of Paper *A* or *B*. This time, assume a *role*; pretend you are someone other than yourself with characteristics you know well. Again, keep your ideas, thesis, organization, and illustrations basically the same as they were in Paper *A* (or *B*); make changes to fit the new "voice" you have assumed in the paper. Here are some role suggestions (you may use others):

a. Your father (or mother)
b. An excited young girl (or boy)
c. Your grandmother (or some other relative)
d. A housewife with no high school education
e. A salesman who never stops selling
f. A person much younger than you

In parentheses immediately below your title, identify the "voice" you are trying to project, like this: (Writer: Agnes, age 12).

D. If you study the techniques you used in B and C, you should be able to write a theme on one of the following:
1. Changing Tone in a Paper
2. Creating Reader Interest in a Paper
3. Some Effects of "I" and "He" in a Paper

You should discuss this paper in class before trying to write it; your instructor may want to give you some additional suggestions.

research and the long paper

hapter 6 brought together the parts of the five-hundred-word theme, provided a diagram showing the interrelationship of the parts, supplied you with a check sheet for the whole paper, and asked you to evaluate a number of complete papers. It also further explored additional problems in tone, reader interest, and point of view—important ingredients in any successful paper. Add to this information that provided by the first five chapters, and you should be able to tackle the long paper, the subject of the present chapter. This point is worth emphasizing: *All the skills and principles you learned to use in writing a short paper apply to a longer one,* no matter what your instructor (or boss) may call it.

WHAT IS A RESEARCH PAPER? Depending on its specific purpose and who will read it, the long paper assumes many names. Here are some of the most common: *research paper, investigative paper, library paper, term report, technical report, problem-solving paper, thesis, dissertation, reference paper.* Although all of these require the skills and principles presented in the first six chapters of this book if they are to be effective and successful, they differ from the basic five-hundred-word theme in a number of important ways.

To begin with, they are longer. Excluding theses and dissertations, which can vary in length from about fifty to several hundred pages, the long papers this chapter prepares you for can range in length from five to fifteen or twenty typewritten pages, depending on your instructor's requirements and the time available for the project. In addition, long papers are usually documented; that is, they contain notes or footnotes referring the reader to the information sources used in preparing the paper. Also, as the word *research* implies, the long paper is a systematic study and investigation of available information in some field of knowledge, and it usually tries to establish certain principles or facts. Some long papers do more than simply discover the facts and present them in a detailed, orderly, objective manner; they can evaluate the facts, provided that the researcher has enough information and insight to make the concluding evaluation. Whether simply informative or evaluative, research is a *way of learning* that you will find useful for the rest of your life. It is a skill, a method of investigating and reporting information you have gathered—from articles, books, pamphlets, questionnaires, libraries, people, government documents, even letters. And, unlike the five-hundred-word theme, whose purpose is to *explain* something, the long paper chooses its purpose to fit the reader's requirements. It can *re-*

port facts and summarize them without making an inference. Or it can, in addition, make an inference from the facts (see p. 17, 112–13) and use this conclusion as a *thesis* for the paper. Or, its purpose may be to *solve a problem* or *answer a question,* providing a solution that the facts convincingly support. To summarize, then, the long paper:

Is often five to fifteen typewritten pages
Uses footnotes (or endnotes) to document the information
Gathers information systematically
Reports the facts without making an inference, or
Uses the facts to come to a conclusion, or
Presents a solution to a problem or an answer to a question

The check sheet that follows provides an overview to guide you through the process of conceiving and writing a research paper.

CHECK SHEET FOR WRITING A RESEARCH PAPER   The following check sheet provides an outline of the information you will be studying in the rest of this chapter, and it presents all the steps you should follow in creating an effective research paper.

CHECK SHEET FOR WRITING A RESEARCH PAPER

I. Seeing the whole paper (Review Chapter 2)	Know what the finished product looks like.
II. Choosing a subject (Review Chapter 3)	1. Discover a suitable subject. 2. Limit the subject with a specific controlling attitude. 3. Write a purpose statement.
III. Getting the facts (Review Chapter 4)	4. Discover suitable information sources. 5. Survey and list the information sources. 6. Take exact, relevant notes.
IV. Organizing the facts (Review Chapter 2)	7. Classify the facts into major subject categories. 8. Outline the paper.
V. Writing the paper (Study Chapters 8, 9, 10)	9. Write the first draft. 10. Revise the paper and make the final copy.

The five major parts of this check sheet (I–V) should be familiar to you. They represent what you have already learned in writing a five-hundred-word theme. Before studying how each of these parts relates to the long paper, you should review the suggested relevant chapter, since much of the discussion of the research paper assumes that you understand the earlier material. Also, note that the three chapters on revision (8, 9, and 10) which follow this one provide useful suggestions on writing and revising your paper to make it more effective. If you follow the ten steps as they are explained below, you should be able to make the transition from the short papers you've been writing to the longer research paper you are now asked to write.

SEEING THE WHOLE PAPER You can't begin to write an effective research paper unless you have a fairly specific idea of the product you want to create. What does it look like? Length aside, how does it differ from the five-hundred-word papers you've been writing? This section will help you visualize the

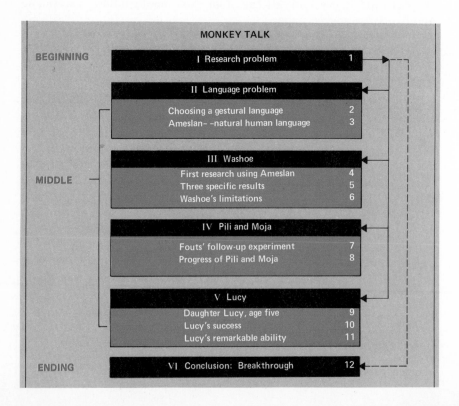

MONKEY TALK

BEGINNING
I Research problem — 1

II Language problem
Choosing a gestural language — 2
Ameslan--natural human language — 3

III Washoe
First research using Ameslan — 4
Three specific results — 5
Washoe's limitations — 6

MIDDLE

IV Pili and Moja
Fouts' follow-up experiment — 7
Progress of Pili and Moja — 8

V Lucy
Daughter Lucy, age five — 9
Lucy's success — 10
Lucy's remarkable ability — 11

ENDING
VI Conclusion: Breakthrough — 12

whole research paper by asking you to study a schematic diagram of the sample paper ("Monkey Talk") on which it is based. Study the following diagram carefully.

Like the five-hundred-word theme, "Monkey Talk" has a beginning, middle, and ending, each serving a specific purpose—to introduce, to develop (support), and to conclude. Although it is not unusual for a research paper's introduction (I) to have more than one paragraph, "Monkey Talk" has only one, and it states what information will be presented in the main body of the paper (II, III, IV, V) to determine the *success* scientists have had in teaching chimpanzees a human method of communication (the problem/thesis).

The three developmental paragraphs of the five-hundred-word theme (see diagram, page 15) have been replaced by ten (numbered 2 to 11), organized into four parts. This middle part of the research paper provides the information needed to answer the question or problem proposed in the introduction. The body of an acceptable freshman research paper should have at least two or three parts, each comprised of three or four paragraphs. Since the main body of "Monkey Talk" has four parts, the two paragraphs of Parts II and IV are probably sufficient. The organization of "Monkey Talk" will become more clear if you review the diagram given in Chapter 2 to help you picture inductive organization (see page 17). Although the writer of "Monkey Talk" decided not to put in concluding statements along the way (at the end of each part), in longer papers or in those presenting much detailed information, these concluding statements become more essential and serve as additional ties to echo the research problem proposed in the introduction.

In the five-hundred-word paper, the ending was a concluding restatement of the thesis and was presented as the last sentence in the third (the final) developmental paragraph. In "Monkey Talk" the ending is a complete paragraph, stating what the research has shown concerning the *success* scientists have had in establishing meaningful two-way communication with chimpanzees. Though only one paragraph here, this conclusion could be two or more paragraphs in a longer research paper with more supporting information.

Now, using this diagram as a guide, read "Monkey Talk" carefully, noting the parts printed in color and how they fit into the overall picture.

MONKEY TALK

1   Can animals talk? This question has always intrigued people.
Today it has pushed researchers to record and study animal sounds
ranging from bird calls to the whistles of porpoises. Although
they have tried to discover how animals communicate to each
other, they have been more interested in learning if meaningful,
two-way communication can be established between man and certain
animals. Of all animals, the chimpanzee seems the subject most
likely to succeed, as recent experiments in teaching chimpanzees
a human method of communication tend to show. To describe this
success, one needs to consider what kinds of language researchers
have used in trying to communicate with chimpanzees and the
nature of the experiments they have devised to try to establish
two-way communication with them.

2   Researchers have observed that "chimpanzees in the wild use
a great many gestures" and hand signals to communicate with each
other.[1] This leads them to assume that a gestural language would
be more natural to chimpanzees than direct verbal communication,
which failed when tried by Keith and Cathy Hayes with a chimp
named Viki. After six years of constant effort, the Hayeses could
get Viki to learn approximate sounds for only three words, papa,
mama, and cup.[2] They concluded that chimpanzees could not master
human speech because of limitations in their vocal mechanisms.[3]
For this reason, researchers chose to use Ameslan, the American
Sign Language of the Deaf.[4]

3   Used by deaf people to communicate, Ameslan is a "natural
human language"[5] in which ". . . gestures made with the hands are
substituted for words and phrases. Many of the gestural signs are
iconics; . . . the sign constitutes a visual representation of its
meaning. For example, the sign for "drink" is made by touching the
mouth with the thumb extended from the fisted hand."[6] In addition

[1] Robert Froman, The Great Reaching Out: How Living Beings
Communicate (Cleveland: The World Publishing Company, 1968), p.
125.

[2] Froman, p. 125.

[3] Duane M. Rumbaugh, "Learning Skills of Anthropoids," in
Primate Behavior: Developments in Field and Laboratory Research,
ed. Leonard A. Rosenblum (New York: Academic Press, 1970), p. 49.

[4] Beatrice T. Gardner and R. Allen Gardner, "Evidence for
Sentence Constituents in the Early Utterances of Child and Chimpanzee," Journal of Experimental Psychology: General, 104 (September 1975), 245; hereafter cited as Evidence.

[5] Evidence, p. 245.

[6] Maurice K. Temerlin, Lucy: Growing Up Human (Palo Alto, Cal-
fornia: Science and Behavior Books, Inc., 1975), p. 116.

to this sign language choice, researchers had to determine whether Ameslan's "touch" or "nontouch" signs would best serve their teaching goals with chimpanzees.[7] Nontouch signs "use either or both hands," but the hands never touch each other or any other part of the person's body, as do the touch signs.[8] This problem was later built into training experiments conducted by Roger S. Fouts, a graduate student working with R. Allen Gardner and Beatrice T. Gardner in Project Washoe.[9]

4   The first researchers to try to teach Ameslan to a chimpanzee were R. Allen Gardner and Beatrice T. Gardner of the University of Nevada. They reviewed the Hayes failure with Viki and decided that since chimpanzees seemed to have the intelligence to communicate, there must be a channel which they could master. They began their experiments with Washoe, an eleven-month-old, wild-born female chimp who lived in a trailer with an environment as stimulating and homelike as possible. The only language Washoe was ever exposed to was Ameslan. Soon Washoe began to use and interpret signs, most of which she learned by training, but others she picked up by observation. She retained the signs learned, and after fifty-one months with the Gardners she had a vocabulary estimated at 132 signs, with a much larger "receptive vocabulary."[10]

5   Three major results of the Gardners' experiments provided evidence that real two-way communication was possible between chimp and man. The first was Washoe's use of the word more. She first learned the sign in context as "more tickling" and then transferred it spontaneously into "more brushing" and "more food" and drink.[11] A second important result of the experiment was Washoe's use of Wh questions, those in the form of what, who, where, and when. Washoe's ability to use and respond to these questions showed a grasp of a basic concept of human communication, the gathering of information.[12] The final result pointing to Washoe's ability to use and understand language was illustrated

---

[7] Roger S. Fouts, "Use of Guidance in Teaching Sign Language to a Chimpanzee (Pan Troglodytes)," Journal of Comparative and Physiological Psychology, 80 (March 1972), 516.

[8] Fouts, p. 516.

[9] Fouts, p. 516.

[10] Evidence, pp. 244-46.

[11] Evidence, p. 247.

[12] P. C. Reynolds, "Social Communication in the Chimpanzee," in The Chimpanzee: Immunology, Infections, Hormones, Anatomy, and Behavior of Chimpanzees, ed. Geoffrey H. Bourne (Basel, Switzerland: S. Karger, 1970), III, 370-71.

when she began combining and recombining signs and responses into meaningful sequences in different situations.[13]

6   Though these accomplishments were extraordinary, they were still limited. Full conversation, as most people understand it, did not occur. As shown in the table below, however, Washoe's answers to specific questions revealed that genuine two—way communication had occurred.[14]

Researchers' Questions	Washoe's Replies
Whose those?	Shoe yours
What color?	Bird white
What that?	Book
What now?	Tickle
Now what?	Time drink
What color that?	Green
What want?	Want berry

As the Gardners point out, Washoe's introduction to Ameslan came when she was already one year old, and her sign—teachers were new to the language.[15] If these experimental handicaps were eliminated, the Gardners believed Washoe's success could be surpassed.[16]

7   These handicaps were eliminated in an experiment involving two chimpanzees named Pili and Moja. Roger S. Fouts, the graduate student who served under the Gardners in Project Washoe, conducted this follow—up experiment. Since age was considered an important factor, Moja was brought to Fouts' laboratory the day after she was born, and Pili arrived only two days after his birth.[17] Both chimps received care similar to that given human infants, including "around—the—clock feedings, diapering, inoculations, . . . and body contact whenever they were awake."[18] Equally important, teachers in the project included fluent sign-ers——deaf persons and persons who had deaf parents.

8   Both Pili and Moja made excellent progress in learning word signs. Both began making recognizable signs when they were about

[13] Evidence, p. 256.

[14] Evidence, p. 250.

[15] Evidence, p. 256.

[16] Evidence, p. 256.

[17] R. A. Gardner and B. T. Gardner, "Early Signs of Language in Child and Chimpanzee," Science, 187 (February 1975), 752; hereafter cited as Early Signs.

[18] Early Signs, p. 752.

three months old. At thirteen weeks, Moja had mastered four
signs: come—gimme, go, more, and drink. Similarly at fifteen
weeks Pili had consistently produced four signs: drink, come—
gimme, more, and tickle. And by the end of six months Moja had a
vocabulary of fifteen signs, while Pili had one of thirteen. By
contrast, at the end of six months' teaching, Washoe could produce only two signs: come—gimme and more.[19] The experiment showed
that exposure to teachers from birth and the use of teachers
fluent in Ameslan greatly improved the language learning potential of chimpanzees.

9 In addition to his involvement in the Washoe and Pili—Moja
experiments, Roger Fouts conducted a third experiment with Lucy,
a chimp raised by Dr. Maurice Temerlin. Although Lucy was already
five years old when she began to learn Ameslan from Roger Fouts,
she had lived so closely with Dr. Temerlin's family that she
already understood and obeyed spoken words. For this reason, Dr.
Temerlin did not believe that teaching Lucy Ameslan would really
improve communication between them.[20] And so Roger Fouts taught
Lucy sign language, at first an hour every day, then twice a week
for an hour each time, "teaching her one sign at a time, . . .
observing any generalization which might occur to new situations."[21]

10 Fouts' success with Lucy was both remarkable and interesting. After five years of training, he had taught Lucy nearly
two hundred signs, established her vocabulary at over one hundred
words, and observed her "creative integration" of signs she had
mastered. Temerlin describes this combination of signs as follows:

> . . . on three different occasions she learned a sign for cry,
> food, and hurt. Then, sometime later, she was shown a radish.
> When she bit into it she signed, "Cry hurt food." After that
> . . . when shown a radish she always signed either "Cry food"
> or "Hurt food" or "Cry hurt food." This is not an isolated or a
> unique example.[22]

Again on different occasions, Lucy learned the separate signs for
food, fruit, candy, drink and cry. In a later session, when Lucy
tasted a piece of watermelon, she promptly signed "Candy fruit."
And before she was taught the sign for onion she pointedly
described it as "That cry fruit."[23] On another occasion, Lucy had

[19] Early Signs, p. 753.

[20] Temerlin, p. 117.

[21] Temerlin, p. 120.

[22] Temerlin, p. 120.

[23] Temerlin, p. 120.

defecated on the floor and was confronted with the mess. First she blamed it on "Sue," then on "Roger"; but after continued questioning, she surrendered with the statement, "Lucy dirty, dirty. Sorry Lucy."[24] She had discovered the talent of evasion and had learned the art of apologizing.

11 This episode and Lucy's ability to invent and combine signs creatively certainly make her a remarkable chimpanzee. Dr. Temerlin is convinced that his daughter Lucy understands and obeys his spoken words. He is now also certain that Lucy uses Ameslan to communicate her feelings, and he provides the following episode to illustrate.

> When she tired of the pictures she put the magazine down, crossed the room, stood before me on two legs wearing her play-face. This conversation ensued, Lucy speaking ASL [Ameslan] while I replied in English.
>
> > Lucy: "Maury, tickle Lucy."
> > Maury: "No! I'm busy."
> > Lucy: "Chase Lucy."
> > Maury: "Not now."
> > Lucy: "Hug Lucy, hurry, hurry."
> > Maury: "In just a minute."
> > Lucy (Laughing): "Hurry, hurry, hug Lucy,
> tickle, chase Lucy."
>
> How could I resist?[25]

Lucy had made her feelings unmistakably clear; she was communicating.

12 Can meaningful, two-way communication be established between humans and chimpanzees? Technical discussion of "evidence for sentence constituents" and other qualities of language communication will continue. But the experiences of these researchers with Washoe, Pili and Moja, and Lucy has convinced them that Ameslan has provided a breakthrough. One is inclined to agree with Duane M. Rumbaugh of the Yerkes Regional Primate Research center, when he says:

> Provided with a language system which its motor capacity can clearly accommodate, only Washoe's natively endowed intellect should stand between it and meaningful, highly informative, two-way communication with man.[26]

And, using two signs she knows well, Lucy could very well add, "Hurry, hurry! Please hurry."

[24] Temerlin, p. 123.

[25] Temerlin, p. 125.

[26] Rumbaugh, p. 50.

SELECTED BIBLIOGRAPHY

Bourne, Geoffrey H., ed. The Chimpanzee: Anatomy, Behavior, and Diseases of Chimpanzees. Vol. 1. Basel, Switzerland: S. Karger, 1969.

Fouts, Roger S. "Acquisition and Testing of Gestural Signs in Four Young Chimpanzees." Science, 180 (1973), 978-80.

——"Use of Guidance in Teaching Sign Language to a Chimpanzee (Pan Troglodytes)." Journal of Comparative and Physiological Psychology, 80 (March 1972), 515-22.

Froman, Robert. The Great Reaching Out: How Living Beings Communicate. Cleveland: The World Publishing Company, 1968.

Gardner, R. A. and B. T. Gardner. "Early Signs of Language in Child and Chimpanzee." Science, 187 (February 1975), 752-53.

Gardner, Beatrice T. and R. Allen Gardner. "Evidence for Sentence Constituents in the Early Utterances of Child and Chimpanzee." Journal of Experimental Psychology: General, 104 (September 1975), 244-67.

Reynolds, P. C. "Social Communication in the Chimpanzee," in The Chimpanzee: Immunology, Infections, Hormones, Anatomy, and Behavior of Chimpanzees, ed. Geoffrey H. Bourne. Basel, Switzerland: S. Karger, 1970, III, 369-94.

Rumbaugh, Duane M. "Learning Skills of Anthropoids," in Primate Behavior: Developments in Field and Laboratory Research, ed. Leonard A. Rosenblum. New York: Academic Press, 1970.

Temerlin, Maurice K. Lucy: Growing Up Human: A Chimpanzee Daughter in a Psychotherapist's Family. Palo Alto, California: Science and Behavior Books, Inc., 1975.

The numbers in color at each paragraph indention don't appear in the original paper, of course; they have been added for quick reference in the discussion which follows. To create a product that accomplishes everything "Monkey Talk" does, you will need to follow the steps on the check sheet on page 173.

CHOOSING A SUBJECT   If you have reviewed the material in Chapter 3, you should find choosing a subject for your research paper an interesting challenge rather than a major stumbling block. To begin with, note that the five steps given in Chapter 3 on page 38 have been condensed into three on the research check sheet:

1. Discover a suitable subject.
2. Limit the subject with a specific controlling attitude.
3. Write a purpose statement.

Let's consider each step closely.

discover a suitable subject

If your instructor doesn't provide a list of general subjects suitable for research, you will have to find your own subject. Although you were cautioned to use only specific *facts* to support the thesis of your five-hundred-word paper (see pages 110–13), you were encouraged to use facts from your personal experience or knowledge. In choosing a general subject for your research paper, again you may select a general subject you are already familiar with; your supporting facts, however, must come from authoritative information sources. If you use the discovery process discussed in Chapter 3 and let your mind actively play with possibilities, you'll find that many of the general subjects listed on page 40 will provide general subject areas suitable for formal research. Here are some with obvious possibilities.

Accidents	Planes
Advertising	Pollution
Animals	Population
Congress	Space
Laws	Television

If you chose *accidents,* for example, you could focus on *major causes* of *automobile* accidents *in the United States*; your research problem would then be to find authoritative books, articles, or government documents that provide factual information to use in your paper. *Advertising* might suggest a research problem in *federal government regulation of deceptive advertising practices in the sale of nonprescription drugs* (or other products). *Pollution* might lead you to investigate the *legal action taken by the federal government to free the air of automobile pollutants* (or pollutants from steel or chemical plants). A little thought about the general subject of population could suggest research into the *success of birth control practices* in a specific country (India or China, for example). And *television* could suggest an investigation of the *effect on preschool-age children* of the *portrayal of violence on television.* The possibilities are almost unlimited, depending on how actively involved you let your mind become and how much personal interest you can generate. You must make the discovery process work for you.

The student who wrote "Monkey Talk" began with the general subject *communication,* became interested in communication between man and other animals, and then zeroed in on the chimpanzee as a suitable subject for research. To be suitable, the limited subject chosen must be one for which factual, authoritative information sources are available, usually in the library. Until the student checked the library, therefore, he couldn't be certain that the chimpanzee subject was suitable. To be safe, you should try to think of several subject possibilities before heading for the library; then, depending on what a quick, first search reveals, you can settle on the subject for your paper. Before making a final decision, note that a subject is *not* suitable for a research paper if:

1. It is based on personal experience alone.
2. All the information about the subject comes from a single reference source (for example, an encyclopedia, or one book, or one article).
3. It is too general to lead to specific research information.
4. It is too technical for you or your reader.
5. Opinion about the subject is wholly subjective (personal) or hopelessly conflicting.

In contrast, a general subject is probably suitable for a research paper if:

1. It is personally interesting to you and your reader.
2. It is discussed in a number of articles and books.
3. It readily suggests a number of meaningful, limited subjects.
4. It can be limited and focused with a specific controlling attitude.
5. It has been investigated objectively (scientifically) and described in factual, nonemotional language.

If you apply these criteria to the general subject of "Monkey Talk," *communicating with chimpanzees,* you'll see that it meets all the requirements.

limit the subject with a specific controlling attitude

From your work on the five-hundred-word paper, you already know why a general subject is unsuitable (see pages 39–50 in Chapter 3). The discussion you have just read about choosing a suitable research subject shows this limiting process in action. If you examine each illustration closely, you'll see at once that both the subject area and the predicate area of the problem statements have been limited.

LIMITED SUBJECT AREA	LIMITED PREDICATE AREA (Controlling Attitude)
Accidents: automobile accidents in the United States	major causes of
Advertising: deceptive advertising practices in the sale of nonprescription drugs	federal government regulation of
Pollution: to free the air of automobile pollutants	legal action taken by the federal government
Population: birth control practices in India	success of
Television: portrayal of violence on television	effect on preschool-age children

To discover a single, limited subject area is to choose for your paper only one subject that cannot be significantly divided further; it is the key to unity of thought. (See pages 39–44 in Chapter 3.) To discover a single, limited predicate area is to decide on a controlling attitude (the "pointer") for your paper that tells the reader what you are going to investigate *about* the limited subject area. (See pages 44–50 in Chapter 3.)

In "Monkey Talk," the last sentence of the first paragraph presents the limited subject area and limited predicate area of the paper. As written by the student, this sentence seems to have two subjects, *kinds of language* and *nature of the experiments devised.* With a little thought, however, he might have written: "To describe this success, one needs to consider the kinds of language researchers have used in experiments devised to try to establish two-way communication with chimpanzees." The two ideas are really inseparable, since you can't talk effectively about the sign language problems without talking about the experiments. The predicate area is clearly stated: *to describe this success.*

write a purpose statement

Writing the purpose statement is the most important and most difficult part of the process, even though this statement probably will not appear in the paper. The purpose statement tells you (and your instructor) that you have carefully thought out the problem and are ready to organize and write the paper. A purpose statement for "Monkey Talk" might read as follows:

> In this paper I will describe the success researchers have had in experiments devised to try to establish two-way language communication with chimpanzees.

In the paper, the student may present this purpose as a simple assertion (as he has done), or he can present it as a problem/question to be answered:

How successful have researchers been in experiments devised to try to establish two-way language communication with chimpanzees?

The student has another option. He can present his purpose as a carefully thought out thesis sentence:

> Although researchers have had extremely limited success in teaching chimpanzees direct verbal communication with humans, they have been very successful in teaching them how to communicate using a human language.

Each of these methods of presenting the purpose—*assertion, question, thesis*—is adequate and effective. The first commits the writer to a straightforward *description* of the experiments. The second implies an inductive approach, a wait-and-see attitude that promises to present the evidence and then conclude (or perhaps evaluate) on the basis of the information presented. The third presents a thesis ("they have been very successful") which will be supported. Each implies a slightly different handling of the information gathered in the research process.

If you examine "Monkey Talk" carefully, you'll see that with only very slight changes in wording (especially at the end of its first paragraph) the paper can be made to fit all three approaches.

exercises

A. Make a list of the most important changes you would have to make in "Monkey Talk" to make it fit the *question approach* and the *thesis approach.* Pay special attention to transitions between major parts (or paragraphs) and to statements that "echo" the question or thesis as the paper progresses.

B. Evaluate the following alternate version of an introductory paragraph to "Monkey Talk" for:
1. First person point of view
2. The personal tone
3. The attempt to gain reader interest
4. The statement of aim in the last sentence
5. The appropriateness of this paragraph in a research paper

MONKEY TALK

I have often wondered what it would be like to talk with animals. What would I learn from a gorilla or baboon? Or an orangutan? Recent experiments in teaching chimpanzees a human method of communication suggest that perhaps my curiosity can be satisfied, at least concerning one animal. In November 1975 the cover of Psychology Today further stirred my interest. It showed researcher Maurice K. Temerlin with his lips only a fraction of an inch from those of a most attentive chimpanzee, and it carried the caption, "The Sexual Coming of Age of My Chimpanzee Daughter Lucy." That settled it. I decided to find out what kinds of language researchers have used to communicate to chimpanzees, the nature of the experiments they have devised to teach chimpanzees to communicate, and how successful they have been so far.

C. 1. Evaluate and comment on the suitability of each of the following as an approach to writing a research paper.

Purpose statement: In this paper I will investigate contemporary readers' responses to Keats's poems when they were first published.
Question approach: How did contemporary readers respond to Keats's poetry when it was first published?
Thesis approach: Although some contemporary readers recognized Keats's poetic ability, most did not react favorably to his poems when they were first published.

2. Which approach gives the writer the greatest freedom in presenting his information? Why?

3. Suggest some other words to replace *investigate* in the purpose statement. Be prepared to discuss the differences in *controlling attitude* implied by your suggested substitutions.

4. Using the question approach, devise a series of questions that might be suitable for a research paper on several of the following general subjects.

Shakespeare's *Julius Caesar*	Any novel
Offshore oil	Corruption
Smoking	I.Q. tests
Urban renewal	Energy sources
Science fiction	Communication

GETTING THE FACTS   If you have reviewed Chapter 4, you will remember that every statement in your research paper should in some way explain or support the controlling attitude toward the limited subject (unity). Your paper must have one subject, one controlling attitude, and one tone (see pp. 65–6). Equally important, you will remember that your paper must also have logical direction, created through interlocking connection within and between paragraphs (coherence). All your facts must be relevant, and you must give them the kind of direction that guides the reader to see and accept their relevance. This section builds on the information you already have on unity and coherence and takes you through the next three steps to follow in creating a research paper:

4. Discover suitable information sources.
5. Survey and list the information sources.
6. Take exact, relevant notes.

Again, we shall consider each step in detail.

discover suitable information sources

Although you can gather information in many ways and from many sources, not all are suitable for the kind of long paper we are discussing in this chapter. For example, professional writers create good research reports from information gained from *interviews,* or direct personal *observation,* or actual *experiments,* or *questionnaires.* These are all important sources of information, but unless your instructor tells you otherwise, you will get your information through *reading* (i.e., "re-searching" what has been written about a specific subject). A check of the bibliography shows that the student who wrote "Monkey Talk" got his information from books and articles describing *experiments* actually conducted by researchers. This kind of reading is the key to writing your research paper. If you need statistics, facts, professional opinions, the testimony of experts, or documents to investigate your subject, you must check articles in reliable magazines, books by experts, various reports or records or government documents. And to find these you must know how to use the library and its resources, especially the following: the card catalog, indexes to magazines and newspapers, abstracts (summaries of articles in magazines), and reference books.

the library card catalog. Your library's card catalog will help you find the information sources you need, *including* the indexes, abstracts, books, magazines, and reference books that will guide you to *additional* information sources. The card catalog is a file of cards identifying everything on the shelves of the library, including books, magazines (usually called *periodicals*), sets of books or reference works, pamphlets, microfilms, microcards, and often other library holdings as well (maps and government documents, for example). For each holding, you will find at least two cards in the catalog, an *author card* and a *title card,* filed in different places. In addition, most catalogs have a *subject card.* As you will see in a moment, this means that you have two or three different ways of finding the item you need. Some libraries file author and title cards in one catalog and subject cards in another, keeping the two groups clearly separated.

To see how the system works, study this illustration of an author card:

```
      QL            2
  1  775       Altmann, Stuart A        3
     A4.8           Social communication among primates, edited by Stuart
                A. Altmann.  Chicago, University of Chicago Press [1967]  4

               5  xiv, 392 p.  illus., plates.  24 cm.

                    Based on an international symposium on communication and social
                    interactions in primates held in Montreal, Canada, Dec. 27-31, 1964,  6
     ALSO IN        during the annual meeting of the American Association for the
     Veterinary L.  Advancement of Science.
        11          Includes bibliographies.


               7  1. Primates—Behavior. 2. Animal communication.     I. American
                    Association for the Advancement of Science. II. Title.

               QL775.A48              599.8                  65–25120
            8                              9                            10
                    Library of Congress            [12]
```

1 Call number in the library being used. You must have this number to find the work.

2 Author's name, with last name given first.

3 Title of the book.

4 Publication data: Place of publication (Chicago), publisher (University of Chicago Press), date (1967).

5 Description of book: 14-page introduction, 392 pages of text, illustrations, special illustrations (plates), 24 centimeters in height.

6 Additional information about the book; the book has extensive bibliographies.

7 Other listings in the card catalog, indicating places to look for this card and related works: Check under *Primates—Behavior* and *Animal communication* in the subject catalog; there is a title card also filed, under *Social communication.* . . .

8 Library of Congress call number for libraries using this system. Smaller libraries usually use the Dewey system.

9 Dewey Decimal call number for libraries using this system.

10 Order number of the card from the Library of Congress, from which additional cards may be bought.

11 Another copy of this book is found in the Veterinary Library at this institution.

√ Indicates that this author card was filed in the *subject* catalog under *Animal communication.* An identical card is filed under *Altmann* in the author catalog.

Knowing your alphabet and how the library uses it to arrange the cards in the catalog will keep you from missing cards by going to the wrong part of the alphabet (often far enough away so that merely flipping through the cards won't help). Here are some basic rules to remember:

1. In titles beginning with *A, An,* or *The,* these are ignored and the card is filed under the next word.
2. The basic arrangement is word by word, alphabetized letter by letter to the end of the word. *Book* World comes before *Book*binding; *New* York and *New* Zealand both come before *Newa*ld and *Newar*k.
3. Initials come before words beginning with the same letter: *ASST Handbook* is filed before *Aakhus,* Theodore.
4. Personal names come before titles beginning with same word: Adam, James, and Adam, William, are both filed before the novel *Adam and Eve.*

When in doubt, ask the librarian for help, for filing can become a very complicated problem. Don't be intimidated by the card catalog;

it is the most powerful research tool you have at your command. Learn to make it serve you well.

indexes. Don't let the word *index* bother you; it comes from a Latin word, *indicare,* meaning "to indicate," usually where to find something. The indexes you must learn to use are simply *alphabetical lists of titles*—usually of the individual items in magazines (articles), anthologies (poems, stories, articles, essays), newspapers (articles), and other collections whose *contents* cannot be located by checking only the card catalog. In some ways, these indexes are even more important than the card catalog, for they indicate where you can find information that you are unlikely to discover in *any other way.* Also, an index will locate articles for you on subjects about which, perhaps, no *book* has been written. Searching *only* the catalog for a book about "teaching chimpanzees how to talk" could lead you to assume erroneously that little or nothing had been written on the subject; almost always, searching the indexes will lead you to usable information.

The most important indexes for your search will provide lists of articles that have appeared in magazines (periodicals, journals). Only one index lists "general magazines" (periodicals in which you would find *general* articles about various subjects). All other indexes are specialized, each one listing only articles concerning a fairly specific subject area. The only general periodical index is *Reader's Guide to Periodical Literature* (1900–   ). Because some popular magazines often publish important technical articles, the *Reader's Guide* is probably a good *starting* place. But because it lists only popular magazines, your search *must* go beyond it, to the specialized indexes and bibliographies. Every subject you can think of (and some you can't) has a specialized index, and many, especially in the sciences, appear as abstracts (brief summaries). We'll take a brief look at abstracts in a moment. The following list includes only a few of the most important specialized indexes:

> *Agricultural Engineering Index*
> *Art Index*
> *Applied Science and Technology Index* (formerly *Industrial Arts Index*)
> *Biological and Agricultural Index*
> *Business Periodical Index*
> *Current Index to Journals in Education*
> *Education Index*
> *Engineering Index*
> *Humanities Index*
> *Science Citation Index*
> *Social Sciences Index*
> *Social Sciences Citation Index*

Because these books list articles from many hundreds of magazines, they are indispensable in any serious research. For example, the *Applied Science and Technology Index* analyzes more than 225 magazines in the fields of aeronautics, automation, chemistry, construction, electricity, engineering, geology and metallurgy, machinery, and physics—and this is a partial list. And the *Engineering Index* covers every aspect of the field, analyzing some 1,500 magazines! Ask your librarian for a list of *indexes* available in your library, and be sure to ask your instructor about the *MLA International Bibliography of Books and Articles on the Modern Languages and Literatures.*

abstracts.   An index simply locates materials; an abstract also locates materials, but in addition it briefly describes the essential points of the article, pamphlet, book, report, or other publication listed. These descriptions are short, often just a single sentence, but frequently as long as several hundred words. Like the indexes, abstracts are also indispensable to serious research, especially since they cover almost every conceivable subject area. Here are a few of the hundreds of abstracts published:

> *Abstracts of English Studies*
> *Biological Abstracts*
> *Chemical Abstracts*
> *Field Crop Abstracts*
> *Forestry Abstracts*
> *Geoscience Abstracts*
> *International Abstracts of Biological Sciences*
> *Metallurgical Abstracts*
> *Petroleum Abstracts*
> *Physics Abstracts*
> *Psychological Abstracts*
> *Sociological Abstracts*
> *Soils and Fertilizers*
> *Vitamin Abstracts*

How many *abstracts* does your library have? Locate two of these publications in the library, take descriptive notes about how they are set up, and bring several short sample entries to class for discussion. What problems did you run into?

other information sources.   Develop the habit of first checking an encyclopedia to see how much basic information you can find in a hurry and how many references you can find in the bibliographies provided at the end of the longer articles.

Encyclopaedia Britannica
Encyclopedia Americana

Check your library to see what publications it has to help in biographical studies.

Current Biography
Dictionary of American Biography
Dictionary of National Biography

What reference works does your library have to help you locate articles about English and American literature? In addition to the *Cambridge Bibliography of English Literature,* what special bibliographies are available to you? Does your library have the *MLA International Bibliography*?

For more information about the library and its resources, try to find a book that tells you more about libraries than this brief summary can suggest. Here are examples of several such books you might look for:

Barton, Mary Neill, and M. V. Bell, *Reference Books*
Galin, Saul, and Peter Spielberg, *Reference Books*
Gates, Jean Key, *Guides to the Use of Books and Libraries*
Shove, Raymond, and others, *The Use of Books and Libraries*

These pages on the library have shown you where to look to discover suitable information sources for your research paper. In summary, your first search steps should include the following:

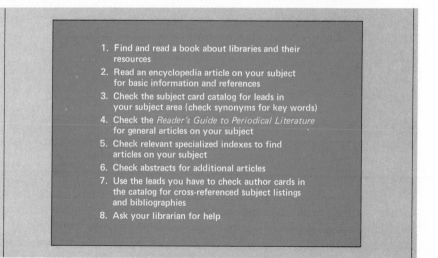

1. Find and read a book about libraries and their resources
2. Read an encyclopedia article on your subject for basic information and references
3. Check the subject card catalog for leads in your subject area (check synonyms for key words)
4. Check the *Reader's Guide to Periodical Literature* for general articles on your subject
5. Check relevant specialized indexes to find articles on your subject
6. Check abstracts for additional articles
7. Use the leads you have to check author cards in the catalog for cross-referenced subject listings and bibliographies
8. Ask your librarian for help

You should now be ready for the next step in getting your facts together.

survey and list the information sources

At this point, your instructor may ask you to submit a *working bibliography*, a tentative list of books, articles, and other sources that you think will be useful in providing the facts you need for the subject of your research paper. Depending on your instructor's requirements, this list may take the form of a *set of three-by-five-inch index cards* (which you should make for yourself in any case), or it may take the form of an alphabetized list on one or more sheets of regular theme paper (see the bibliography following "Monkey Talk" on page 181). To compile this list, you will have to make a separate card for each bibliography item you discover that seems relevant to your subject. Be selective; list only those works that seem specifically relevant, otherwise your list will seem padded and will certainly be too long. On each card, carefully write all the information you need, following exactly the order and the form that the reference will have in the bibliography at the end of your paper (this will make the final compilation much easier, for you can then simply transfer the information directly into the bibliography for your paper). The two sample bibliography cards (below, and on p. 194) follow the form used in the bibliography of "Monkey Talk."

A BOOK

> Froman, Robert.
>
> The Great Reaching Out: How
> Living Beings Communicate.
>
> Cleveland: The World Publish-
> ing Co., 1968.

Later, when your instructor has approved your bibliography cards (or your list), you will add to them the call numbers you find in the card catalog. Then, as you check each source to see if it is relevant and suitable, you may add a brief comment to remind you of the

> Fouts, Roger S.
>
> "Use of Guidance in Teaching
> Sign Language to a Chim-
> panzee (*Pan Troglodytes*)."
> *Journal of Comparative and
> Physiological Psychology*,
> 80 (March 1972), 515-22.

first impression you got when you scanned the information. If any source seems clearly useful, you should read it and begin to take notes, summarizing, quoting, and paraphrasing information you hope to use in the paper.

take exact, relevant notes

The key to taking notes is your *controlling attitude.* If this attitude is clear and limited properly, you should be able to tell what information to take from your source. If you have written a careful purpose statement, it will provide two useful guides to taking notes:

1. An exact, limited controlling attitude
2. The basic approach to developing this attitude

If you check the purpose statements given for "Monkey Talk" (p. 185), you'll see that all three have a clear controlling attitude: "the success researchers have had" (assertion), "How successful have researchers been?" (question), and "they have been very successful" (thesis). The key to note-taking is the word *success;* the student would look for information that could be used to show the results or success of the teaching experiments. Also, the way in which each purpose statement is worded influences the way in which the information will be used in the paper. The *assertion* statement says the paper will *describe* this success; the *question* version implies that the results will be examined and then a *conclusion* will be reached (perhaps with an *evaluation* added); the *thesis* version clearly presents a specific *thesis* to be *supported by evidence* in the paper. Early in your investigation, decide exactly what you hope to show and how you plan to go about it; these two factors will influence the information you choose from the sources, how much you will need, how detailed you must be, and how you use the information in the paper.

Write your notes on a three-by-five-inch card, with the information source clearly indicated. For example, look at paragraph four of "Monkey Talk." As footnote 10 suggests, all the information in this paragraph, including the two quoted words, comes from one source. The note card with the necessary information might look like this:

All these facts and the phrase "receptive vocabulary" will be found on pages 244–46 in the article by the two Gardners in the *Journal of Experimental Psychology* (indicated by the word *Evidence*). The notes simply list the facts considered relevant. Almost no quotation marks are needed because nothing substantial is quoted *as phrased* in the original source. Note, however, that even though no quotation marks appear, *all* borrowed facts must be documented if you are to avoid the charge of plagiarism. You must indicate where all the *ideas* come from, whether you quote directly or not. If you make your notes brief enough and then phrase your sentences from these notes without looking at the source, you aren't likely to duplicate the exact phrasing of the source. The result should be a summary or paraphrase similar to paragraph 4. Your instructor may require more than the one footnote the student used to tag his paragraph, though here they are probably unnecessary.

Once you have gathered all the information you think you'll need, move on to the last two phases of the research project—organizing the facts and writing the paper.

In any long paper a major problem is to organize the gathered facts into major units (parts) and subunits (usually paragraphs), and then to devise an outline to guide you in the actual writing process. This process is represented by steps seven and eight on our check sheet:

7. Classify the facts into major subject categories.
8. Outline the paper.

classify the facts into major subject categories

The greater the number of facts, the greater the need for careful, efficient classification. (Review Chapter 3, pages 57, 59, and 61.) Most information can be classified (i.e., arranged and organized) in many ways, depending on the writer's purpose and controlling attitude. Information about *shirts*, for example, can be classified according to *material, color, use, cost.* In "Monkey Talk" the information is classified by experiment, the easiest and most obvious grouping. Could it be reorganized and presented in some other way? Would the paper work if all the information were presented about each of the following: *language used, participants, success*? What problems would this arrangement create? What information would be included in a major unit (of three or more paragraphs) describing Washoe, Pili and Moja, and Lucy *only as participants*?

The aim of classification should be to decide from your note cards what major parts the paper is to have and what paragraphs will comprise each part. For each part and each paragraph a "pointer" or controlling attitude determines what information you will include. Your aim is to make certain that each part and each supporting paragraph has unity. The result of classification should be a preliminary outline of the paper. For "Monkey Talk," this preliminary outline might look like this:

Paper's purpose—success (teaching chimps a language)
Language problem
Experiment one—method, participants, results
Experiment two—method, participants, results
Experiment three—method, participants, results
Conclusion—success described

If your classification is effective, you should be able to translate these preliminary notes and your note cards into a more detailed outline.

Whether your instructor requires it or not, devise a good topic outline for your paper, including enough detail so that major parts and paragraphs can be seen at a glance. A good outline will keep you on track as you write the paper, though you should be prepared to change the outline if, during the writing process, you discover something relevant and important you have omitted. When you are finished the paper, rewrite the outline to make it represent exactly what you have written. Turn in the outline with the paper so that it can help guide the reader through your paper. Study the form and the details of the following topic outline for "Monkey Talk," using it as a basis for the outline of your own paper. For additional information about outlining, study pages 57, 59, 62, and 150.

```
TOPIC OUTLINE FOR RESEARCH PAPER


Title: MONKEY TALK

Problem/Thesis:   Although researchers have had extremely limited
                  success in teaching chimpanzees direct verbal
                  communication with humans, they have been very
                  successful in teaching them how to communicate
                  using a human sign language.

  I. Problem: Success Communicating with Chimpanzees

 II. The Language Problem
     A. Choosing a gestural language
        1. Gestures of wild chimpanzees
        2. Failure of direct verbal communication
        3. Researchers choose Ameslan
     B. Ameslan--a natural human language
        1. Iconics
        2. Touch and nontouch signs
        3. Designing training experiments

III. Experimental Research--Washoe
     A. Washoe--first research using Ameslan
        1. Finding the right channel
        2. Washoe and her learning environment
        3. General results
     B. Washoe's success--three specific results
        1. Using the word more
        2. Using Wh questions
        3. Combining and recombining signs
     C. Washoe's limitations
        1. Limited two-way communication
        2. Sample from the Wh questions
        3. Additional problems for future research
```

IV. Experimental Research--Pili and Moja
    A. Fouts' follow-up experiment
       1. The age factor
       2. Human environment
       3. Fluent signers
    B. Progress of Pili and Moja
       1. At the age of three months--first signs
       2. At thirteen to fifteen weeks
       3. After six months
       4. Improved results

V. Experimental Research--Lucy
    A. Daughter Lucy, age five years
       1. Family relationship
       2. Temerlin's skepticism
       3. Fouts' training method
    B. Lucy's success
       1. After five years of training
       2. Combining signs
       3. Evasion and apology
    C. Lucy's remarkable ability
       1. Communicating feelings
       2. Illustrative dialogue
       3. Conclusion

VI. Conclusion: Communication Breakthrough
       1. Unresolved problems
       2. Three successful projects
       3. Meaningful, informative two-way communication

WRITING THE PAPER Of the ten steps listed on the check sheet for writing a research paper, only two necessary and important procedures remain:

9. Write the first draft.
10. Revise the paper and make the final copy.

If you've been attentive and interested, the actual composing process has been going on in your head ever since you began gathering facts. And, when you began classifying the information on your note cards, you may very well have begun jotting down sentences or writing leads for you to follow. At this point, however, you must concentrate on the actual writing itself.

write the first draft

Some instructors require a first draft of the paper to be turned in with the final copy. Comparing the two versions can show a reader how your mind actually worked with the available information, how carefully you revised your first version. If the two versions are exactly alike in wording, you probably didn't put the revision process to work, but merely recopied the original.

set up the footnotes as you write. One useful purpose of the first draft is to set up the footnotes within the paper. Here's one of the best ways to handle the problem (the illustration is from Paragraph 3 of "Monkey Talk").

Used by deaf people to communicate, Ameslan is a "natural human language"[5]

---

[5] Evidence, p. 245.

---

in which ". . . gestures made with the hands are substituted for words and phrases. Many of the gestural signs are iconics; . . . the sign constitutes a visual representation of its meaning. For example, the sign for 'drink' is made by touching the mouth with the thumb extended from the fisted hand."[6] In addition to

---

[6] Maurice K. Temerlin, Lucy: Growing Up Human (Palo Alto, California: Science and Behavior Books, Inc., 1975), p. 116.

---

this sign language choice, researchers had to determine whether Ameslan's "touch" or "nontouch" signs would best serve their teaching goals with chimpanzees.[7]

---

[7] Roger S. Fouts, "Use of Guidance in Teaching Sign Language to a Chimpanzee (Pan Troglodytes)," Journal of Comparative and Physiological Psychology, 80 (March 1972), 516.

This method allows you to identify and number your information sources right in the text as needed, with all the required publication data copied *exactly* as it appears on the note card and as it will appear in the footnote. You could accomplish the same purpose by using brackets [ ] or double parentheses (( )) around the citation. Since the Temerlin reference (Note 6) is more than five typed lines, it probably should be single spaced, separated from the main text, and indented (see note 22 in Paragraph 10). Traditional form requires a reference like note 5 to appear as a footnote, but it could be put right in the text within parentheses and without a footnote, as follows:

> Used by deaf people to communicate, Ameslan is a "natural human language" (Evidence, p. 245) in which ". . . gestures

If your instructor asks you to use this form of *internal documentation,* note that it can cut down drastically on the number of footnotes. If you used this method in "Monkey Talk," only *six* footnotes would remain! If you use internal documentation, it appears *within* the sentence (before the period) when it is run into the text, and *outside* the sentence (outside the period) with indented quotations, as follows (see notes 23 and 22):

> . . . she pointedly described it as "That cry fruit" (Temerlin, p. 120).
>
> either "Cry food" or "Hurt food" or "Cry hurt food." This is not an isolated or a unique example. (Temerlin, p. 120)

check spacing and form for accuracy. The first draft is also the best time to get the spacing and form of all footnotes and bibliography items accurate. Both the illustrations just discussed and "Monkey Talk" show footnotes and bibliography items in the form you will follow. However, to help you work with citations containing special problems, a basic approach to acceptable form can be a useful guide. Whether in a bibliography entry or in a footnote, all the citation information fits the following *three-part pattern,* in the order shown in the diagram on page 201. The first illustration in this diagram shows the basic punctuation between the three units for bibliography form (I) and footnote form (II) when the reference source is a *book.* Note that in footnote form (II), no punctuation is placed between units *B* and *C.* When the reference source is an *article* (as in the second illustration), there is only one change in this basic punctuation pattern—in footnote form (II), a comma is placed between units *B* and *C.* Below the two illustrations, each reference source is shown exactly as it would appear in the typed paper. In addition to these differences in punctuation between the three parts, study the final typed versions for the differences shown in the check list for documentation form.

Although this summary of bibliography and footnote form does not cover all the problems you are likely to encounter, it does provide the basic approach used in deciding the form of all entries. A useful

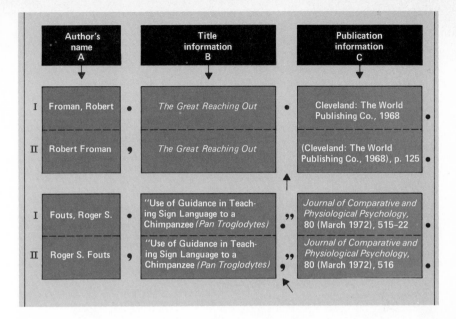

Author's name A	Title information B	Publication information C
I Froman, Robert •	*The Great Reaching Out* •	Cleveland: The World Publishing Co., 1968 •
II Robert Froman ,	*The Great Reaching Out*	(Cleveland: The World Publishing Co., 1968), p. 125 •
I Fouts, Roger S. •	"Use of Guidance in Teaching Sign Language to a Chimpanzee *(Pan Troglodytes)* " •	*Journal of Comparative and Physiological Psychology,* 80 (March 1972), 515–22 •
II Roger S. Fouts ,	"Use of Guidance in Teaching Sign Language to a Chimpanzee *(Pan Troglodytes)* " ,	*Journal of Comparative and Physiological Psychology,* 80 (March 1972), 516 •

Here's the actual spacing in final typed form:

(Bibliography)

I Froman, Robert. The Great Reaching Out. Cleveland: The World Publishing Co., 1968.

(Footnote)

II ¹ Robert Froman, The Great Reaching Out (Cleveland: The World Publishing Co., 1968), p. 125.

(Bibliography)

I Fouts, Roger S. "Use of Guidance in Teaching Sign Language to a Chimpanzee (Pan Troglodytes). "Journal of Comparative and Physiological Psychology, 80 (March 1972), 515–22.

(Footnote)

II ⁷ Roger S. Fouts, "Use of Guidance in Teaching Sign Language to a Chimpanzee (Pan Troglodytes)," Journal of Comparative and Physiological Psychology, 80 (March 1972), 516.

way to solve additional problems is to ask your instructor for a journal to use as a model, which you can then consult for your specific difficulties by checking its footnotes (or endnotes). In the humanities, the journal most widely used as a model is probably *PMLA,* in which the footnotes appear at the *end* of each article, simply titled

CHECK SHEET FOR DOCUMENTATION FORM

BIBLIOGRAPHY FORM	FOOTNOTE FORM
1. First line begins at the margin.	1. First line begins five spaces in from the margin with a raised numeral, *followed by one space.*
2. All other lines are indented, usually five spaces.	2. All other lines return to the margin.
3. Author's last name comes first, followed by a comma.	3. Author's first name comes first (or his initials).
4. *Two* spaces separate the author's name (A) from the title (B).	4. *One* space separates the author's name (A) from the title (B).
5. *Two* spaces separate the title (B) and the publication information (C).	5. *One* space separates the title (B) and the publication information (C).
6. For a book, do not place parentheses around the publication information (C).	6. For a book, place parentheses around the publication information (C).
7. For a book, the place of publication (city) comes before the publisher's name and is followed by a colon.	7. SAME FORM, except for parentheses (see 6).
8. For an article, give the inclusive page numbers in the magazine (515–22).	8. For an article, give only the number of the page on which the quoted information appears (516).
9. Magazine sources require no publication place or publisher's name, but give the volume number, the date, and inclusive page numbers, with the abbreviation *pp.* omitted: 80 (March 1972), 515–22.	9. SAME FORM, except give only the number of the page on which the source information appears, with the abbreviation *p.* omitted: 80 (March 1972), 516.
10. An article in a *book* that is part of a series of volumes is followed by *in*.	10. SAME FORM. See footnote 3 of "Monkey Talk."

"Notes." In any case, bibliography and footnote form must fulfill the requirements of the reader (your instructor, or the editor of the journal in which the paper appears). In the sciences and in engineering, documentation form varies considerably from field to field, so that choice of a specific journal to follow as a model is extremely important and should be attempted only with permission of your instructor. Your instructor will also tell you whether you should use footnotes or endnotes, a "selected bibliography" or "list of works cited." Never simply pad your bibliography by adding works that you have neither consulted nor cited. If you compare the bibliography of "Monkey Talk" with the footnotes, you will discover that the student has listed in the bibliography two works consulted but not actually cited.

write with your controlling attitude in mind.   As you write the first draft, keep the controlling attitude clearly in mind. Somewhere in each major unit, this attitude should be "echoed" (restated) or in some way implied. You can easily spot these "echoes" in the topic outline of "Monkey Talk": *success* (I), *failure* (II), *success, results, limitations* (III), *progress, results* (IV), *success, remarkable ability* (V), *breakthrough, two-way communication* (VI). The result will be a series of reminders to your reader that you have indeed delivered what your introduction promised. In addition, the echoes will improve the coherence of your paper, since they serve as interlocking connections to guide the reader through the paper. If you write your first draft with care, with special attention to the controlling attitude, unity, coherence, and documentation, you will find that writing the final version is much easier.

make the final copy

As with the five-hundred-word theme, revision of the first draft should be used as an opportunity to correct errors in mechanics, documentation, form, and wording. Delete or condense as you think necessary, add explanations where clarity is questionable, or additional evidence where support of a thesis seems inadequate. Check for wordiness, jargon, trite expressions, and the "who-which-that disease," as well as for faulty punctuation and spelling. Look for passive-voice constructions that add unnecessary words, and for problems in grammar. These and other problems you will find discussed in Part 2 of this book, "Revision—Mechanics and Style."

In appearance, your final paper should look like "Monkey Talk." Here are some final guidelines to follow.

1. Type, using double spacing for the text and single spacing for footnotes. Use good white paper (not erasable bond).
2. Prepare a title page with the following information on it: paper title (all caps), your name a few lines below the title (upper and lower case), the course, the instructor's name, and the date (placed in the lower third of the page).
3. Include a topic outline with a thesis or purpose statement at the beginning.
4. Repeat the paper title on the first page of the text (all caps). Count, but do not number this page.

5. Beginning with page 2, place the number of each page at the top (usually lined up with the right margin).

6. Place the bibliography, with entries alphabetized according to authors' last names, at the end of the paper on a separate page, and number it also.

7. If footnotes rather than endnotes are used, be sure to allow adequate space at the bottom of each page, and place the footnotes as shown in "Monkey Talk."

8. Unless your instructor requires it, do *not* place your paper in a slippery plastic folder or any other cumbersome folder; use a paper clip to hold the pages together.

questions for discussion of "monkey talk"

Although "Monkey Talk" is an acceptable paper, it has a number of weaknesses you need to be aware of. The following questions and comments have been designed to provide material for class discussion and questions about your own research paper.

1. *Title.* The title seems to be intentionally misleading, since the paper isn't about monkeys. Would the title be improved if the words *success* and *chimpanzees* were used? The student argued that he used the title to create interest. Does it work for you? Is it appropriate in a paper of this kind? Find out if your instructor would accept similar titles.

2. *Thesis.* In the topic outline, the purpose of the paper is presented as a thesis; in the introductory first paragraph the purpose is in the form of an assertion. Would use of the thesis approach in Paragraph 1 improve the paper? Which approach provides the better blueprint? Could a blueprint be added using the thesis approach (perhaps in an earlier sentence in the paragraph)?

3. *Introduction.* How does the student try to gain reader interest and acceptance? In a research paper aimed at publication, what purpose could the interest/acceptance approach serve? Ask your instructor if you are expected to work at this problem in your research paper.

4. *Body—Part 2.* Does the paper clearly tie the sign-language problem to the controlling attitude (*success*)? Is all the information in Paragraphs 3 and 4 really needed? Could these two paragraphs be combined without damaging their effectiveness? How much background information should a research paper contain?

5. *Body—Three Experiments.* Does the paper provide enough information to be convincing? For example, only the Hayes experimental failure is mentioned (Paragraph 2). Were there other failures? Has there been more language research with chimpanzees than that described in the three experiments? Perhaps a whole paragraph could be devoted to the work done prior to the three experiments described in the paper? The student was highly selective in choosing information for the paper, rightly omitting all technical data. For example, the Gardners' article on "sentence constituents" talks about "semantic range" and "criterion

reliability," classifying Washoe's signs into categories (modifiers, markers, verbs, locatives). Perhaps some nontechnical summary of this information would make the student paper more convincing, since it raises the question of what can be considered genuine language communication.

6. *Conclusion.* In a long paper, the conclusion should do more than merely echo or restate the thesis. In "Monkey Talk," several additional sentences in the last paragraph could be used to point to the progressive success achieved in the experiments described. In a more complex paper, this kind of recapitulation is probably a necessity, since it usually brings together many facts in summary form. In "Monkey Talk," the final quotation seems almost thrown in, since it is about Washoe only and probably belongs in Paragraph 6. The quotation's point about "highly informative, two-way communication" could then have been used as an echo and to tag Lucy's success as well as that of the experiments in general. Do you think the student's final attempt at creating interest in the last sentence is successful?

7. *Documentation.* Is the documentation adequate? For example, compare footnotes in Paragraphs 4 and 10. Which paragraph seems more authoritative? Throughout the paper, do the footnotes always indicate clearly what facts are being used from the sources cited? And, as suggested earlier, the use of internal documentation would have drastically cut down on the number of required footnotes, streamlining the whole process.

8. *Bibliography.* Since the student decided to include several works consulted but not cited, he probably could have included several more to emphasize his selectivity. If your instructor requires you to list only works cited, you must exclude all others from the bibliography.

In spite of its weaknesses, "Monkey Talk" is an acceptable paper. Its subject is limited, its controlling attitude is clearly focused on "success," its information comes from seven different sources and isn't available in only one. It is long enough (actually nine typed pages), uses footnotes to document the information, gathers information systematically from various sources, reports the facts, and concludes that the experiments have been successful. A glance at the outline shows that it is thoughtfully organized with a specific purpose in mind. Most paragraphs in the paper begin with a transitional statement to tie them to preceding information, providing coherence. And, successful or not, the writer tries not to be dull. The paper honestly tries to meet the criteria for a long paper that this chapter has described.

TWO

REVISION–MECHANICS AND STYLE

The preface tells you that your writing will take on strength and life if you practice the two basic skills emphasized in this book—clearly and systematically explaining a main point with specific supporting evidence and projecting a convincing attitude with self-confidence. "But why," you may be asking, "aren't my papers more convincing? Why can't I sit down and *just write*?" You *can* make your papers more convincing, but no one can sit down and "just write"—freely, easily, seemingly without thought and preparation, and without rewriting. Good writing requires patience and discipline. And it requires time. Even professional writers find writing hard work, and they know the value of revision—the subject of Part 2 of this book.

To help you develop your revision skills, Chapter 8 asks you to review material not usually considered part of rhetoric—the mechanics of grammar, punctuation, and spelling; Chapter 9 provides additional aids to strength, clarity, and direct expression (diction); and Chapter 10 presents important guides to the revision of sentences. Part 2 also discusses two subjects that traditionally belong in rhetoric—intention and audience (tone), and style. Because, in one sense, even the mechanics of writing can be considered elements of style, effective revision of mechanical details will contribute positively to the final writing style you will develop. In fact, before you are finished with this book, you will realize that nearly everything you've studied is in some way related to style. With this idea in mind, style is finally defined as the individual, *personal* way in which you use your own knowledge to present your chosen subject to a specific audience in a "voice" appropriate to a particular communication situation. And isn't this really the aim of all effective communication? Isn't this the "art of discovering the most effective means of communication in a particular situation"?

mechanics: grammar, punctuation, spelling

efore tackling some of the most common problems in mechanics, let's briefly consider the revision process as it applies to your five-hundred-word theme or research paper.

the importance of revision

Like the prewriting process (thinking, discovering, planning, organizing), revision requires concentration and time. Though writers often tend to neglect these two phases of the writing process, both are vital to effective communication. Professional writers welcome revision because it provides them with additional opportunities to polish their style, to make their work stand out. Their writing carries a *personal mark,* not accidentally, but because they consciously revised it to make it do exactly what they wanted it to. These last three chapters ask you to revise *seriously* to achieve the two broad purposes you are striving for:

1. Strength, clarity, and directness of well-supported thought—getting the reader to say, "I understand."
2. A *tone* of self-confidence and conviction—getting the reader to say, "I agree."

The first of these purposes depends partly on the mechanics of grammar, punctuation, and spelling. But both depend largely on appropriate word choice (diction) and effective sentence structure, as you will see in Chapters 9 and 10. Equally important, the revision process allows you to become more conscious of your own style and of ways to improve it.

from rough draft to final copy

The first complete copy of your theme or paper is the rough draft. Although this is often the copy some students turn in, it is only the first stage of the actual writing process described in the early chapters of this book. With a completed rough draft, you will have managed merely to get your ideas organized and your supporting evidence down on paper. At this point you'll need some systematic revision, perhaps consulting the check sheets on pages 157, 201–02, and 203. Here is a summary list of things to look for:

1. Reread your paper slowly, systematically, and thoroughly, moving from the title to the last word in the conclusion or bibliography.

210

2. Check the introduction to see if the thesis (or problem statement) is clear and focused with a specific controlling attitude.

3. Check each paragraph to see that the topic sentence and the support clearly reflect the thesis.

4. Compare your paper with its outline to see that only relevant ideas and paragraphs are included.

5. Check each developmental paragraph for unity, making sure it concentrates on only the main idea of the topic sentence.

6. Check for coherence *within* paragraphs and transitions *between* them, providing transitions where you've neglected them.

7. Study the introduction to see if reader interest and acceptance can be improved, changing words that don't seem to fit the tone you are trying to project. (See check sheets, pp. 283, 312.)

8. Look for vague, general words, substituting concrete, specific ones where necessary. (More information on diction is presented in Chapter 9.)

9. Check closely for problems in grammar, punctuation, and spelling, with special attention to subject-verb agreement, pronoun reference, illogical sentence fragments, run-on sentences, and dangling modifiers (reviewed for you later in this chapter).

10. For a research paper, recheck footnote and bibliography form, accuracy of page references, and basic typing requirements. (See pp. 201–02, 203.)

After you are satisfied that you have made all necessary revisions, recopy (or retype) the paper. Give this second copy the same close scrutiny you gave the first and don't hesitate to make additional changes where necessary. You may need to make still another copy before you are satisfied that you have written a paper as exact in idea and as polished in expression as you can make it. Never turn in a paper that has not gone through this revision process or get someone else to do all the revising for you.

When you are satisfied that the revison is as good as you can make it, recopy it as neatly as possible (or type it). Although manuscript neatness is not a virtue in itself, you shouldn't make your paper difficult to read; there is no need to prejudice your reader (in this case your instructor) against your ideas with a messy-looking paper. Remember, if your reader is an employer, he won't tolerate messy work. Whether you write or type, get into the habit of making the final copy a finished product you can be proud of.

After you've had some experience, you should become so conscious of the elements that go into the making of a good paper that you'll be able to avoid some of the effort of revision by using greater care in the rough draft. This kind of added care will greatly improve your writing performance on essay exams in a short, fifty-minute class period.

GRAMMAR

Most of the chapters in Part 1 conclude with a brief section of Review Terms, usually divided into a unit of rhetorical terms followed by a list of grammatical terms. In fact, you couldn't really understand the early chapters without some knowledge of grammar. So don't worry; you already know a great deal of grammar. The main purpose of the following unit on grammar is to review the major problems that repeatedly occur in most writing. But before beginning this review, complete the pretests on grammar and punctuation to see if you can spot and correct the basic problems they cover. You can then test yourself again after you've completed the chapter. Your teacher may want you to complete the spelling pretest also at this point.

grammar pretest

Most (not all) of the sentences given below contain *only one* of the following grammatical problems:

0. Sentence contains no grammatical problems.
1. Subject and verb don't agree.
2. Pronoun does not agree with its antecedent.
3. Dangling modifier—verbal phrase doesn't clearly refer to any word in the sentence.
4. Misplaced modifier—word or word-group needlessly separated from the term it modifies.
5. Sentence fragment—incomplete grammatical construction not clearly connected to other meaning in context.
6. Run-on (fused) sentence—sentences run together with no conjunction or punctuation between them.
7. Faulty verb form—illogical shift in tense.
8. Faulty parallel structure—unequal grammatical elements placed in a series.

Use the numbers (including "0") given above to identify the one grammatical problem in each sentence below. First decide what problem the sentence has, and then place in the blank provided to the left of each sentence the *one* number from the above list that best identifies the grammatical problem. If the sentence has no problem, place a "0" in the blank. *Note:* Your instructor may ask you to provide a correction below each sentence, especially if you don't know the grammatical terms used in the list.

Example: _3_ By studying regularly, your grades can be improved.

Correction: By studying regularly, *you* can improve your grades. Since the verbal phrase *by studying regularly* does not clearly refer to any word in the sentence, you would place the number 3 in the blank. In the correction, the verbal phrase modifies *you.*

_____ 1. An addition should include a new kitchen, dining, bathroom, and recreational facilities.

_____ 2. Assuming this hypothesis to be true, the conclusions can be justified.

_____ 3. Place the one number from the above list that best identifies the grammatical problem in the blank provided to the left.

_____ 4. An important quality of a teacher is their ability to awaken intellectual curiosity in students.

_____ 5. To grow good tomatoes, support the vines with stakes.

_____ 6. Each of the students tried to follow their teacher's instructions.

_____ 7. The repeated use of too many unnecessary words irritate even the most patient reader.

_____ 8. I already have many interesting ideas about college. Although, I haven't yet visited a college campus.

_____ 9. I already had many interesting ideas about college, although I haven't yet visited a college campus.

_____ 10. Some call poetry nonsense others say it helps develop our moral sense.

_____ 11. Investigation revealed that neither the students nor the teacher was to blame.

_____ 12. Investigation revealed that neither the teacher nor the students were to blame.

_____ 13. Don't panic. *Choose.* Reject any notions that you have nothing to write about.

_____ 14. The first thing you'll have to learn is to think for yourself upon entering college.

_____ 15. No group of students represent the whole school.

_____ 16. Watch a young pedestrian trying to coax his reluctant mutt across a car-filled street. Frightening. And dangerous.

_____ 17. After sowing the seed, the ground should be raked and rolled lightly.

_____ 18. Taking a bus to campus every day is expensive and an inconvenience.

_____ 19. To build good cabinets, well-kept, accurate tools are needed by a carpenter.

_____ 20. Right where I want to put the driveway is a huge oak tree and a two-ton rock.

_____ 21. If you don't learn to concentrate when you study, it will probably make you get lower grades. This can be very discouraging.

_____ 22. Hazel kept a record of all the boys she had known in a little red notebook.

_____ 23. Larry let me believe I had first chance at the job. But without definitely committing himself.

_____ 24. If the board of directors controls the school system, they may vote themselves a pay raise.

_____ 25. After removing the crucibles from the oven, they are placed in a desiccator to cool.

What we call grammar is simply a description of the way a language works. Grammar describes how the structured parts of a language—especially its words and sentences—use the vocabulary of that language to communicate meaning accurately and acceptably. What is "acceptable"? Even though you may have become accustomed to speak of "good" grammar and "bad," the communication situation determines what is acceptable usage in written and spoken communication. The spoken language, for example, takes great liberties with grammar and varies considerably from community to community and from group to group within a community. The written language, where you might expect greater conformity to what is generally "acceptable," also varies from writer to writer, again depending on the demands of the communication situation.

However, consider these statements:

> It don't matter to me.
> He ain't bad for a beginner.

Anyone with a high school education should recognize the first statement as grammatically unacceptable because the verb *do* takes the form *does* with *he, she,* and *it.* A verb must *agree* with its subject. To some readers, the second statement will seem "acceptable" in certain informal situations; to most, however, *ain't* is a grammatically unacceptable form in all communication situations. Although speakers and writers do take liberties with language, they avoid constructions that are clearly ungrammatical or nonstandard usage.

Now consider the following statement:

> Assuming this hypothesis to be true, the conclusions can be justified.

At first glance, many readers would say that the statement is "acceptable." But is the statement clear? Who is doing the *assuming? Justified* to whom? Here are several possible interpretations of the statement:

> If I assume this hypothesis to be true, I can justify my conclusions.
> If a person assumes this hypothesis to be true, he can justify his conclusions.

This confusion arises because *assuming* does not clearly *modify* any word in the original sentence; it isn't grammatically tied to any word. Careful speakers and writers avoid these dangling modifiers and strive for unmistakable clarity because they don't want to be misunderstood.

After a brief review of grammar, this unit concentrates on writing that is clearly ungrammatical or nonstandard, on the kind of grammar that muddies or wipes out meaning and can lead to misunderstanding between the sender and the receiver of a message. Let's begin with a brief look at how the English language works, since that is what grammar is all about.

learn how language works

You will eliminate many of your grammatical and punctuation problems and greatly improve your ability to communicate complex ideas if you:

> Understand the components of basic sentence *patterns* and how their *signaling systems* work.
>
> Know the basic *functions* that single words and longer components can perform within a sentence.
>
> Practice rearranging, changing, and *combining* the components and basic sentence patterns to communicate complex ideas.

These processes represent three basic ways of describing how language works. The first concentrates on the ways in which we organize the components into a few basic *structures,* the second describes what *functions* the components perform, and the third shows how a few basic patterns can be *recombined* to create very complex structures. Though you may not know it, you are already quite familiar with all three methods. The aim here is to help you become more conscious of your skills so that you can avoid the common word-blocks to clear, effective communication.

understand the basic terms and basic
sentence patterns

Grammatically speaking, we can communicate with one another because we have learned through personal experience to use words as "labels" for persons, actions, things, ideas, places, events, and all the other elements of the world around and within us. We learn the labels and the patterns first by imitating what we hear as children and then, later, by imitating what we see in written form. Once we have learned to speak and to read, we already know the grammar of the language, though we may not know the terms used by grammarians to describe the communication process. You may have experienced this difference as you worked the grammar pretest, probably recognizing some of the problems without really knowing what to call them. Your first goal, then, should be to understand these terms; your second will be to understand the basic sentence pattern and its components.

Knowing the terms will pay off in the revision process if you systematically search the first draft of your paper for the grammatical problems described by these terms. Also, you need them throughout this book, as a check of the review terms at the ends of Chapters 1 through 5 will show. Similarly, understanding how the components of an English sentence work together will help as you write the first draft of your paper and then again as you revise it. Equally important, however, *practice* in expanding, combining, and repeating these components and the basic sentence pattern will improve both the clarity and the maturity of your writing style.

understand the basic terms

Recheck the review terms at the end of the first four chapters, and you will see that most of the grammatical terms you need to know have already been used in this book. *Any good dictionary will define these terms for you.* Like all words, those used to describe how language works are simply "labels" for things we want to communicate. In grammar, these labels are for *words* and their *functions* in communication. Consider this simple *sentence:*

6 2 3   3   1   3   1   5   4 6 4   1
In their first English class, college students quickly learn to write themes
 7 6 4   2
and to revise them.

We can "label" each word in this sentence according to the function it performs *in this sentence;* i.e., how it relates to other words. If the function of the word changes, then the grammatical label may change, as in the following illustrations:

 1   4
love is blind; I *love* freedom
 3   1
college students, students in *college*
6   5
in class, come *in.*

The numbers above the words point out those with similar grammatical functions and represent nearly all the basic terms you must know. Here are some simple definitions for these "basic parts of speech" (as traditional grammarians refer to them).

1

nouns.   Any word that names something is labeled a noun. Nouns that name a general class of things are labeled *common nouns;* boy, girl, city, house, nation, class, student, theme, noun, verb (the last two words name groups of words). Nouns that name particular persons, places, or things are labeled *proper nouns:* Larry, Hazel, Houston, Texas, City National Bank, Abraham Lincoln, Africa, Mars (a planet), *David Copperfield* (a book). Nouns that name a group of persons, places, or things as if they were a single unit are labeled *collective nouns;* crowd, bunch, flock, family, herd, audience, committee, jury. When phrases (any word-group) and clauses (any SVC word-group) function as nouns, they are labeled *noun phrases* or *noun clauses:*

Larry liked *riding his motorcyle.*	(Noun *phrase,* naming what Larry liked to do)
What you did before class is not relevant	(Noun *clause,* identifying something done)

2

pronouns.   Words that substitute for nouns ("take their place") are labeled pronouns. The noun a pronoun substitutes for ("stands for") is called the *antecedent,* and the relationship between pronoun and antecedent must be unmistakably clear from the context. Depending on whether they function as subjects or objects (see the SVC pattern), or indicate possession, pronouns change their form, as shown by these *personal pronouns:*

SUBJECT	OBJECT	POSSESSION
I ⟶	me ⟶	my, mine
we	us	our, ours
you	you	your, yours
he	him	his
she	her	her, hers
it	it	its
they	them	their, theirs

Depending on their functions, pronouns may be grouped as follows:

Personal (substituting for the names of persons): see table above
Relative (linking subordinate clauses): who, whom, whose, which, that, whoever, whomever
Demonstrative (pointing to an antecedent): this, that, these, those, such
Indefinite: any, each, few, anyone, everyone, no one, some, someone

3

adjectives. Any word or word-group that modifies a noun is labeled an adjective. To *modify* is to describe or in some way change the meaning of a word. *The, a,* and *an* are usually called adjectives, though they are often referred to as *articles.*

> *The deep-green* sea roared against *the black, jagged* rocks.
> *The* end *of the movie* provides *the* key *that solves the mystery.*

The first illustration contains a compound adjective and a series of adjectives; the second contains an *adjective phrase* and an *adjective clause.*

4

verbs. Verbs are words that express action or motion (*walk, run, kill, jump*), being (*am, become*), or state of being (*suffer, rejoice, please, delight*). Verbs requiring an object to complete their meaning are called *transitive verbs* (he *lifted* the weight; she *hit* the ceiling); those that require no object to complete their meaning are called *intransitive verbs* (she *talks* constantly; he *works* well; she *talks,* he *works,* they *play*). Verbs are said to be in the *active voice* when their *objects receive* the action, and in the *passive voice* when their *subjects receive* the action:

> He *hit* the ball; the ball *was hit* by the batter.

Note that the noun *ball* functions first as the object of *hit,* and then as subject of *was hit.* Subjects and verbs must *agree*: I *begin,* he *begins,* they *begin*; I *am,* she *is,* we *are*; he who *fights* and *runs* away may live to fight another day; these men *have sacrificed* for us. Subject-verb agreement is one of the most frequent grammatical problems in student writing. Related verb forms include *present participles* (verb + *ing*), *past participles* (verb + *ed* in regular verbs), *infinitives* (to + verb), and *gerunds* (present participles that function as nouns).

5

adverbs. Adverbs are words that modify verbs, adjectives, or other adverbs. Most adverbs function to describe or qualify time (when?), place (where?), direction (in what direction?), degree (how much? how little?), or manner (how?). A phrase or clause may function as an adverb.

When?—Now, immediately, today, ago, yesterday, soon, tomorrow, always, ever, never.

Where?—Above, below, near, here, there, where, upstairs.

In what direction?—Forward, onward, away, left, north.

How much? how little?—Far, little, very, completely, barely, nearly, scarcely.

How?—Gladly, carefully, nicely, sadly, learnedly.

Adverb phrase—Hazel arrived *after Larry.*

Adverb clause—We know the value of rain *when the fields are dry.*

Adverbs—I *slowly* moved *forward, carefully* turned *left,* and *soon* discovered the raccoon *nearly* hidden *in the bushes.* (Note the adverb phrase.)

6

prepositions. Words that link nouns or pronouns to the rest of the sentence are called prepositions. A preposition and its *object* are called a *prepositional phrase,* which functions usually as an adjective or an adverb. The oldest English prepositions include: after, at, but, by, down, for, in, of, over, since, through, to, under, with.

Because of the storm, half *of* the students came *to* school late.

By late morning, she finally arrived, walked *to* her seat, and removed her books *from* the bottom *of* her bag.

The second illustration has three prepositional phrases that function as adverbs and one that functions as an adjective.

7

conjunctions. Conjunctions are words that join single words, phrases, or clauses, and sometimes paragraphs. Coordinating conjunctions join elements of equal grammatical rank; subordinating conjunctions join unequal grammatical elements.

> *Coordinating:* and, or, but, nor, yet, for
> *Subordinating:* if, unless, because, since, for, as, that, though, although

Some conjunctions appear in pairs (correlative) that join equal elements: *both . . . and, neither . . . nor, either . . . or.*

> Investigation revealed that *neither* the students *nor* the teacher was to blame.

Faulty parallel structure occurs when the words, phrases, or clauses joined by coordinating and paired conjunctions are of unequal rank.

An English sentence is not just a string of words stuck together at random. It follows a basic pattern, in which certain components fit together in an orderly sequence.

1	2	3
SUBJECT	VERB	COMPLEMENT
S ———————→	V ——————→	▶ C
Students	write	themes.
(doer/actor)	(action)	(receiver/object)
(noun function)	(verb function)	(completing function)

Although this illustration simplifies the process, it represents the basic **SVC** pattern from which all sentences can be built. This is true because the 1–2–3 order can be varied, each component can be expanded into a complex word-group, and the basic pattern can be expanded and repeated in various ways.

1. using word-groups to expand components. The following sentences have word-groups functioning as subject, as verb, and as complement.

> *What you did before class* is not relevant.
> The game *will be starting* soon.
> Larry liked *riding his motorcycle.*
> Hazel learned *how to influence her friends.*

2. using combination (coordination) to expand components. A sentence can be expanded by combining (coordinating) several components or complete SVC patterns. To combine or coordinate components requires the repetition of grammatically equal units, whether words, phrases, or clauses. The result will be *parallel* (balanced) structure.

> *Swimming* and *jogging* can improve *blood circulation* and *breathing.*   **(S+S V C+C)**
>
> Hazel knew *what she wanted* and *how to get it.*   **(S V C+C)**
>
> The players *won their game* but *lost the series.*   **(S VC+VC)**

220

Larry wanted to wait until September, but Hazel insisted on a July wedding. **(SVC+SVC)**

What she wanted, Hazel knew; *how to get it*, she hadn't figured out. **(CSV; CSV)**

Notice that in the last illustration the usual SVC order is changed for special effect and the two basic sentence patterns are exactly parallel in structure, part for part as well as in the order of parts.

3. using subordination. Any component of the SVC pattern can be expanded or modified by a word or word-group subordinated to it. In the following sentence, the basic SVC pattern (independent clause) is *players lost series,* with the beginning word-group as a subordinate modifier.

Although they won their last game, the fired-up *players lost* the *series* which they tried so hard to win.

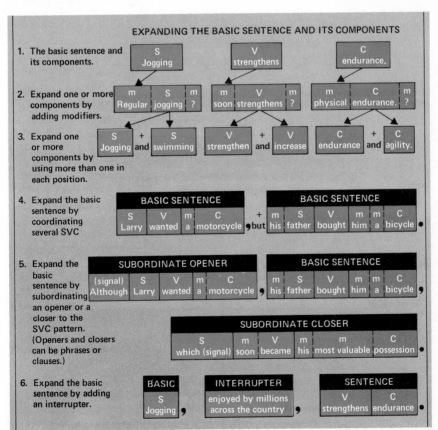

What does the subordinate clause at the end of the sentence modify? The sentence combines three SVC groups. What are they? What two words serve as "signals" to the reader?

In most sentences you will almost automatically "hear" the SVC pattern at work. More important, listen for it and make it work for you. Use the pattern to expand simple sentences into complex ones; experiment with the SVC *order* to gain special effect in appropriate situations; coordinate, subordinate, modify, combine. Building sentences can become a fascinating game, for the combinations are virtually limitless. If you can really hear the components repeated in a sentence, you'll become aware, also, of a fundamental basis for parallel structure: Several components or SVC patterns coordinated in a series. Although the diagrams on page 221 on Expanding the Basic Sentence summarize the most important ways to expand components and combine SVC patterns, in Chapter 10 you'll find additional comments on the SVC pattern and how to make it work for you, especially when you add modifiers before or after any of the components (pp. 290–309).

exercise

Your instructor may ask you to do the exercises on pages 298 and 308, which provide basic sentence patterns for expansion and subordination.

Now, with the basic terms and the basic sentence patterns clearly understood, you should be able to master the following problems in grammar with very little difficulty.

GRAMMATICAL WORD-BLOCKS TO ACCURATE COMMUNICATION Only a handful of grammatical problems account for most of the questionable constructions in student papers. About half of them require an understanding of basic grammatical terms, and the rest require knowledge of the SVC pattern and how it works. All these problems appear in the list at the beginning of the grammar pretest (p. 212).

agr

agreement—subjects, verbs, nouns,
pronouns

Agreement is the grammatical relationship between words that change form, usually to indicate number (singular or plural) and person (first person, *I, we*; third person, *he, she, it, they*). In addition, a few nouns and pronouns change form to indicate *case*—whether they are functioning as subjects, objects, or possessives (see the examples under pronouns). When using these words with changing forms, you must match singular with singular, first person with first person, plural with plural. Here are the major problem areas in agreement.

agr 1

make the verb and its subject agree in number.   In revising your work, check the subject-verb relationships in the SVC pattern to be sure they agree. If you have trouble finding the subject of a sentence, first find the verb, since it describes action and is usually easy to spot. Then you should be able to discover what is doing the acting—your subject. *Most* of the time, you automatically use a singular verb with a singular subject (or a plural with a plural) because the construction is firmly established in your speech patterns:

> *Singular:*   The bird sings, the girl talks, I am, it flies.
> *Plural:*   The birds sing, the girls talk, we are, they fly.

But your sentences are almost never this simple, so that you can easily become careless in making subjects and verbs agree. The following illustrations identify the chief causes of faulty subject-verb agreement.

a.

Watch the *-s ending*. With subjects (nouns) the *-s ending* is a plural form; with verbs it is a singular form. Check yourself by *quickly* scanning the following pairs of subjects and verbs, to spot those with faulty agreement: *I don't, we don't, they don't, he don't, the student writes, the woman writes, it don't, Hazel don't, women writes, changes comes, changes come, he come late, they came late, he says, I says, the jury votes, scientist ask.*

b.

Don't be misled by plural words placed between the subject and the verb.

> *Faulty:*   Every *magazine* in those racks *are* coming apart.
> *Revised:*   Every *magazine* in those racks *is* coming apart.
> *Faulty:*   Repeated *use* of too many long words *irritate* me.
> *Revised:*   Repeated *use* of too many long words *irritates* me.
> *Faulty:*   The *student* as well as the *teachers were* pleased.
> *Revised:*   The *student* as well as the *teachers was* pleased.

c.

Two subjects joined by *and*, regardless of their number, require a plural verb.

> Faulty: A *hammer* and *saw is* in the tool chest.
> Revised: A *hammer* and *saw are* in the tool chest.
> Faulty: A limping *halfback* and a tired *end was* all that separated him from the goal.
> Revised: A limping *halfback* and a tired *end were* all that separated him from the goal.

d.

All indefinite pronouns take singular verbs: *each, neither, either, anybody, anything, someone, somebody, another, everything, nobody, nothing.* Each of these is (not *are*) singular in meaning, even when connected to a plural word (*each* of the girls *is, neither* of the men *is* a pro).

> Each *has* his preference; nobody *shirks* his duty.
> Either *is* acceptable; nothing *is* absolute.
> None of these students *is* a failure.

Although you will often hear the expression *none of them are,* you'll find that careful speakers and writers use the singular, *none of them is.* In fact, *none* is frequently plural, depending on the meaning of the rest of the sentence:

> None *are* so cruel as those who don't feel.
> None *is* so cruel as he who does not feel.

Other indefinite pronouns that can be either singular or plural are *any, all, more, most,* and *some*: Some of the pie *is* better than none; when hope is lost, all *is* lost; some of the students *are* bound to pass; when nations make war, all *are* involved.

e.

Double check correlative pronouns. *Either . . . or* and *neither . . . nor* take a singular verb if both subjects are singular. When one subject is plural, the verb usually agrees with the subject nearer to the verb.

> Neither the student nor the teacher *is* to blame.
> Neither the teacher nor the students *are* to blame.
> Neither the students nor the teacher *is* to blame.

Either you or I *am* mistaken.　(Correct)
Either you *are* mistaken or I *am*.　(Better)

The best solution to these troublesome contrasts is to keep the plural subject next to the plural verb. With some constructions, rewriting the sentence to avoid the problem may be the best solution.

f.

Collective nouns take singular verbs. Because they are singular units with legitimate plural forms, collective nouns (*jury, committee, herd, family, kind, group, audience, majority*) require singular verbs unless the meaning of the sentence clearly demands the plural.

A *jury decides* a man's guilt; the *jury are* individuals who decide a man's guilt.
The *committee plans* to act; the *committee are* unable to agree on a plan of action.
This *kind* of potato *is* best for baking.　(Permissible)
These *kinds* of potatoes *are* best for baking.　(Permissible)
These potatoes *are* best for baking.　(Preferable)

The British use a plural verb with most collective nouns, but American writers tend to make the distinctions suggested above.

Like collective nouns, numbers denoting a fixed quantity usually take singular verbs because the quantity is usually considered to be a unit.

A *hundred dollars is* worth working for.　(A unit)
A *hundred dollars are* counted carefully.　(Individual dollars)
Forty students is too many for one class.　(A unit)
Forty students make a lot of noise.　(As individuals)

g.

Double check agreement when the verb precedes the subject. When the verb comes before the subject, check the subject component carefully before deciding on number.

Faulty:　In the room there *is* a desk for the teacher and seats for all the students.　(Desk and seats *are* in the room.)
Faulty:　His chief support *are* his sister and brother. (The subject of the sentence is *support*.)
Faulty:　There is his sister and brother to support him.　(Sister and brother *are* the subject.)
Revised:　His brother and sister *are* his chief support.

h.

Nouns with plural forms but singular meanings usually take a singular verb. The following nouns are regularly singular: *acoustics, aesthetics, civics, economics, linguistics, mathematics, measles, mumps, news, physics.* Unless the sentence meaning demands a plural form, these nouns are followed by singular verbs.

> Acoustics *is* an interesting study.
> The acoustics of the auditorium *are* excellent.
> Mathematics *is* a science; physics *is* a science.
> Athletics *provide* good exercise. (Various games)
> Athletics *builds* firm muscles. (Activity in games)
> Measles *is* a disease; mumps *is* a disease.
> The statistics *were* assembled; statistics *is* a science.

When subject-verb agreement becomes a problem, think and use your common sense. Be clear on the SVC pattern first, determine the exact meaning, and make the subjects and verbs agree. If you revise hastily (or not at all), you won't discover the problems and your reader will evaluate you and your work accordingly.

agr 2

make pronouns agree with their antecedents.   Pronouns stand for the nouns or ideas they represent and, therefore, must agree with *them* in number. Relative pronouns (*who, which, that*) functioning as subjects must *clearly refer to and agree* with their antecedents. Also, since pronouns change their form with their case (subject or object), you must be clear on their function in the SVC sentence pattern; they can function as either subject or complement (object). Some problems in pronoun agreement occur because the noun to which the pronoun refers appears earlier in a sentence and too far away from its pronoun for the reference to be unmistakably clear. Or the pronoun may refer to either of two antecedents ambiguously. Occasionally the same pronoun (often *it*) may appear several times in a sentence but will refer to different antecedents. Part of the difficulty is that pronoun agreement and reference may be so clear in the writer's mind that he doesn't see the ambiguity. Here are some illustrations of faulty pronoun agreement for you to study and correct by matching the pronouns with their antecedents.

A discouraging *student* trait is *their* emphasis on grades.
Each of the students tried to follow *their* teacher's instructions.
When a *boy* or *girl* enters college, *they* find it different from high school.
The school is old. The rooms are small and poorly lighted, with worn out

desks and faded chalkboards. The library is like a small closet. However, *it* is still in good condition and should not be torn down.

Larry is the student *whom* I think *will succeed.*

If the *administration* wants the support of the *students, they* should listen to *their* problems.

Hazel missed her exam, *which* caused much comment.

If *you* break the law, *you* may be arrested.

He gave the information to John and *I.*

In the book *it* says that pronouns must agree with antecedents.

Copyright © 1977 by Field Newspaper Syndicate, Chicago, Illinois.

mod

check modifiers for clarity of connection. Whether it consists of one word or a word-group, a modifier must be clearly tied to the word it describes or explains. Since the meaning of an English sentence depends largely on the position of its parts, careless placing of a modifier can change or obscure the meaning. And, as with pronouns, too wide a separation of the modifier from the word it describes can create confusion or unintended humor.

mod 1

clarify dangling verbal phrases. Study the following illustrations, noting two basic processes at work in the clarified versions: (1) adding words to clarify the relation of the verbal phrase to the rest of the sentence, and (2) rearranging words so that modifiers are next to the components they describe.

Confused:	*Before going to work,* the truck is washed.
Clear:	Before *I* go to work, *I* get the truck washed.
Clear:	Before going to work, *the men* get the truck washed.
Confused:	Sentences gain clarity *by eliminating wordiness.*
Clear:	*Your* sentence will gain clarity if *you* eliminate wordiness.
Clear:	To give sentences clarity, eliminate wordiness. (*You* is understood before *eliminate.*)

Confused:	*When picking a location to camp,* there are several factors to consider.
Clear:	When *you* pick a camp site, consider several factors.
Confused:	*To write well,* good books must be read.
Clear:	To write well, *you* must read good books.
Confused:	*After sitting there awhile,* it began to rain.
Clear:	After *I* had been sitting there awhile, it began to rain.

mod 2

place modifiers next to the words they describe.   Because position is a key to meaning in the English sentence, you can change meaning unintentionally by carelessly placing a modifier. The modifier *only* is a good example:

> She said that she made *only* one mistake.
>
> She said that *only* she made one mistake.
>
> She said *only* that she made one mistake.
>
> *Only* she said that she made one mistake.

Sometimes careless positioning of a modifier will make it seem to refer to two things at the same time. Here are some "squinting modifiers":

> She agreed *on the next day* to help me.
> The motorcycle which was whining *noisily* roared up the road.
> Larry promised *when he was on his way home* to stop at the store.
> They decided *when both teams lost* to begin recruiting.
> Several students *I know* missed two major quizzes.

In all these sentences the italicized modifiers should be positioned to project one meaning only. You should be able to write at least two unmistakably clear sentences for each illustration.

frag

*complete the meaning of all grammatical
fragments*

You must complete grammatical fragments so that they are *independent*. They must communicate a *complete* thought even if part of the SVC pattern is missing. Often a fragment results when you use a *verbal phrase* as if it were a complete SVC pattern:

> They had a great time at the lake. *Swimming near the shore and fishing off the pier.*

Student athletes want to do well. *To succeed not only as athletes but also as scholars.*
She made little progress. Finally *giving up all her efforts.*

The italicized fragments can be corrected in several ways. Each verbal phrase can be *expanded* into a complete SVC pattern with the addition of a subject and verb: *they swam and fished, they wanted to succeed, she finally gave up.* Often the fragment can be *tied* simply to the rest of the sentence:

> *Swimming near the shore and fishing off the pier, they.* . . .
> *Student athletes want to succeed not only as.* . . .
> *She made little progress, finally giving up.* . . .

Occasionally you may want to *subordinate* one of the ideas involved:

> *Because she made little progress*, she finally gave up. . . .

If you do subordinate, be careful not to use a subordinate clause as if it were a complete (independent) sentence:

Larry had some definite ideas about college. *Although he had never been on a college campus.*

In this example, replace the period with a comma and tie the subordinate clause to the independent clause. And, since it modifies the subject *Larry*, it is probably better positioned at the beginning of the sentence next to the word it modifies. Some subordinate clause fragments sound deceptively complete:

> *When several students asked for make-up quizzes.*
> *Which isn't true of the last examination I took.*

Placed within the context of a paragraph, these subordinate clause fragments could easily be mistaken for complete, independent sentences. The *signal word* at the beginning of the **SVC** pattern should alert you to the subordination.

run-on

learn to spot and correct run-on sentences

If you carelessly run together two independent **SVC** patterns without joining them with conjunctions, you will create run-on (fused) sentences:

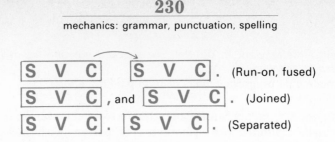

Here are some examples:

Carol has her mind made up nothing you can say will change it.

Clearly, this is the $\boxed{S \quad V \quad C} \quad \boxed{S \quad V \quad C}$. pattern, with

no punctuation and no conjunction. Suppose you added a comma:

> *Carol has her mind made up, nothing you can say will change it.*

Although this version recognizes the two **SVC** patterns, it has not corrected the problem. Instead, the version has become a *comma splice* (a splice is a connection or joining):

$$\boxed{S \quad V \quad C}, \quad \boxed{S \quad V \quad C}. \quad \textit{(Wrong; comma splice)}$$

The original run-on sentence can be corrected in four ways:

1. $\boxed{S \quad V \quad C}$, and $\boxed{S \quad V \quad C}$. (Coordination)

2. $\boxed{\text{Although} \quad S \quad V \quad C}$, $\boxed{S \quad V \quad C}$. (Subordination)

3. $\boxed{S \quad V \quad C}$; $\boxed{S \quad V \quad C}$. (Coordination)

4. $\boxed{S \quad V \quad C}$. $\boxed{S \quad V \quad C}$. (Coordination)

Following these four patterns, correct the Carol run-on in four ways.

> *Wrong:*   *Water skiing is great fun, however try it only if you can swim.*
>
> *Correct:*   *Water skiing is great fun; however, try it only if you can swim.*
>
> *Correct pattern:* $\boxed{S \quad V \quad C}$; $\boxed{\text{however,} \quad S \quad V \quad C}$.
>
> *Correct:*   *I seldom eat avocadoes; **in fact**, I don't like them.*

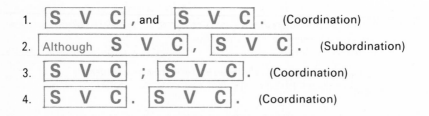

verb

If you understood the unit in Chapter 4 on "Coherence through Consistent Point of View," (see p. 78), you should have little trouble with shifting verb tenses. There you learned that sentences in a paragraph won't *interlock* properly if the verb's *tense* changes from sentence to sentence. Here you are reminded to be *logical* and *consistent* in all time references. You are already familiar with *present, past,* and *future* forms of hundreds of common verbs (I *walk,* he *walks*; I *walked,* he *walked*; I *will walk,* he *will walk*). Wherever possible, use these as models to guide you with verbs you have trouble with, keeping a list of *principal parts* for review purposes (*write, wrote, written; choose, chose, chosen; drink, drank, drunk*). Then consider the following guidelines.

verb 1

make verb tenses logically fit time references. Verb tenses change to indicate time references extending from the *present* (here and now) back into the *past* (yesterday, last year) and forward into the *future* (tomorrow, next year).

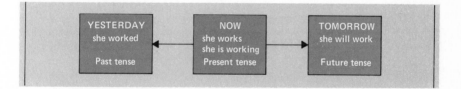

1. *Present.* Use present tense to indicate action going on *now,* in the present: She *works* (*is working*) at a dress shop; She *works* every day (customary, habitual action). Also, use the present tense to describe events in stories or plays, or other literary works: When Juliet *wakes* in the tomb, she *finds* Romeo dead; the friar *begs* her to leave. Additional uses of the present include the following:

   Aristotle *knew* the world *is* round.   (Timeless truth or fact is in present tense, even though main verb is past)

   I *start* my vacation next Tuesday.   (Present used instead of future, *will start.*)

2. *Past.* Use the past tense for all action taking place *before* the present and not extending into the present.

   I *saw* her at the dress shop last year.
   She *worked* at the dress shop.   (Does she work there now?)

I *watched* television last night and *saw* a fine movie. (Both verbs are past tense.)

3. *Future.* Use future tense for all action expected *after* the present. Future time can be expressed in several ways.

She *will work* at the dress shop next week. (Straight future.)
She *is going to work* at the dress shop next week. (Future expressed by *is going*.)
When she *works* at the dress shop next year, she will earn more. (Future expressed by present tense.)

We need to consider two more verb tenses, represented by the following: *she has worked* and *she had worked*. Here's where these fit on the time scale.

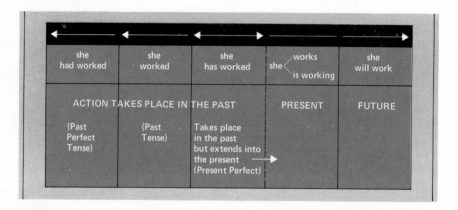

Here are sentences which show all five tenses in action:

By the end of last year, she *had worked* at the shop for three years. She *worked* nearly every night last month, she *has worked* every night this week, she *is working* tonight, and she probably *will work* every night next week.

Although these are unusual sentences, they illustrate the time references governing the sequence of tenses. The two added tenses in the illustration are called the present perfect and the past perfect.

4. *Present Perfect.* Use the present perfect tense for past action extending into the present. In the illustration, *she has worked* refers to past action taking place before "tonight" (i.e., "every night this week"). But the action also extends into the present, since "she is still working." Here's another example: She *has phoned* me many times.

5. *Past Perfect.* Use the past perfect tense for past action *completed before some specified time* in the past. In the illustration, *she had worked* is correct because it refers to past action completed "by the end of last year" (all in the past). Here's another example: I *had talked* to her several times before I *left* the house.

6. *Future Perfect.* Use the future perfect tense for action *to be completed before* some *specified time* in the *future*. Example: She *will have worked* four years at the dress shop by December. The future perfect tense has not been shown on the time chart because it is rarely used.

verb 2

keep a list of troublesome principal parts. A good dictionary gives you the principal parts of verbs immediately following the main entry: *see* (main entry, present stem, infinitive form as in *to see*), *saw* (past tense), *seen* (past participle, when different from the past tense, as in *had seen* and *have seen*), *seeing* (present participle). Most verbs are *regular*, forming the past by simply adding *-d* or *-ed* to the infinitive form (*work, worked, tame, tamed, hire, hired, talk, talked*). The verbs you are likely to have trouble with are *irregular*, changing their infinitive form for past tense and past participle (as the verb *see* does in the illustration above).

Use a dictionary to look up the principal parts of the following troublesome irregular verbs.

begin	do	run
blow	drink	shrink
choose	get	sing
come	lead	swim
dive	ring	swing

Once you have looked up these principal parts, practice writing for each verb the five tenses shown on the time scale above.

parallel structure

correct faulty parallel structure

Faulty parallel structure can occur when a series of words or word-groups (phrases or clauses) are joined by conjunctions. Though not a serious grammatical problem, faulty parallelism can easily obscure meaning and mess up the natural flow of words in a sentence. You will find illustrations of this problem in Chapter 10 on sentence revision under *coordination* (pp. 298–306). The signal words for coordination are coordinating conjunctions, *and, or, but, nor, for, yet.* You have already seen these at work in combining sentence components to achieve *balanced,* complex sentences (pp. 86 and 220). Here you are reminded only that any three or more equal grammatical elements can appear in a series—nouns, verbs, participles, clauses, prepositional phrases, or any sentence component. Here are some illustrations.

Faulty: The instructor told the students *to study* the chapter, *to take notes* on it, and *that they would be tested* on the material.

Correct: The instructor told the students *to study* the chapter, *to take notes* on it, and *to prepare* for a test on the material. (Three parallel infinitive phrases)

Awkward: I shall consider the *origin* of the ecology movement and *how it has progressed.*

Better: I shall consider the *origin* and the *progress* of the ecology movement. (The subordinate clause has been replaced by a noun.)

Awkward: Carol is *attractive, aggressive,* and *has brown hair.*

Better: Carol is *attractive, aggressive,* and *brown-haired.*

Awkward: I like a mystery story *with exciting action* and *which keeps me guessing.*

Better: I like a mystery story *which has exciting action* and *keeps me guessing.* (*which* is understood before *keeps.*)

punctuation pretest

Most (not all) of the examples given below contain one (occasionally more) of the following punctuation problems:

0. Sentence has no punctuation problems.
1. Period needed: run-on sentences.
2. Comma needed as coordinator—items in a series.
3. Comma needed as coordinator of independent clauses (SVCs).
4. Comma needed to set off dependent *opener.*
5. Comma needed to set off dependent *closer.*
6. Comma(s) *not* needed with restrictive interrupter.
7. Comma(s) needed with nonrestrictive interrupter.
8. Comma splice: full stop *or* conjunction needed with independent clauses (SVCs).
9. Semicolon needed to separate independent clauses (SVCs) *or* for clarity.
10. Semicolon fault: semicolon used between components of unequal grammatical rank.
11. Colon needed as anticipator.
12. Apostrophe needed for possession.
13. Apostrophe needed for omissions *or* other special uses.
14. Apostrophe is misplaced *or* not needed at all.

Use the numbers (including "0") given above to identify all punctuation *errors* in the sentences below. First decide what punctuation error(s) the sentence has; then place in the blank provided to the left the numbers from the above list that best identify all the punctuation *errors*. If you think the sentence has no punctuation problem, place a "0" in the blank. *Note:* Your instructor may ask you to provide a correction within or below each sentence, especially if you don't understand the descriptions of punctuation uses given in the list.

Example: _4_, _5_, _5_ As he fell Larry grabbed the branch which broke off in his hand sending him plunging into the cold water.
Correction: As he fell, Larry grabbed the branch, which broke off in his hand, sending him. . . .

Three commas are needed: one to set off the dependent opener, one to set off the first dependent closer (a *which*-clause), and one for the final dependent closer (a verbal phrase). The numbers in the blank name the problems; the correction shows how the punctuation would be placed.

_____ 1. Carols mind is made up nothing you can say will change it.

_____ 2. Although they were no longer interested the students did well.

_____ 3. All students who cut this weeks classes unnecessarily will be penalized.

_____ 4. The old car badly in need of a paint job was not hard to sell.

_____ 5. An old car badly in need of a paint job may be hard to sell.

_____ 6. The old car is badly in need of a paint job, therefore it will be hard to sell.

_____ 7. Its a students right to ask questions the teachers job is to answer them.

_____ 8. The student's right is to ask questions, they can't learn much unless they do.

_____ 9. This chapter discusses three subjects grammar, punctuation and spelling.

_____ 10. The boy's faces showed alarm, they were afraid of the snakes tight coil and chilling rattle.

_____ 11. Their faces showed no alarm; although they were afraid of the huge rattlers' sound.

_____ 12. She could think of only one thing marriage.

_____ 13. The committee consisted of Ralph Brigand, the president of the Snook Bank, I. M. Stealing, the manager of the phone company, and the mayor.

_____ 14. None of the boys dated Marilyn; although she was intelligent, alert, and too readily available.

_____ 15. None of the boys dated Marilyn; she was intelligent, alert, and too readily available.

_____ 16. None of the boys dated Marilyn; although she was intelligent and alert, she was too readily available.

_____ **17.** Football requires the best in strength and endurance; track, the best in speed and agility.

_____ **18.** Football requires the best in strength and endurance, track requires the best in speed and agility.

_____ **19.** The fierce rain filled the gutters with water causing them to overflow onto walkways driveways and lawns.

_____ **20.** She will see if she uses common sense that she has made a mistake her best choice wouldve been to attend summer school.

_____ **21.** An interrupter, which immediately follows and restricts the meaning of the subject, should not be set off with commas.

_____ **22.** An interrupter, which often appears immediately after the subject, may also be inserted between the verb and completer.

_____ **23.** Closers can also be afterthoughts; ideas that expand the sentence definitions that clarify a word in the sentence.

_____ **24.** Mr. Jones's mind is made up and nothing you can say will change it.

_____ **25.** The opener can be any word, phrase or dependent clause its followed by a slight pause and lowering of the voice.

PUNCTUATION

Listen carefully to the way you talk, and you'll soon discover that you punctuate by using *pauses* and the *sound* of your voice. Although the pauses are sometimes hardly noticeable, at other times they are very definite. Have you noticed that at times the sound of your voice seems to go higher? The key to punctuation is to translate these sounds and pauses into a written form that accurately conveys your intended meaning. That's what punctuation marks are all about. They take the place of voice signals that contribute to meaning and prevent misunderstanding.

For example, when you ask a question, the sound of your voice usually goes *up* and you *pause.* When you translate this into written form, how do you signal your reader that you are asking a question? When you begin a sentence with an opener, you normally pause slightly. Or, if you interrupt the flow of a sentence, again you usually pause slightly. But when you complete a sentence, the pause is more definite and the sound of your voice goes down. If you check the sentences in this paragraph, you'll see that most of them illustrate the use of the punctuation mark they are describing. Begin to study punctuation, therefore, first by *listening;* then use your knowledge of grammar and sentence components to discover why some sentence structures require special punctuation signals while others don't. This unit will review the following punctuation signals: period [.], comma [,], semicolon [;], colon [:], and apostrophe [′].

Use the period to signal a full stop for the end of a sentence. In speaking, you signal this stop by a definite pause and a lowering of the sound of your voice. Keep in mind the SVC sentence pattern, and you should be able to place the period stop signals in the following series of sentences:

She came to school early preparing for her quiz before class was important she discovered while studying how much she already knew learning this gave her more confidence therefore she did well

Counting the period at the very end, you should have five. Which SVC components have been expanded into word-groups? Would you place a comma before the word *therefore?* (See pp. 229–30 on run-on sentences and comma splices.)

Like the period, the question mark (?) and the exclamation mark (!) also signal full stops. If your sentence is to be understood as a question, use the question mark, which signals a rising sound in the voice as well as a definite pause. *Do you understand?* As its name suggests, the exclamation point "exclaims": it signals an increase in loudness of voice and a full stop signal. *What a mess!* Use the exclamation mark only for truly important emphasis.

the comma—pause within the sentence

The comma is probably the most used and most abused punctuation signal. Like all punctuation signals, it is important because it clarifies meaning by indicating relationships between sentence components within the SVC pattern. In speaking, you signal the comma with a slight pause and a slight lowering of the sound of your voice. If you doubt this, read this sentence aloud, listening for each pause, noticing the sound of your voice. To understand the way in which the comma signal functions, you need to remember the SVC pattern and know how its components can be expanded (see pp. 220–21). Most comma signals function in one of four ways—coordinators, openers, closers, or inserters.

the comma as coordinator. As used here, the word *coordinator* means to join single words or word-groups (phrases or clauses) of the same grammatical rank. The comma signal *plus* a coordinating conjunction (*and, but, or, nor, for, yet*) tells the reader that the grammatical elements belong together as a series or group. Here are some examples.

For breakfast he ate *bacon, eggs,* and *toast.*   (Three nouns)

Before every exam, she *read, studied,* and *summarized* each chapter in the book.   (Three verbs)

It was still raining, and Larry was *wet, irritable,* and *exhausted.*   (Three completers; two SVC patterns)

Notice that the comma signals two kinds of coordination in the last illustration:

Use a *comma plus a coordinating conjunction* to join two independent SVC patterns:

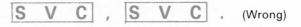

If you use only the comma to join two independent SVC patterns (omitting the conjunction), you will create a *comma splice,* an error you should avoid:

$$\boxed{S \quad V \quad C} \; , \; \boxed{S \quad V \quad C} \; . \quad \text{(Wrong)}$$

In the unit on the run-on sentence (p. 230), you've already seen this illustration of the comma splice:

and

Carol has her mind made up, ↑ nothing you can say will change it.

To correct this error, insert the coordinating conjunction as shown. Remember, too, that you can't use a conjunctive adverb (*however, also, furthermore, moreover, still, then*) as a coordinating conjunction. The result will still be a comma splice:

Carol has her mind made up, *furthermore* nothing you can say will change it.   (Wrong; comma splice)

In summary, use of the comma as coordinator can be illustrated by two simple diagrams:

a, b, and c   Use commas to coordinate three or more words with the *same* grammatical function, and three or more phrases or clauses with the *same* grammatical function. (See also pp. 298–306)

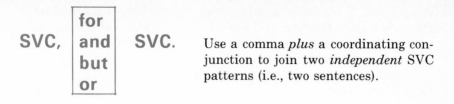

SVC, [for / and / but / or] SVC.   Use a comma *plus* a coordinating conjunction to join two *independent* SVC patterns (i.e., two sentences).

the comma as opener.   Use the comma to signal an opener preceding the basic SVC pattern, especially if the meaning is ambiguous or can be misunderstood. Here's the diagram:

[opener] , SVC.

The opener can be any word, phrase, or *dependent* (subordinate) clause. *In speaking,* you would normally pause slightly and lower your voice slightly after the opener (as in this sentence, after *in speaking*). Here are some additional illustrations of openers:

At the beginning of the semester, the students were eager to learn.   (Introductory prepositional phrase)

However, by the end of the term they had lost their enthusiasm.   (Conjunctive adverb begins and pauses. Would you put a comma after the word *term?*)

Although they were no longer interested, the students did well.   (Introductory subordinate SVC pattern; i.e., a dependent clause)

For example, everyone received at least a *B* grade in the course.   (Short, interruptive phrase followed by a pause)

During the night she heard strange noises.
At noon everyone went to the cafeteria.   (Short prepositional phrases that aren't interruptive are seldom followed by a comma)

the comma as closer.   Use the comma to signal a *closer* following the basic SVC pattern, especially if the closer is interruptive. Here's the diagram:

SVC, [closer] .

The closer can be any word, phrase, or *dependent* (subordinate) clause. Look at the openers in the above illustrations, *for example.* You could put all of them at the end of the sentences following the SVC patterns, *though not all would be preceded by a comma.* In which would you use the comma signal to indicate an interruptive pause? Closers can also be afterthoughts, *ideas that expand the sentence, definitions that clarify a word in the basic SVC pattern.* In the preceding sentence, did you notice the way in which two closers were used to clarify the meaning of *afterthoughts?* Here are some additional illustrations:

Monday was a hot day, *hotter than predicted.*   (SVC + closer)

As he fell, Larry grabbed the branch, *which broke off in his hand, sending him plunging into the cold water.*   (Opener + SVC + two closers—one a dependent clause, the last a participial phrase)

You'd better study your math for tomorrow, *just in case we have a quiz.*   (SVC + dependent clause as a closer)

It was an easy quiz, *much easier than I thought it would be.*   (SVC + dependent clause as a closer)

The closer in the last illustration is so parenthetical that it could be enclosed in parentheses ( ). Some writers would put a dash before *just in case* (in the third sentence) to indicate a more abrupt pause than the comma signals.

the comma as inserter.   Put commas on *both* sides of a nonrestrictive interrupter *inserted into* the SVC pattern. Most examples will follow this form:

S, interrupter , VC.

The interrupter can be a word, a phrase, or a dependent SVC pattern (clause). An interrupter, *which usually appears immediately after the subject,* may also be inserted between the verb and the completer. An interrupter *that immediately follows and restricts the meaning of the subject* should not be set off with commas (as in this sentence). An interrupter *that immediately follows the subject, therefore,* may or may not be set off by commas, depending on its relation to the subject. In the preceding sentence, *that follows the subject* is a restrictive interrupter with no comma preceding it. But the word *therefore,* as a nonrestrictive interrupter, is set off by two commas. Here are some additional illustrations:

All students *who cut classes unnecessarily* will be penalized.   (Restrictive interrupter, *defining which students* will be penalized)

The students, *who had cut classes regularly,* knew they would be penalized. (What idea is emphasized in this sentence? How is it different from the sentence which follows?)

The students *who had cut classes regularly* knew they would be penalized. (Read the sentences *aloud* and listen for the difference.)

The students knew, *however,* that they would be penalized.

(SV , interrupter , C.)

Hazel, *the banker's wife,* works as a secretary.   (Nonrestrictive appositive)

Larry, *not his brother,* will pay for the damaged car.   (Nonrestrictive contrasted phrase)

His son *Larry* will pay for the damaged car.   (Restrictive appositive; i.e., not "his son John")

Houston, *Texas,* is the site of the Astrodome.   (Texas may be thought of as equivalent to the nonrestrictive clause *which is in Texas.*)

"I believe," *she said,* "that you have no choice left."   (*She said* is an interrupter inserted into dialogue.)

"That's it," *she said.* "You have no choice left."   (*She said* functions as a sentence closer; *you* begins a new sentence.)

She will see, *if she uses common sense,* that he has made a mistake.
(S V , | subordinate clause interrupter | , C.)

You should be able to see from these illustrations that a *restrictive* interrupter (no commas) is essential to the *meaning* of the basic SVC pattern, limiting or defining the meaning in some way. The *nonrestrictive* interrupter (a *pair* of commas) provides related, additional information but does not *limit* or define the meaning of the basic SVC pattern.

the semicolon—stop signal that ties

The semicolon signals a *full stop* between independent SVC patterns closely tied in meaning. Use the semicolon where you could also substitute a period; other uses are uncommon. Here's your pattern:

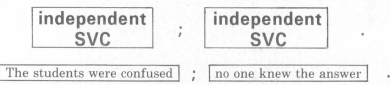

As you can see, the semicolon "ties" the two statements together, as a coordinating conjunction would; it links only *independent* SVC patterns (i.e., two independent clauses). To use the semicolon between SVC patterns of unequal grammatical rank results in a lopsided construction, sometimes called a semicolon fault. It is lopsided because the semicolon, like the period, signals a full stop and a lowering of the voice, after which we normally expect an independent SVC pattern. Read the following illustrations aloud, comparing the punctuation signals:

None of the boys dated Marilyn; although she was intelligent, alert, and too readily available.   (Semicolon fault)

None of the boys dated Marilyn; she was intelligent, alert, and too readily available.   (Correct)

None of the boys dated Marilyn; although she was intelligent and alert, she was too readily available.   (Correct)

In the first illustration, the semicolon ties a *dependent* SVC pattern to an independent one; in the second, it ties together two independent SVC patterns. In the third, however, you have three SVC patterns, one of them dependent. Which is it? How can you tell? Justify the punctuation in the third illustration. What comma "rule" governs the comma after the word *alert?* Could a period replace the semicolon in the first illustration? Apply this test to the following illustrations to discover which uses of the semicolon are acceptable.

A fierce rain filled the gutters with water; causing them to overflow onto yards and walkways.

Although Agnes did her best to explain her failure in math; her parents still scolded her severely.

The astronaut was not merely following instructions; he had to use his own judgment repeatedly.

Steve didn't work very much; in fact, he hardly ever worked.

He has his mind made up; therefore, nothing you say will change it.

Football requires the best in strength and endurance; track, the best in speed and agility.

Football requires the best in strength and endurance; but track requires the best in speed and agility.

The committee consisted of Ralph Brigand, the president of the Snook Bank, I. M. Stealing, the manager of the phone company; and the mayor.

The last illustration is a special case: occasionally you need semicolons to clarify a series of words or word-groups confused by too many commas. Where else would you place a semicolon in this sentence?

the colon—a pause that points

The colon signals a pause that anticipates; it points forward, usually to a list of items to follow. This is what the colon does: it directs attention forward. You also know the colon in the *Dear Sir:* that begins business letters, where it seems to say, "Read on." The following examples show the colon's several functions:

This chapter discusses three subjects: grammar, punctuation, and spelling.   (Correct)

This chapter discusses grammar, punctuation, and spelling.   (Better)

She could only think of one thing: marriage.   (Correct)

She could think only of marriage.   (Better)

Remember this: Don't panic.   (Correct)

The following cities have smog problems: Los Angeles, New York, Pittsburgh, and New Orleans.   (Correct)

You could also use either a comma or a dash in the third example, making it less formal.

the apostrophe—the mark of possession or omission

The apostrophe's use will be simpler if you remember that it usually signals possession (*one student's exam, many students' exams*) or omission (*it's* for *it is, '79* for *1979*). To indicate possession, always begin with this pattern:

[word]'s

Whether your word is singular or plural, one word or a compound, first name or last name, write it down first, and then add *'s,* as shown in the diagram. As the following examples show, this method doesn't always work; however, it does help prevent some common errors with plurals and compounds, and it makes it easy to see whether your ending is *'s* or *s'*. Study the examples below carefully, noting where the *s* has been dropped. Can you see the pattern for dropping this *s?*

SINGULAR	PLURAL
one [girl]'s mother	many [girls]'s mothers
one [man]'s tie	many [men]'s ties
a [lady]'s hat(s)	many [ladies]'s hats
a [woman]'s face	many [women]'s faces
a [boy]'s book	a [boys]'s book
a [box]'s lid	many [boxes]'s lids
[James]'s book	[Dick and Jane]'s book
[Mr. Jones]'s house	the [Joneses]'s house
[brother-in-law]'s wife	two [brothers-in-law]'s wives

As you can see, the system works reasonably well. Very few singular forms containing an *s* or *s*-sound deviate from the rule. Two examples are *Moses* and *Jesus,* which drop the *s,* with possessives of *Moses'* and *Jesus'*. Say the word aloud, and if the combination of *s's* makes the word unpronounceable, drop the final *s*. The same holds true for plurals with *s* endings: *ladies, boxes, Joneses*. If you know the plurals of compound words (*mothers-in-law, courts-martial, sisters-in-law*), adding the *'s* should be easy. Last names are also easy if you form the plurals first and then add *'s*, deciding whether to keep the *s* by pronouncing the name: *Smiths', Browns', Jameses', Pettits'* (all plurals). Notice that *Dick and Jane's book* means one book shared (owned) by two people, but *Dick's and Jane's clothes* means individual ownership.

Some words are already possessive and need no apostrophe: *its, his, hers, theirs, ours, whose.* Remember that *it's* always means *it is* and *who's* always means *who is.* And don't try to make a noun plural by adding *'s:* one *try* and many *tries* (not *try's*), one *cry* and many *cries* (not *cry's*).

Use the apostrophe to indicate omitted letters or numerals: *can't, didn't, he's* (he is), *'79* for *1979* or *'76* for *1776, o'clock* (for *of the clock*), *it's* (for *it is*), *you're* (you are). Finally, the apostrophe with *s* is often used to indicate the *plurals* of letters, numerals, symbols, and words referred to as words: Jane never crosses her *t's*, her *9's* look like *7's*, and her *and's* usually are *&'s*. An alternate method for these plurals is to omit the apostrophe: *t*s *q*s and *and*s.

spelling pretest

A. Most (*not all*) of the word-groups below contain one *or more* spelling errors. To the left of each word-group, identify each misspelled word by placing an X under the number corresponding to the word. If you think the word-group has no misspelled words, place an X in the "0" column.

0	1	2	3	4	5

1. ceiling 2. arguement 3. unecessary 4. seize 5. evened

1. neice 2. conceive 3. weild 4. grief 5. irresistible

1. adviseable 2. desireable 3. detestable 4. blameable 5. analyse

1. disappear 2. mileage 3. noticeable 4. serviceing 5. reprieve

1. mother-in-laws 2. conferred 3. occurred 4. regretting 5. conscientious

mechanics: grammar, punctuation, spelling

0	1	2	3	4	5

1. mistatement 2. acheive 3. temperment
4. benefited 5. leveling

1. blaming 2. height 3. foreign 4. eighth
5. propelling

1. accommodate 2. accidentally 3. supersede
4. precede 5. exceed

1. defenite 2. occasionally 3. incidentally
4. allotted 5. discription

1. the Kellys (plural) 2. trys 3. attorneys
4. heroes 5. echos

1. judgement 2. duly 3. disservice
4. changeable 5. hoeing

1. valleys 2. mispronunciation 3. niece
4. taxis 5. crammed

1. advise (noun) 2. advise (verb) 3. chose (past
tense) 4. chose (present tense) 5. irritible.

1. repitition 2. surprize 3. permissable
4. familiar 5. similiar

1. perscription 2. seperate 3. benificial
4. forty 5. dissipate

1. irresistable 2. hypocrisy 3. goverment
4. hinderance 5. desirable

1. sacrilegious 2. playwright 3. embarrassed
4. procedure 5. psychological

1. preference 2. prefered 3. supress
4. mischievious 5. devide

1. useage 2. doseage 3. sacrafice 4. occassion
5. dependant

1. allottment 2. hypocrit 3. desease
4. laborously 5. gaiety

1. payed 2. villian 3. exercise 4. professor
5. tommorrow

B. To the left of each word-group, identify the CORRECT spelling by placing an *X* under the number corresponding to the word that fits the given definition. If you think there is no correct answer, mark the "0" column.

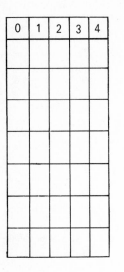

the RESULT (noun):
  1. affect 2. effect

to ACT UPON, to INFLUENCE:
  1. affect 2. effect

to MAKE HAPPEN, BRING ABOUT:
  1. affect 2. effect

RULE OF ACTION, GENERAL TRUTH:
  1. principal 2. principle

HEAD PERSON:
  1. principal 2. principle

FOREMOST, MOST IMPORTANT (adjective):
  1. principal 2. principle

REFERENCE TO, MENTION OF (something):
  1. illusion 2. allusion 3. delusion

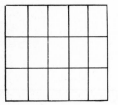

FALSE IDEA, MISCONCEPTION:
  1. illusion 2. allusion 3. delusion

A FIXED MISCONCEPTION:
  1. illusion 2. allusion 3. delusion

HE HAS A GUILTY:
  1. conscious 2. concious
  3. conscience 4. concience

HE IS AWAKE, OR:
  1. conscious 2. concious
  3. conscience 4. concience

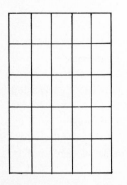

to GIVE AN EXAMPLE:
  1. site 2. cite 3. sight

a LOCATION OR PLACE:
  1. site 2. cite 3. sight

ACT OF SEEING, SOMETHING SEEN:
  1. site 2. cite 3. sight

WRITING MATERIALS:
  1. stationary 2. stationry 3. stationery

NOT MOVING:
  1. stationary 2. stationry 3. stationery

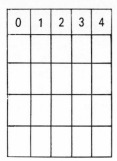

0	1	2	3	4

ROUGH, UNEVEN:
1. course 2. coarse 3. corce

a WAY, PATH, or DIRECTION:
1. course 2. coarse 3. corce

to GO BEFORE:
1. procede 2. proceed 3. precede 4. preceed

to MOVE FORWARD, ADVANCE:
1. procede 2. proceed 3. precede 4. preceed

to SUFFER THE LOSS OF:
1. loose 2. lose

NOT TIGHT, FREE:
1. loose 2. lose

AN ASSEMBLY:
1. counsel 2. council 3. consul

ADVICE (noun):
1. counsel 2. council 3. consul

to ADVISE (verb):
1. counsel 2. council 3. consul

SPELLING

Why improve your spelling? And does it matter outside the classroom? To begin with, hundreds of personnel managers across the country list careless spelling as the single most irritating problem in job applicants' letters. They routinely reject job applicants with obvious spelling problems. Also, careless spelling may very well reflect careless work habits or lack of self-pride—qualities few employers will tolerate. Clearly, accurate spelling is important.

As with punctuation, to improve your spelling, you will have to get your eye to cooperate with your ear; what you see on the page should represent the sounds you hear. This cooperation will succeed, however, only if you give it a chance to work for you. To succeed, you will have to develop a positive, ongoing attitude toward spelling accuracy. Become aware of accurate pronunciation and match it with the written word. Hear the word, say the word, write the word. Learn some basic guides to spelling improvement and put these to work for you. Also, you will want to keep a list of your special spelling problems. More important, however, classify your special words into groups, each group representing a basic problem shared by all the words in that group. This process should let you concentrate on only a few basic principles rather than individual words, greatly simplifying the amount of remembering you have to do. Use the problem areas discussed in this unit as the bases for classification, beginning your list with the words you miss in the spelling pretest. Later, add words collected from your daily reading and writing. After you have studied the material in this unit and the words on your list, check your progress by working the spelling test at the end of this chapter. And, most important of all, be sure you own a good dictionary. Look up all words you are uncertain of and check the special section on "Spelling" (it gives you all the "rules").

sound and sense in spelling

Words come *before* spelling rules. The rules are only guides, *inferred* (see p. 112) from groups of words sharing spelling similarities. Classifying your personal spelling problems should lead you to *infer* "guides" to improve your spelling habits.

sound. The inability to translate the spoken word into its current, accepted written form causes *all* spelling errors. With certain words, however, pro*nun*ciation itself is the key to the misspelling. As you study the words in this unit, therefore, pro*noun*ce every syllable in a word; don't add any that aren't there. *EnvIRONment* and *FebRUary* are good examples of words in which careless spoken and written omissions occur. *Athlete* (not *athelete*) and *mischievous* (not *mischie-VIOUS*) are good examples of words that tend to be given syllables that aren't there. As your first step toward improved spelling, classify the following words into two groups—those to which you *add* syllables, and those from which you *omit* syllables; circle the part of each word that represents its problem area.

accidentally	generally	probably
athlete	government	quantity
candidate	grammatically	recognize
disastrous	hindrance	remembrance
drowned	lightning	representative
entrance	literature	sophomore
environment	occasionally	umbrella

Some important pronunciation/spelling problems are also suggested by these words: *irrelevant, perspiration, prescription, cavalry.* What happens when you spell these words? Can you find others like them? Using sound as your basis, devise a way of remembering the spelling of *definite* and *repetition.*

words that sound alike. Some words sound alike but don't look alike; more important, they mean different things. Students most frequently misspell words found in these two word-groups:

their teacher	*two* books (not three)
I went *there*	*too* many books
they're (they are)	go *to* the game

Keep a list of sound-alike words that give you trouble. Begin by reviewing the meaning of each word in every group of *homonyms* (sound-alikes) given below.

accept, except	lose, loose
advice, advise	passed, past
affect, effect	precede, proceed
choose, chose	principal, principle
cite, sight, site	quiet, quite
coarse, course	right, rite, wright, write
conscience, conscious	sense, since
council, counsel	there, their, they're
decent, descent, dissent	threw, through
formally, formerly	to, too, two
irrelevant, irreverent	weather, whether
its, it's	whose, who's
lead, led	your, you're

Keep your ear and eye alert for other homonyms (there are a great many others); add them to this list as you find them.

prefixes. A prefix is a syllable added to the beginning of a word to modify or change its meaning. Almost always the prefix is simply *added* to the beginning of the word; both the prefix and the word are retained completely in the resulting word, thus:

[prefix] + [word] = new word
[un] + *necessary* = *unnecessary*
[il] + *logical* = *illogical*

It's less important to remember where these prefixes came from than to know how to spell them and how they change the meaning of the word they're added to. Most of those in the present grouping have a negative effect: they usually mean *not* + the *word*. Here are the ones you will run into most often: *dis-, il-, im-, in-, ir-, mis-, un-.* If you simply write down the prefix first, then add the word, you shouldn't have trouble deciding where the "double" letters appear (and don't appear) in the following words: *disappear, dissimilar, disservice, dissatisfy, disappoint, illegal, illegible, illogical, immaterial, immoderate, immoral, immortal, immovable, inappropriate, innumerable, irrational, irreconcilable, irregular, irrelevant, irreligious, irresistible, misspell, misfire, misspeak, mistype, misbehave, misstatement, missent, misunderstand, unnamed, unnatural, unnecessary, unnerved, unnumbered, unpinned.*

suffixes.   A suffix is a syllable added to the *end* of a word to modify or change its meaning. Here you will be concerned with a very limited but most important group of suffixes—those that begin with a vowel, including the *-ing* used to form present participles of verbs and the *-ed* used to form past participles. These are the important ones: *-able, -ible, -ing, -ed, -ance, -ence, -er.* Is it *occured* or *occurred?* What's the difference between *striped* and *stripped?* Is it *shipper* or *shiper?* You will bring thousands of words under control if you remember the following three and what happens to them when you add one of the suffixes beginning with a vowel:

1. Ship   + -ed = Ship*p* ed   (*ALWAYS* double the consonant.)
2. Occur + -ed = Occur*r* ed (*ALWAYS* double the consonant.)
3. Color + -ed = Colo*r* ed   (Do *not* double the consonant.)

Let's examine each of these to be sure we have the word-class spotted.

1. *Ship.* One syllable, ends in a single consonant. The doubling rule applies to *all monosyllabic* words ending in a single *consonant*, if a suffix beginning with a vowel is added. Note the number of words involved: *shipped, shipping, shippable, shipper; cram, crammed, cramming, crammable, crammer; drop, dropped, dropping, droppable, dropper.* And there are thousands of monosyllabic words: *spin, span, sin, sun, stop, crop, mop, tan, ban, mar, bar,* etc.

2. *Occur.* More than one syllable, the accent (stress) on the *last* syllable (the one next to the suffix we'll be adding). The doubling rule applies to all words of *more* than one syllable also __IF__ they end in a single consonant and the accent is on the last syllable. Read the following words aloud and listen to where you place the *stress* (accent): *occur, allot, repel, infer, refer, excel, dispel.* As long as the stress remains on the last syllable, the consonant doubles; but note what happens here: *infer, inferred, inferring, inferrable, inference.* In the last of the series, the stress has shifted: from *in*__FER__ to __IN__*ference,* which has only one *r.*

3. *Color.* More than one syllable, ends in a single consonant, stress is *not* on the last syllable: __COL__or, __COL__ored, __COL__oring, __COL__orable. All words like *color,* then, do *not* double that last consonant. This word-group is unusual, however, since the doubled consonant is also accepted for many of the words: __BEN__efit, __BEN__efited or __BEN__efitted; __COUN__sel, __RI__val, __MOD__el, __MAR__vel, __TRA__vel, and __YO__del all have the alternate spellings.

Still, the rule applies, and you can never go wrong when you do run into words (like *color*) for which there is no alternate spelling: E̲ven, E̲vened, E̲vening, E̲vener.

Other suffix "rules" can be as useful as these three. Some of them involve single letters: *c* and *g* become soft when followed by an *i* or *e,* as in *slice, city,* and *age;* for this reason, the *k* is added to *mimicKing* and *picnicKing,* to maintain the hard sound. But *change* and *notice* already have the *e* to keep the sound soft and, therefore, must retain it, even when a suffix beginning with a vowel is added, as in *chanGEable* and *notiCEable.*

final e and common sense. Many suffixes take care of themselves if you use common sense when adding them. For example, you'll have less trouble with the *-ally* suffix if you first check to see if the word has an *-al* form:

$$
\begin{aligned}
\text{accident} \;+\;\; &-al = \text{accident}al \;+\;\; -ly = \text{accident}ally \\
\text{occasion} \;+\;\; &-al = \text{occasion}al \;+\;\; -ly = \text{occasion}ally \\
\text{incident} \;+\;\; &-al = \text{incident}al \;+\;\; -ly = \text{incident}ally
\end{aligned}
$$

What should you do when the word ends with an *e?* Here are two simple guides:

1. *Retain* the *e* when adding a suffix beginning with a consonant: *care + FUL = careFUL; care + LESS = careLESS; rude + NESS = rudeNESS.*
2. *Drop* the *e* when adding a suffix beginning with a vowel: *come + ING = comING; desire + ABLE = desirABLE; ride + ING + ridING.*

Common sense should take care of such exceptions as *hoeING* and *awFUL.*

-cede, -ceed, -sede. These troublesome endings will be easier to handle if you remember just a few words. Look at *superSEDE.* It is the only word in English with the "seed" ending spelled *sede.* Like *hypocrISY,* it's in a class by itself. Only three words end in *ceed: exCEED, proCEED,* and *sucCEED.* All others ending with the "seed" sound are spelled *cede,* as in *preCEDE, reCEDE,* and *interCEDE.* The word *proCEDure* doesn't even qualify as an exception, since it doesn't end with the "seed" sound.

-able, -ible. There are also "rules" describing the spelling patterns of *-able/-ible* words, but the best of these depend on a knowledge of Latin. However, some major *-able/-ible* grouping can still readily be suggested with a handful of words:

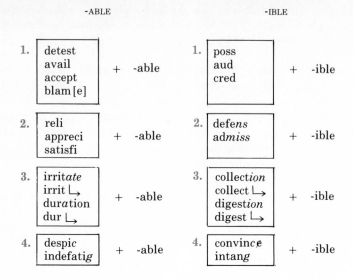

You should be able to infer the "rules" from these examples.

USE THE *-ABLE* SUFFIX WHEN:

1. The base is a complete word.
2. The base ends in *i*.
3. The base also forms a word with the *ay* sound in it.
4. The base ends in a hard *c* or *g*.

USE THE *-IBLE* SUFFIX WHEN:

1. The base in an *in*complete word.
2. The base ends in *ns* or in *miss*.
3. The base word also forms an *ion* word *directly*.
4. The base ends in a soft *c* or *g*.

But note the following exceptions: *equitable, formidable, memorable, probable; irresistible, contemptible, discernible, flexible.*

-yze, -ise, -ize.   You are likely to run into only two words ending in *yze: analYZE* and *paralYZE.* Those ending in *ise* include *surPRISE, exerCISE,* and *comproMISE,* representing the three groups of the most common *-ise* words, *-prise, -cise,* and *-mise.* Most other words ending with this sound have the *ize* ending: *criticIZE, emphasIZE, realIZE, recognIZE, stabilIZE.* Only a few words don't fit the pattern: *advertise, merchandise, despise, chastise, franchise.*

the ie/ei rule.   For these words, remember the old rhyme:

I before *e*
Except after *c,*
Or, when sounded like *ay*
As in *neighbor* and *weigh.*

What the rhyme says is that when the sound is *ee*, write *ie* (except after *c*, when you write *ei*, as in *receive*).

Here are a few examples. In all the following words, the sound is *ee*, hence the spelling is *ie* (because no *c* is involved): *yield, wield, relief, pierce, niece, grief, field, chief.* In the following words, however, even though the sound is *ee*, we must shift to *ei* because a *c* is involved: *receive, perceive, deceive, conceit, ceiling, conceive.* And here are words in which the sound is NOT *ee* and, therefore, *ie* can*not* be used: *weigh, sleigh, vein, heir, neighbor, reign, height, eight, foreign.*

Exceptions: either, weird, seize, forfeit, protein, counterfeit. Memorize these; the rule doesn't apply to them.

Clearly, so brief a look at spelling as this cannot discuss more than a few "rules"—those generalizations inferred from an examination of words with similar problems. From the discussion, however, you should be able to devise a classification scheme of perhaps a half-dozen categories to represent your personal problems in spelling. With a little ingenuity, you can probably come up with "rules" or remembering devices of your own. If the device works, use it.

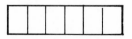

spelling review test

A. Most (*not all*) of the word-groups below contain one *or more* spelling errors. To the left of each word-group, identify each misspelled word by placing an *X* under the number corresponding to the word. If you think the word-group has no misspelled words, place an *X* in the "0" column.

0	1	2	3	4	5

1. cieling 2. arguement 3. unecessary 4. seize
5. evened

1. peirce 2. cheif 3. weird 4. inumerable
5. dissappoint

1. court-martials (plural) 2. occuring
3. regrettable 4. concientious 5. counseled

1. inferrable 2. inference 3. stopping
4. benefiting 5. servicing

1. disappear 2. disatisfy 3. mispell 4. ilegal
5. reign

1. defendible 2. defensible 3. correctable
4. predictible 5. desireable

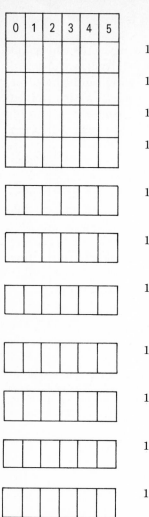

0	1	2	3	4	5

1. temperment 2. acheive 3. misstatement
   4. height 5. foriegn

1. accomodate 2. accidently 3. supercede
   4. preceed 5. excede

1. irritible 2. defenite 3. paralyze 4. emphasize
   5. surprize

1. allotted 2. discription 3. incidently
   4. evidently 5. repitition

1. conceivable 2. convenience 3. privilege
   4. separate 5. predominant

1. atheletic 2. disasterous 3. optomistic
   4. hinderance 5. occurrence

1. advise (noun) 2. advise (verb) 3. chose (past tense) 4. chose (present tense) 5. it's (possessive)

1. the Kellys (plural) 2. the Kelly's house (plural, possessive) 3. trys 4. attornies 5. heroes

1. familiar 2. similiar 3. hypocrasy
   4. brother-in-laws (plural) 5. valleys

1. criticisim 2. conscientious 3. mischievious
   4. embarassed 5. sacrilegious

1. exagerate 2. surpress 3. catagory 4. fourth
   5. fourty

B. To the left of each sentence, place an *X* under the number corresponding to the word on the right that fits into the blank.

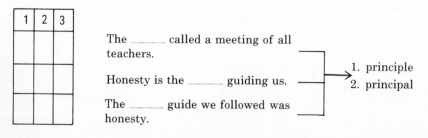

1	2	3

The _____ called a meeting of all teachers.

Honesty is the _____ guiding us.

The _____ guide we followed was honesty.

1. principle
2. principal

1	2	3

Bad study habits _____ grades adversely.

The _____ of bady study habits is poor grades.

1. effect
2. affect

He projected an _____ of honesty.

She made an _____ to the coming party.

Hitler had a _____ of racial supremacy.

1. allusion
2. illusion
3. delusion

I'm barely _____ in the morning.

His _____ kept him honest.

1. conscience
2. conscious

The _____ for the building was cleared.

The building was a beautiful _____ .

Be sure to _____ an illustration.

1. cite
2. site
3. sight

The _____ was filled with trees and traps.

The material had a _____ texture.

1. coarse
2. course

The animal was finally _____ .

Her dress was long and _____ .

Because he studied, he could not _____ .

1. lose
2. loose

Last night I _____ not to study.

Today I _____ to rest.

Tomorrow I will _____ a new plan of action.

1. choose
2. chose

The teacher provided good _____ to the students.

The students had a _____ to represent them.

The teacher promised to _____ the students.

The _____ consisted of students and teachers.

1. council
2. counsel
3. consul

Most (not all) of the sentences given below contain *only one* of the following grammatical problems:

0. Sentence contains no grammatical problems.
1. Subject and verb don't agree.
2. Pronoun does not agree with its antecedent.
3. Dangling modifier—verbal phrase doesn't clearly refer to any word in the sentence.
4. Misplaced modifier—word or word-group needlessly separated from the term it modifies.
5. Sentence fragment—incomplete grammatical construction not clearly connected to other meaning in context.
6. Run-on (fused) sentence—sentences run together with no conjunction or punctuation between them.
7. Faulty verb form—illogical shift in tense.
8. Faulty parallel structure—unequal grammatical elements placed in a series.

Use the numbers (including "0") given above to identify the grammatical problem(s) in each sentence below. First decide what problem(s) the sentence has; then place in the blank provided to the left of each sentence the numbers from the above list that best identify the grammatical problem(s). If the sentence has no problem, place a "0" in the blank. *Note:* Your instructor may ask you to provide a correction below each sentence, especially if you don't know the grammatical terms used in the list.

Example: _3_ By studying regularly, your grades can be improved.

Correction: By studying regularly, *you* can improve your grades. Since the verbal phrase *by studying regularly* does not clearly refer to any word in the sentence, you would place the number 3 in the blank. In the correction, the verbal phrase modifies *you*.

_____ 1. Each of the astronauts tried to follow their trainer's instructions.
_____ 2. The investigation revealed that neither the president nor his assistants was to blame.
_____ 3. The investigation revealed that neither the assistants nor the president was to blame.
_____ 4. After completing the experiment, the desk should be cleared by each student.
_____ 5. No group of strikers represent the whole union.
_____ 6. Some say politics are dirty others say politics help develop good character.
_____ 7. Although no longer interested, I thought the students still did well.
_____ 8. The student's right is to ask questions they can't learn much unless they do.
_____ 9. To succeed in college, a well disciplined, active mind is needed by the student.

_____ **10.** The constant repetition of spelling rules help students improve their spelling.

_____ **11.** If the board of directors controls the school system, they may vote themselves a pay raise.

_____ **12.** The dentist did his job quickly, competently, and hardly working.

_____ **13.** Carol let him believe he had first chance at the job. But without definitely committing herself.

_____ **14.** When only a small girl my mother took me to Houston.

_____ **15.** Keep your eyes and ears open. Never allowing your attention to relax.

_____ **16.** Although not many of the class went, those who did found the lecture heavy, dull, and the acoustics in the hall adequate, though not everything could be heard.

_____ **17.** Neither Agnes nor Carol have completed their work.

_____ **18.** The teacher, as well as the students, uses the chalk board.

_____ **19.** He said he had read the poems of Dickinson and Cummings, and the novels of Hemingway.

_____ **20.** My best friend and adviser has gone.

_____ **21.** I already had many interesting ideas about Houston, although I haven't yet visited the city.

_____ **22.** Right where I want to put the driveway is a huge oak tree and a two-ton rock.

_____ **23.** Riding the bus to school every day is inconvenient and expensive.

punctuation review test

Most (not all) of the examples given below contain one (occasionally more) of the following punctuation problems:

0. Sentence has no punctuation problems.

1. Period needed: run-on sentences.

2. Comma needed as coordinator—items in a series.

3. Comma needed as coordinator of independent clauses (SVCs).

4. Comma needed to set off dependent *opener.*

5. Comma needed to set off dependent *closer.*

6. Comma(s) *not* needed with restrictive interrupter.

7. Comma(s) needed with nonrestrictive interrupter.

8. Comma splice: full stop *or* conjuction needed with independent clauses (SVCs).

9. Semicolon needed to separate independent clauses (SVCs) *or* for clarity.

10. Semicolon fault: semicolon used between components of unequal grammatical rank.

11. Colon needed as anticipator.

12. Apostrophe needed for possession.

13. Apostrophe needed for omissions *or* other special uses.

14. Apostrophe is misplaced *or* not needed at all.

Use the numbers (including "0") given above to identify all punctuation *errors* in the sentences below. First decide what punctuation error(s) the sentence has; then place in the blank provided to the left the numbers from the above list that best identify *all* the punctuation *errors*. If you think the sentence has no punctuation problem, place a "0" in the blank. *Note:* Your instructor may ask you to provide a correction within or below each sentence, especially if you don't understand the descriptions of punctuation uses given in the list.

Example: <u>13, 12, 1, 12</u> It's a student's right to ask questions˄ the teacher's job is to answer them.

Correction: It's a student's right to ask questions; the teacher's job is to answer them.

One apostrophe is needed in *it's* to indicate omission (13); two apostrophes are needed to indicate possession: *student's* (12) and *teacher's* (12). The example consists of two run-on sentences (1), which require a period to separate them; or, as the correction shows, a semicolon can be used to separate the two independent SVCs (9). Errors in order: 13, 12, 1/9, 12.

_____ **1.** Although they were no longer interested; the students did well.

_____ **2.** All students, who cut this weeks classes unnecessarily will be penalized.

_____ **3.** As he fell Larry grabbed the branch; which broke off, in his hand sending him plunging into the cold water.

_____ **4.** Hazels decision was final nothing he did was able to change it.

_____ **5.** College freshmen seem to think of only one thing sex.

_____ **6.** The student who is honest and motivated, will succeed.

_____ **7.** Bill King, who is highly motivated will succeed.

_____ **8.** The teacher explained or rather tried to explain why a students' study habits are important.

_____ **9.** An old car badly in need of a paint job may be hard to sell.

_____ **10.** My old Ford badly in need of a paint job wont be hard to sell.

_____ **11.** As they all know the students right is to ask questions, the teachers job is to try to give them answers.

_____ **12.** This chapter the last in the book discusses three subjects grammar punctuation and spelling.

_____ **13.** None of the girls wanted to date Roger; although he was good looking and sharp, he was coarse and far too aggressive.

_____ **14.** None of the girls wanted to date Roger; although he was good looking, sharp and too aggressive.

_____ **15.** The movie was a winner in adventure, in suspense in conflict.

_____ **16.** Football requires the best, in strength and endurance; track, the best in speed and agility.

_____ 17. An interrupter which immediately follows and restricts the meaning of the subject, should not be set off with commas.

_____ 18. An interrupter, which often appears immediately after the subject may also be inserted between the verb and completer.

_____ 19. Prominent citizens were on the committee I. M. Stealing, the manager of Snooks bank, Ralph Brigand, the president of the phone company, and the mayor.

_____ 20. Three girls—Agnes, Hazel and Jane—were sitting in the principals office wondering what would happen to them planning the right apology.

_____ 21. The opener can be any word, phrase or dependent clause its followed by a slight pause a lowering of the voice.

_____ 22. The students were delayed because of heavy traffic but they made it to Professor Foxs ten oclock class the most important one of the day.

_____ 23. He paused, he aimed, he fired.

_____ 24. Jack won the mile Hazel won the hundred-yard dash and Jim easily won the broad jump.

_____ 25. The girls' faces showed alarm, they were pale and wide-eyed.

revising
your paper–diction

$h$ave you really thought about the way words work? If someone says, "Living in the city is great," are you certain you understand what he means? At first, the words *living, city,* and *great* seem to be reasonably clear. But *are* they? If you take another look at the problem suggested by the cartoon on page 5, you should be able to come up with questions about each word and discover problems in meaning. Choosing specific rather than general words and pointing them unmistakably is a skill you can learn and develop, provided you aren't satisfied with the first word that comes to mind. You can say, "I like my steak medium rare"; or, you can revise this and announce, "I prefer sirloin to T-bone steak, and I like it grilled—charred on the outside, hot, juicy, and pink within."

Revising your diction in this way after you've completed the first draft of your paper will pay off. You'll learn to get rid of lazy verbs and tired expressions, to eliminate the *who-which-that* disease and the involutions of passive constructions, and to delete irritating ten-dollar words in simple, fifty-cent situations. You'll discover how to make words comfortable in each communication situation by projecting a suitable tone. You'll choose cautiously from such alternatives as *concede, admit, confess, acknowledge* and *clever, sly, cunning, shrewd, calculating, smooth.* Revise your diction, and your writing will gain directness, clarity, and strength. Choose each word for maximum reader impact; then watch for and enjoy the results. Make revision a creative game.

AIDS TO STRENGTH, CLARITY, DIRECTNESS

By all means enjoy the game. Here are some creative plays you may have forgotten.

change the passive voice to active voice

English verbs have two voices—active and passive. For example, consider these sentences:

Andy | hit the ball.

The ball | was hit by Andy.

The first sentence is in the active voice. The subject of the sentence, *Andy,* is doing the hitting, the action expressed in the sentence. The second is in the passive voice. The subject of this sentence, *ball,* is *receiving* the action. Or, to put it another way, the first sentence (active) follows the normal word order for English sentences—subject, verb, complement, or *actor, action, receiver of action.* The second sentence (passive) turns this normal word order around. What was the complement of the first sentence becomes the subject in the second sentence. Its order is *receiver of action, action, actor.*

Look at this example.

---

(1) To call a telephone on your own party line proceed as follows: Lift the receiver and wait for dial tone. (2) The regular seven-digit number of the desired station is dialed, the busy signal will be heard, and the calling party then places the receiver on the hook. (3) The desired station is then signaled. (4) After a reasonable time, remove receiver and start talking.

The writer of these directions has shifted from active to passive and back to active in four brief sentences. The resulting jumble is enough to cause telephone subscribers to hesitate making calls on their own party lines. The first sentence is in the active voice. The subject *you,* the actor, is understood. *You* are to lift the receiver and *you* are to wait for the dial tone. The second sentence, however, shifts to the passive. There is no one dialing, and no one is hearing the busy signal. The last part of the second sentence shifts again to active voice. The calling party acts. Again, in the third sentence, no one is signaling the desired station, and the sentence is passive. The final sentence returns to the active voice with an understood *you* as the actor. These directions do not communicate clearly. If the understood *you* had acted throughout (that is, if the author had remained in the active voice), there would be no confusion about following the directions. Here is a revision of the paragraph.

---

(1) To call a telephone on your own party line proceed as follows: Lift the receiver and wait for the dial tone. (2) Dial the regular seven-digit number of the desired station, listen for the busy signal, and then place the receiver on the hook. (3) Signal the desired station. (4) After a reasonable time, remove the receiver and start talking.

The passive voice isn't always inappropriate, of course, or there would be no need to have it in the language. But you must be careful to use it appropriately and unobtrusively. If, for instance, you do not know who performs the action, or if the actor is too unimportant to the thought of the sentence to be worth mentioning, you could appropriately use the passive verb. If you write, "Highway 6 was completed last May," no one is likely to insist that you change this passive construction into an active one by naming the engineering firm that built the road. But you probably do not need to leave this sentence in the passive voice. You can easily make it a phrase and put it into a longer, active sentence, for example: "Highway 6, completed last May, has increased trade in Boonville by fifty percent," or "Completion of Highway 6 last May boosted trade in Boonville."

This example acceptably uses the passive voice:

After the operation, Ernest was moved to his room and was given a sedative by the nurse who was to watch over him during his long convalescence.

In this sentence, we can take it for granted that a doctor performed the operation and that an orderly moved Ernest to his room. There is no point in mentioning them, for they are unimportant in this context. Notice that the remainder of the sentence continues in the passive, *was given by the nurse,* instead of *the nurse gave.* This use of passive is appropriate because to change it to active would change the point of view in mid-sentence. To make it active you would have to change this part of the sentence to an independent clause preceded by a comma: . . . room, *and the nurse who was to watch over him during his long convalescence gave him a sedative.* A second objection to this active form of the verb is the distance between the subject of the clause, *nurse,* and its verb, *gave.* Ordinarily, they should be as close together as possible. Here they are too far separated.

You can use the passive, then, when the actor is unknown or unimportant or when the active voice would interfere with style or cause a clumsy construction. Usually you should change any passive sentences to active ones. Sometimes students use passive constructions to avoid using the first person *I.* For example, sentences such as this one appear frequently: *C. Goehring's* Life in the Jungle *was selected for a book report because of the interest of its subject matter to this reader.* Note that no one has selected a book in this sentence. *This reader* may have, but who is he? Better by far to say in a forthright manner: *I selected C. Goehring's* Life in the Jungle *for a book report because its subject matter interested me.* Furthermore, do not refer to yourself in writing as "the author" or "this writer." Trying to avoid the first person almost always leads to a poor use of the passive or to clumsy circumlocutions.

These examples of poor use of the passive come from student papers.

Coffee had to be drunk and cookies eaten before games were played. (No one in this sentence is doing anything. Change to something like: The visitors had coffee and cookies before playing checkers and monopoly.)

Games to be played were checkers and monopoly. (Again, no one is playing the games. Make it active this way: They will play checkers and monopoly.)

8:15 was shown by the clock on the wall. (Very simple to change. The sentence shouldn't start with numbers, and the clock should be doing the action expressed here, so make it the subject of the sentence: The clock on the wall showed 8:15.)

exercises

A. Change any passive construction to active in these sentences.

1. Her skirts were always too short, Jane's parents insisted, and when she got a veto on her white leather suit, tears were shed, enough to fill Thompson's creek.
2. When the fourth child came, all plans to move to Bardtown in the spring were given up by the Guy family.
3. More than ten pounds of fish and sixteen sacks of ten-cent peanuts were consumed by the two dieters per week on their carbohydrate diet.
4. In 1910, his case was called incurable by every doctor in the north woods of Maine.
5. "All that I hope to be, I owe to my beloved oilwell," was the twist Miss Susie gave the Lincoln quote.
6. The centerpiece was arranged by the office secretary, while doughnuts and coffee were set out on card tables in the foyer by the clerk-typist.
7. Plans to attend the first session of summer school were made by the Douglass girls.
8. The hay was thrown over the fence by Farmer Swenson, whose cows were then called by their owner to "Come and get it!"
9. J. R.'s closet held more than fifty sports shirts, but every time, he chose the blue-gray plaid.
10. The house on Suffolk Street was pink and brown with a most vulgar green on the roof, and the color combination was loudly bemoaned by the neighborhood, as it was by the new owner.
11. Facts could not be ascertained, and so no decision was reached by the Committee to Remove Uncooperative Members from the club rolls.
12. Lee pranced home to stun his father with the news that he would be blasted off to California for the summer with the guys.
13. Complaints were heard by the young man when he announced to his parents that he had just quit his new job.
14. The mystery of the missing hymnals was finally solved by the rector at the Saturday meeting of the acolytes.
15. Because of the development of seven new cavities, the afternoon was unpleasantly spent in the dentist's office.
16. Excellent recommendations were given on the application sent by the artist from Arkansas.

17. The practice was continued until the target was hit by every marksman.
18. On November 15, agreement was reached among the Brechner Boulevard neighbors over rights to the water tank.
19. Amazing progress has been made by the Bell County Chamber of Commerce.
20. All the potato salad, as well as the Greek olives and the pickles, was eaten before mid-afternoon.

B. Write a set of instructions for one of the following:
   1. Tying a shoe lace
   2. Brushing teeth
   3. Making a paper hat (plane, boat)
C. Exchange instructions for B with someone in your class. Then, following your classmate's instructions *exactly,* perform the steps. Make a list of problems you discover.

avoid listless verbs

"Listless verbs" are sluggish, uninteresting, and inexact. They deaden your writing. As you revise, change as many of these as possible to lively verbs with exact meanings.

are	go
is	say
it is	see
had	there are
has	there is
have	

Look at the verbs shown in color in this paragraph:

> The Volkswagen is unexcelled for dependability. It is well-behaved under driving conditions in which other cars are kept off the road. Unlike conventional cars with their engine over the front wheels, the VW engine is in the back, which gives superior traction to the rear wheels. As a result, the VW can climb steep, slippery hills with ease or it can go with sureness through ice, snow, mud, and sand. Furthermore, other cars are easily out-performed by the VW even under the most extreme temperature conditions because there are no radiator problems in the VW. The VW engine is air-cooled; thus there are no leaks, rust, or anti-freeze problems peculiar to conventional cars. Any time, summer or winter, day or night, the VW is ready to go anywhere.

Every verb in this paragraph, with the exception of *gives* and *climb,* appears on the list. Further, a poor use of the passive also appears in mid-paragraph. Can you spot it? It marks a change in point of view.

This paragraph as it stands is not the worst one ever written, but making it better is simple. Just change the verbs (automatically taking care of the passive construction).

> Unexcelled for dependability, the Volkswagen behaves well under driving conditions that frighten other cars off the road. Unlike conventional cars with their engines over the front wheels, the VW, with its engine's weight in the back of the car, allows the rear wheels superior traction. As a result, the VW climbs steep, slippery hills with ease or cruises securely through ice, snow, mud, and sand. Further, the VW outperforms other cars even under the most extreme temperature conditions, because it needs no radiator. The air-cooled engine thus develops no leaks, rust, or antifreeze problems peculiar to conventional cars. Any time, summer or winter, the VW stands ready for anything.

In this revision, none of the listless verbs appear. No change in point of view mars the paragraph's coherence. No weak use of the passive confuses the reader.

Occasionally, you will find it necessary to use some of the listless verbs. Fine! As long as you don't overuse them to the point that your writing becomes boring. A good rule to follow is: *Change any verb that does not draw a picture.*

exercise

Change all colorless verbs in these sentences to stronger, active ones.

1. The tour conductor said that we could not lean over the wooden railing.
2. There is a fat little green pig with roses on his back placed on the dresser.
3. The painter came down the shaky ladder and put his pan and brush down on the floor in disgust.
4. The driver drove his truck down the road, passing cars on the icy road very carelessly.
5. The girl was crying when she said that the police were after her.
6. The governess could see the dusting powder all over the floor, and some of it was on the bedspread and some on the study table.
7. Sylvia gave a loud cry when she realized that the telephone call was long distance from her sister Laura in Philadelphia.

8. Every time one of the carbonated drinks was opened, out came a gush of purple pop with a hissing noise, and I had to put it down and run to keep from getting wet from the spray.

9. Jackson had a stomachache, so he said, and he told us that there were six other leading athletes who had stomachaches, too.

10. We went first to Los Angeles and then went on to Kansas City, not getting to the convention until Thursday afternoon.

examine all uses of "who" and "which"

The overuse of *who* and *which* weighs writing down with deadwood—unnecessary words. These words introduce dependent adjective clauses. Reducing the clauses to phrases almost always results in economy in wording and an increase in interest. Look at this example.

Smith's *Guide to Spain,* which was first written over fifty years ago, has gone through nine revisions, of which the latest was in 1978.

If you drop the first *which* and the first *was*, along with the *of which* and the same listless *was*, you will have a stronger, more economically worded sentence that sounds more direct.

Smith's *Guide to Spain,* first written over fifty years ago, has gone through nine revisions, the latest in 1978.

In the next sentence, the *who* is unnecessary.

Jack Jones is a man who calls every trick.
(Let us assume from his name that Jack Jones is a man. Then strike *is a man who*, and you have cleared away four words of deadwood. Yet the meaning is intact.)
Jack Jones calls every trick.

In the next sentence, the *which* is unnecessary.

Peterson's poem, "The Way to Heaven," is a poem which needs no explanation.
(As in the previous sentence delete *is a poem which* and you have eliminated a weak *is* and an unnecessary *which*.)
Peterson's poem, "The Way to Heaven," needs no explanation.

Note the number of *who's, which's,* listless verbs, and other deadwood in this paragraph.

```
 1        The university catalog can be used to good advantage by
 2    the freshman who is bewildered by university life. It is
 3    revised every year in order that it will be up-to-date.
 4    First of all, there is in this catalog a list of all the
 5    courses which are offered by the university. These courses
 6    are arranged alphabetically by department in order that the
 7    student may choose which courses he wants to take. It is also
 8    from this list of courses of each department that a degree
 9    plan for the student can be devised, which will be within the
10    limits of the regulations of the university.
```

Line 1:
Listless verb, *can be used*.

Line 2:
A *who* followed by the listless verb *is*. Write *freshmen bewildered by university life* and avoid both. *It is* at the beginning of the next sentence needs revision. Why not leave this whole sentence out and substitute the one word *current* before *university* in the first line?

Line 3:
Listless verb *will be*. Problem avoided if you delete this whole sentence as suggested.

Line 4:
First of all. Do not use this expression. If you must use a *first*, be certain you also use a *second*. In any case, delete *of all*. Do not use *firstly* or *secondly* at any time.

Line 5:
Which followed by listless verb *are* needs examination. Listless verb *are* needs revision.

Line 6:
In order that. Do not use this phrase; . . . *to allow students a choice of courses* is better here.

Line 7:
Which avoided by the revision suggested for line 5. *It is,* at the beginning of the next sentence, needs to be removed by revision.

Line 8:
Of courses of each department has too many *of's*. Remove one *of* by writing *of departments' courses*.

Line 9:
Listless verb *can be* needs changing. *Which* followed by listless verb *will be* also needs revising.

Line 10:
Of the regulations of the University. Delete one *of* by writing *of university regulations*.

All lines:
The passive construction in every sentence underlies most of the problems in the paragraph. The active voice usually will eliminate *which, who,* and listless verbs.

Here is a revision of the paragraph. Notice the difference in length with the deadwood deleted.

> The current university catalog offers help for bewildered
> freshmen. It lists all university courses alphabetically by
> department, allowing the student, if he follows university regu-
> lations, to choose his own courses and devise his own degree plan.

Look now at a paragraph by Robert Louis Stevenson. Here no *which* or *who* clutters the thought. No overuse of listless verbs deadens it. Some passive constructions appear. Can you spot them? Verbs are italicized.

These long beaches *are* enticing to the idle man. It *would be* hard to find a walk more solitary and at the same time more exciting to the mind. Crowds of ducks and sea gulls *hover* over the sea. Sandpipers *trot* in and out by troops after the retiring waves, *trilling* together in a chorus of infinitesimal song. Strange seatangles, new to the European eye, the bones of whales, or sometimes a whole whale's carcase, white with carrion gulls and poisoning the wind, *lie* scattered here and there along the sands. The waves *come* in closely, vast and green, *curve* their translucent necks, and *burst* with a surprising uproar that *runs* waxing and waning, up and down the long keyboard of the beach. The foam of these great ruins *mounts* in an instant to the ridge of the sand glacis, swiftly *fleets* back again, and *is* met and buried by the next breaker.[1]

Three listless verbs appear in this paragraph—*are* in the first sentence, *be* in the second sentence, and *is* in the last sentence, and these are all passive. But these are the only listless verbs and the only passive constructions in the paragraph. Notice the preponderance of strong active verbs—*hover, trot, lie, curve, burst, runs, mounts, fleets.* Note also the absence of *which* and *who.*

exercise

Revise the following sentences to eliminate *who, which,* listless verbs, and other deadwood.

1. Bill decided to take the road to the east, which would get him to Troy fifteen minutes sooner.
2. Grace sold the book which had been given to her last Christmas in order to buy a ticket to Calico Rock.
3. Geoffrey Chaslin, who played the lead in *A Man for All Seasons,* which is a play about Sir Thomas More, visited London last year in order to become better equipped to play the role.

[1]Robert Louis Stevenson, in "The Old Pacific Capital," first published in *Frazier's Magazine,* November, 1880.

4. His grandfather, who is also his godfather, gave him an air rifle, which his parents stole and hid, he said.

5. The tall elm tree, which had replaced the scrubby oak, lost all its leaves and turned sick, which worried Frances, who had done all she could to keep the homestead pretty.

6. She decided to wear the black and white piqué, which her mother made and which was far prettier than any of the others wore, which included Sharon, whose dad is Dean of Everything on campus.

7. He went through all the cancelled checks of the Bank of Commerce in order to try to find the one which he had sent to the mortgage company to make his house payment for the month of January.

8. Joe McCown is the man who contributed all his ranch income to the orphan whom the police found in the house which was deserted. (*Note:* If you have to use them, how do you decide between *who* or *whom*? It is simple. *Who* and *whom* will be found only in dependent clauses. Remove the clause from the sentence and substitute *he* or *him* in place of the *who* or *whom*. If *he* fits, then *who* is proper; if *him* fits, choose *whom*. For example, in this sentence *who* is found in the clause *who contributed his ranch income.* If you try both *he* and *him* in place of the *who,* you will find that only *he* will fit properly: *He contributed his ranch income.* So *who* is correct here. *Whom* is found in the clause *whom the police found.* You will find that only *him* can be substituted for *whom: The police found him.* So *whom* is proper in this clause. If the subject is plural, substitute *they* for *who* or *them* for *whom.*)

9. The choice which was made was between Bill and him, neither of whom had any experience in typing, which was required of the person who was to be employed. (Is this *whom* proper?)

10. There is no reason for the chairman, who is Vanessa Jones, to take offense at the motion, which is aimed at electing a vice-chairman who is to help her with her duties.

avoid anything trite

Some words and phrases are used so much they become worn out. Yesterday's slang, for instance, is trite today. Not many of you would want to "cut a rug" or to "put a bee" in someone's "bonnet," nor would many now use a phrase like "crazy, mixed-up kid." These are out of date. The same happens to certain combinations of ordinary words, as in these sentences.

He not only started sweeping like mad, but also gave me a list of items to buy for the party, such as the following: party hats, confetti, horns, and so forth. These things proved to be so much fun that we had a ball.

The trite words and expressions are listed below.

not only . . . but	and so forth
like mad	proved to be
such as	we had a ball
the following	items

eliminate or replace exhausted phrases

An exhausted phrase is just that—worn out from too much use. It is also often a lazy expression, stuck in by the writer unthinkingly. Usually you can either eliminate these lazy, worn out phrases or replace them with a single, strong word. Each sentence below contains at least one exhausted phrase, italicized for emphasis. Avoid them and others like them.

Due to the fact that I had gained too much weight in the past month, I turned down his invitation to dinner. (Always substitute *because* for *due to the fact that*. It works every time.)

This apathy has spread over the *entire world*. (Why not just *world*?)

Our ever-growing population will be a problem in *just a few short years*.

To this rule I was no exception.

We crossed the street *in order to* avoid meeting him. (We crossed the street to avoid meeting him. Always delete *in order*.)

In this fast-moving world, the scientist must *keep abreast* of technological advances.

In this land of ours today, no one can really be a *rugged individualist*.

So for many years to come we will feel the effect of Watergate.

Yes, truly it can be said that young people today are rebellious.

Ours is becoming a *push-button society*.

Texas Avenue will soon reach the limit of its capacity, *as far as traffic is concerned*. (A particularly poor one.)

These tired expressions take up valuable space without adding anything to the thought. Avoid them *like the plague* (another one!).

Exercise your mind by playing with the following exhausted phrases. First, think of a sentence containing the phrase; then see if you can replace it with a stronger equivalent, if possible only one word.

in the event of (that)	with reference to
make contact with	in the near future
at all times	without further delay
in view of the fact that	stunted in growth
during the time that	in order to
in many cases	in most cases
for the purpose of	in this case
at the present time	in all cases
despite the fact that	will you be kind enough to
due to the fact that	on the grounds that

Here are some sample sentences to get you started.

Don't panic in the event of a fire.
I shall try to make contact with you by Thursday.
In view of the fact that you failed math, you must go to summer school.

exercises

A. Pick out all trite and exhausted words and phrases in this paragraph.

> Yes, truly the American way is the one which is best suited
> to serve the needs and desires of the people of this far-flung
> world of ours today. Even if one of the various and sundry philo-
> sophies which oppose our way of life were to win out and conquer
> our country as well as all others, there are various means through
> which we could make a comeback. We could pull the rug out from
> under our enemies by stirring up a hornet's nest of far-flung,
> ever-increasing destruction of enemy material, that is, as far as
> their supply lines are concerned—trains, airplanes, and so forth—
> so that they would not have a leg to stand on, as far as fighting us is
> concerned. It would, therefore, prove to be the case that in order to
> keep us under their thumb, our enemies would have discovered that
> they have bitten off more than they can chew and would be facing an
> impossible task.

B. Rewrite these sentences to remove exhausted words and phrases.
1. She had clearly suffered the ravages of time.
2. We sat under the sheltering arms of the gnarled old oak.
3. Would you believe half a million trading stamps?
4. He is twenty-three and not getting any younger.
5. Heaven only knows and time will tell which way the cookie crumbles.
6. She is the motherly type and talks to me like a Dutch uncle.
7. She left no stone unturned to find happiness at any price.
8. He felt a fierce loyalty for his native Arkansas.
9. The little children played at games and such until dinner.
10. Restitution will be made by June 20.
11. When we asked him about the missing cookies he looked as guilty as the cat that ate the canary.
12. When the going got rough, Becky decided to turn the job over to Susan.
13. He soon discovered that a rolling stone gathers no moss and settled down to a steady job.
14. In my opinion, I think he was just whistling in the dark all the time he was smiling like a Cheshire cat.
15. On the other side of the ledger is the fact that he was driving like a bat when the accident occurred.

avoid forcing your reader to love it

If you grow too enthusiastic about your subject, you may stretch the credibility of your readers. By making excessive statements intended to convince them of the worth of your subject, you are, in effect, attempting to force them to fall on your side. These sentences do just that:

Horseshoes is a delightful game that can always be enjoyed by everyone, young and old. (Maybe horseshoes is delightful, but there is *no* game that everyone will always enjoy).

There's nothing as exciting as a good football game. (To some people there may be activities that are considerably more exciting—reading a book, for instance.)

Irma's Last Love is the most fascinating book ever written. (To the writer, but perhaps not to the reader.)

No one will regret making this trip into the depths of Devil's Canyon. (Not even someone who slips and breaks a leg on the descent?)

The point: Don't tell your readers how wonderful something is; make them *feel* it through the quality of your writing. Then you won't need to tell them.

do not preach

"Preaching" usually takes the form of moralizing in writing. Rarely do readers want a lecture on what their moral positions should be or on what they should believe. If you present convincing evidence, you will not have to state the moral conclusions for the reader. Look at these examples of student moralizing.

Young people should try to understand their parents.
If we all love our country, no foreign ideology can ever take us over!
Everyone should strive to live a more moral life.
Students, awaken! We must not let our sacred traditions be taken away from us.

Examination of these "preachy" sentences discloses the use of certain words that make the sentences preachy. These words divide naturally into two classification.

1. *false words.*

always	everything
ever	never
every	nobody
everybody	no one

When you use these words without qualification you say something about everyone or everything in a class. Almost no conclusion about everyone or everything can be valid. You can write that everyone must die some day or that everyone has been born; but otherwise, someone, somewhere, proves the exception to most statements about *all* people. (Note that this last sentence did not say that someone proves the exception to *all* statements about all people.) The ridiculousness of using these words becomes apparent when you see a sentence such as this one:

Everybody always likes everything about every film that Hitchcock makes, and no one ever criticizes his techniques.

2. *commanding words.* Such words as *must, ought to, should,* and *had better* demand obedience to the writer. Such admonishment is more likely to make the reader resentful of your ideas than receptive to them.

avoid stilted wording and "false tone"

When writers try to impress their readers by using big words and flowery phrases inappropriately, they create stilted writing. They go out of their way to make a simple statement complicated by using longer words and more words than the thought warrants. The result is lack of communication because ideas are obscured rather than clarified by the clutter of words. Look at these examples and their simplifications:

The consumption of alcoholic beverages among the younger generation is escalating. (Young people are drinking more.)
Felicitations on the auspicious occasion of your natal day. (Happy birthday.)
I desire to pen my memoirs. (I want to write an autobiography.)
He matriculated with the earnest desire to graduate in three years, but due to certain problems that presented themselves, he was forced to accept a grade of failing in two courses of study and finally found it necessary to withdraw from two others, which left as a remainder only one course, on which his instructor awarded him a grade of C−. (Although he wanted to graduate in three years, he failed six hours, dropped three, and barely salvaged three in his first semester.)

You can frequently improve the "false tone" created by certain words simply by substituting stronger, one-syllable equivalents. Supply stronger substitutes for the words in this list.

assist	utilize
demonstrate	discontinue
permit	transmit
inquire	endeavor
procure	purchase
indicate	sufficient
terminate	encountered
ascertain	employs

What, for example, could you do with the following sentences to eliminate the "false tone"?

Please permit me to assist you by demonstrating the proper procedure.
We endeavor to ascertain the truth and to utilize it in creating public confidence.
I purchased sufficient food for the picnic.

exercise

Revise all moralizing and stilted wording in these sentences.

1. The surgeon hesitated, her features drawn and sorrowful, as she approached to verify our deep and foreboding premonition that the immediate ancestor of our parent was expected to expire before the sun rose to shine upon the world again.
2. Everyone should consume some of the leafy green products of the garden every day because of their nutritional value.
3. The happy cries of the darling children reached the ears of their delighted parents.
4. Despite warnings of friends and family, of the government, and even of the tobacco manufacturers themselves, Hubert continued to partake of tremendous amounts of nicotine.
5. His employment was terminated due to the fact that his employer felt that an excessive number of hours per day were being spent in other than gainful pursuits.
6. She has the ability to discuss at length any topic of conversation that is introduced, despite the fact that she sometimes is less than expert in the field under discussion.
7. And so in conclusion, let me say that we should all strive in unison to extirpate from our society the evils of gambling.
8. The babe still lay quietly, lost in slumberland, as the wee hours of the morning ticked on and sounds of dawn reached the ears of the drowsy parents.

avoid "fine writing"

Some beginning writers believe that a fancy and elaborate style is elegant. Be warned that it is not. For instance, a freshman English student had difficulty understanding why her instructor marked her down when she wrote the following:

Lush, well-maintained grounds combine with the harmonic grace of the buildings to give a deep majestic glow to the grounds. Flying everywhere, beautiful birds lend their melodious tones, while squirrels flit from tree to tree, chattering ecstatically.

In trying to be artistic, the student said nothing. English instructors usually call this "fine writing," and they are not giving it a compliment. A good rule to follow is this: Write briefly, plainly, and sensibly. Don't put on airs or use flowery words. Say what you mean. Be direct.

avoid unessential "ly" words

Most "ly" words are adverbs and modify verbs or adjectives. When used to modify verbs, "ly" words often allow authors to deaden their writing by selecting listless verbs instead of searching for strong active verbs to make their writing more specific. For instance, you could write "He ate voraciously," but "He gobbled his food" draws a better picture. Sometimes the "ly" words are unnecessary, as in these sentences:

I have completely exhausted my supply. (Delete *completely*. If you have exhausted it, it is exhausted. There is nothing more to say.)
There was really no reason for his success. (Delete *really*. It is a filler word, as are most of the "ly" adverbs.)
His remarks were truly nonsense. (Delete *truly*. If they were nonsense, that is all there is to it. Another word used as a filler.)

Here are some "ly" words you probably should avoid. Check your papers to be certain you don't overuse these words.

absolutely	positively	truly
completely	purely	undoubtedly
extremely	really	unfortunately
fortunately	surely	unquestionably
hopefully		

avoid vague words

Like some exhausted or lazy phrases, vague words are those the writer uses from habit, or without thought, as substitutes for specific words with exact meaning. Vague words carry little meaning because they are general. For instance, this sentence says nothing: "The many different factors involved created various problems for many people." This sentence communicates nothing specific to the reader and there is no point in writing it.

Here is a list of vague words to avoid. When you are tempted to use one of them, mark it out and select a more specific term.

a lot	factor	many	pretty
aspect	field (of)	much	provide
characteristic	innumerable	nice	several
consideration	interesting	people	thing(s)
contains	item	pertains	variety
deal	large	phase	various
different	lots of		very

Most beginning writers have to make a special effort to avoid the words on this list, but eventually the effort will pay off. Remove these words from your vocabulary. Otherwise, you may end up saying nothing, as did the students who wrote these sentences:

There are lots of ways to consider making a living.
There are many and various sweaters to be made in all sizes and colors.
The many different aspects of socialized medicine are interesting.

INTENTION AND AUDIENCE—TONE   As the heading to this section suggests, tone has to do with the intentions of the writer as found in his finished work and as perceived by his readers (audience). Another way of looking at tone is to think of it as the writer's "voice"; in your papers it is your "voice" as your readers hear it, and it may not be the "voice" you intended at all. Once you freeze a word on paper, it loses much of the added power it would normally have if you spoke it. For example, try to *hear* how each of the following would *sound* if spoken according to the instructions given:

1. Good bye. (firmly, straightforwardly)
2. Good bye. (softly, almost with fear)
3. Good bye. (whispered, with love).
4. *Good bye!* (loudly, meaning "get lost")
5. Good *bye.* (loudly, to people at distance)

Not everyone would say these in exactly the same way. Still, it is

B C.   By JOHNNY HART

SOURCE: Used by permission of John Hart and Field Enterprises, Inc.

obvious that a writer loses some "voice power" when he puts his words down on paper. An added problem, too is that readers may not hear what a writer intends. We read into things, we hear what we want to hear. Inexperienced writers often try to supply this missing intention by using adverbs excessively (as you learned earlier in this chapter).

You can see, then, that tone involves the three-part relationship represented in this diagram:

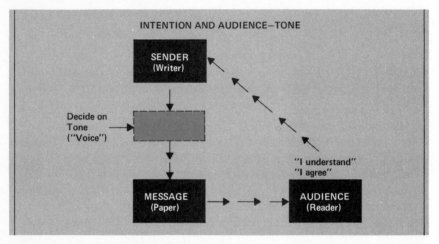

The diagram suggests that you, as the writer (sender), need to decide on the tone or "voice" you will try to project in your paper (message); then you must make sure it is this tone that accompanies your message to the reader (audience). In the classroom, the reader (usually your instructor) will let you know that he "understands" and "agrees"; or he may disagree with you, and ask you to add more factual support. With published papers the information returning to the writer (through sales, criticisms, personal comment, perhaps) is less certain.

Tone is related to changes in the sound of the voice in speech, where it is usually easy to spot a tone that is approving (or disapproving), serious (or humorous), personal (or impersonal), direct (or sarcastic), formal (or informal), calm (or excited), and so on. It is this tone in a work that helps a writer control the reader's attitude toward the ideas presented. If you recheck the section on introductory paragraphs, you'll find that you already know much about tone—how to get the interest of readers, how to get them to accept you and your ideas (see pages 101 to 108). Study and apply this definition of tone:

Tone consists of those qualities in a work through which a writer hopes to get a specific response in his reader.

"Qualities" implies logical thought as well as the psychological appeals used to create reader interest and to get reader acceptance. And since the "qualities" in question must be conveyed by words, they must be your starting point in controlling and projecting the tone you want your reader to hear. If, for example, you wanted your writing to project a quality of seriousness, you would use informal language and humor only with caution, or not all. Similarly, a work can't be personal in tone if its language is formal and technical.

This chapter has already shown you many ways inexperienced writers unknowingly create an undesirable "false" tone by using passive voice, listless verbs, too many adverbs, trite expressions, "fine writing," and *who* or *which* constructions that lead to "deadwood." The following illustrations have been chosen for study because in each the writer has tried to create a specific tone, which he carefully maintains throughout the work. To shift tone can damage or destroy unity, since a consistent tone helps hold the thoughts together. The comments on each selection point out some of the qualities of *thought* and *diction* that help create its specific tone. Also, all are introductory paragraphs, chosen because a writer must establish tone and interest at once if he is to keep his readers moving into the work. The first is by a student; all the others are by professional writers.

A.

Of all the *enemies* of mankind that have ever existed upon the face of the earth, there are some that simply *do not deserve* to be here. Ranked third in the all-time top ten *worst enemies*, just behind the *devil* himself and the *notorious snake*, is the cockroach. This *disgusting* little insect far exceeds his nearest competitor, the mosquito (who, for the sake of *those who may be curious*, could manage only an eighth-place finish behind such *powerful contenders* as *rats, buzzards, lions*, and *piranha*) because of his superior size and strength, and his *too-horrible-for-words* appearance. The cockroach should be *wiped out* at Glory U. because he is an eye sore, he *interferes* with one's learning, and he is a *hazard* to one's health.

Even a quick check of the italicized words in this paragraph reveals a negative tone: *enemies, worst, notorious, disgusting, horrible, eye sore.* This student clearly dislikes cockroaches; his thesis is that this insect "should be wiped out," and his paper develops the reasons pointed to in the rest of the thesis statement. But there is more to the success of this paragraph than a clear statement of disapproval. How, for example, has the student prevented the passage from becoming too serious? Do you think this passage would be as effective if both the subject and the tone were serious? He maintains the tone of playful seriousness throughout the paper with such comments as:

"one of the little monstrosities galloping across the room," "he may be seen a few feet away just sitting and staring," "squatting in the corner surveying the situation," and "converge upon him armed with sticks, shoes, books, chairs." Professional humorists are well aware that exaggerating little things usually creates humor; do you think this student has carried exaggeration too far?

B.

> I am a gun nut, I suppose. My father made me a gun nut. He taught me how to shoot, and ever since what I would really rather be doing than anything else is shooting at small, innocent birds.[2]

You could never tell from introductory Paragraph *B* that Stewart Alsop is seriously attacking computerized bureaucracy. There is no thesis statement at the beginning, only a calculated tone of sarcastic playfulness created at once by the first sentence. The first sentence of the second paragraph echoes this tone: "To the non-gun nut, this may seem as mysterious as the nuttiness of the young does to the middle-aged." Maintaining his tone, he leads the reader surely toward the thesis (about half-way through) with the following statement: "What, indeed, you gonna do? So I took off most of an afternoon to be fingerprinted for J. Edgar Hoover's files, a messy and demeaning business." Only in the next-to-last paragraph does he give his reader a thesis:

> But surely there is a better way. Surely it is better to go to the root of the evil. Invention should have halted with the flush of the toilet a century ago—what sensible man has a good word to say for the ballistic missile or the bomb, or even for the automobile, and the airplane? But the worst invention of the lot was the computer.[3]

But the tone of sarcastic playfulness persists, partly because of exaggeration and partly because readers can't be expected to remain wholly serious as they read about the "flush of the toilet." Notice, too, that the first-person "I," used throughout, disappears in this paragraph. Why has the writer left it out?

C.

> When I hear about some *flagrant violation of human rights* in a far-flung place on the globe I react violently as any free, red-blooded American

---

[2]"A Call to Revolt" by Stewart Alsop, from *Newsweek,* December 22, 1969. Copyright Newsweek, Inc., 1969. Reprinted by permission.
[3]*Ibid.*

does. I get filled with righteous indignation. I get stirred. I get—*I
get nervous is what I get.*[4]

Example *C* is the introductory paragraph to a short political article
on the tense peace in the Middle East. Again the author chooses
to withhold his thesis and concentrate on getting the reader interested
and sympathetic. Aside from the personal "I," how does Goodman
Ace keep you smiling as he heads toward a rather serious comment
on peace? What is the effect of the contrast between the two comments
in italics? The rest of Ace's article illustrates that *serious* commentary
can be made while using a humorous or sarcastic tone—a difficult
art, perhaps best illustrated in some of the writing of Jonathan Swift.

A main function of the "I" in Paragraphs *B* and *C* is to create
a personal tone that can readily be turned into playfulness. Properly
used, the "I" usually adds a feeling of first-hand observation; but
it can be used to gain interest for very serious observations without
the sugar-coating of humor seen in these first paragraphs. Here are
some examples.

D.

A few mornings ago I rescued a bat from a swimming pool. The man
who owned the pool—*but did not own the bat*—asked me why. That
question *I do not expect ever to be able to answer,* but it involves *a
good deal. If even I* myself could understand it, *I* would know what
it is that seems to distinguish *man* from the rest of *nature,* and why,
despite all she has to *teach* him, there is also something he would
like to *teach* her *if he could.*[5]

Paragraph *D* begins a fairly long paper on nature, the individual,
and the species. The author concludes that nature has a "passion
for mere numbers," disregarding individuals, and that some men have
also become too "careful of the type" and too "careless of the single
life." Only when the readers reach the last two paragraphs of the
paper do they fully see the author's main point. In what ways does
the author try to keep the paper from becoming too formal? What
might you conclude about this writer's intention and tone from the
italicized words? How does he create reader interest? How does the
writer get you to think of him as serious, thoughtful, and questioning?

[4]From "Peace Is Hell," by Goodman Ace. Copyright 1967 by Saturday Review Co. First appeared
in *Saturday Review,* August 5, 1967. Used with permission.

[5]From *The Desert Year* by Joseph Wood Krutch. Copyright 1952 by Joseph Wood Krutch. Reprinted
by permission of William Morrow & Company, Inc.

E.

A couple of years ago I became involved on a panel for the Western Psychological Association which was about *something called* "The Psyche of a Scientist." It turned into a *kind of* psychodrama because *here were* all these psychologists, sociologists, and anthropologists, but I was the only *real live* scientist. The *tribe* I belong to is called biochemistry, which is sort of a subgroup in the *pecking order* of science somewhere below physical chemistry and above geology. And what *I* was listening to was a fantasy, or, *you might say,* the results of a *con job* by the *natives* on some *poor hapless explorers* who did not understand the *terrain* at all.[6]

The author of Paragraph *E* is beginning an outspoken attack on certain practices in the "science jungle," concluding (several pages later), "Until we become aware of these evils of big science we cannot hope to eradicate them." Judging from the words in italics, what would you conclude about the tone of this introductory paragraph? Which of the following descriptive terms would you use to describe the tone: *impersonal, objective, personal, formal, informal, casual, serious, direct, indirect, sarcastic.*

F.

I feel that this award was not made to me *as a man,* but to *my work*—a *life's work* in the *agony and sweat* of the *human spirit,* not for glory and least of all for profit, but to create out of the materials of *the human spirit* something which did not exist before. So *this award is only mine in trust.* It will not be difficult to find a dedication for the money part of it *commensurate* with the purpose and significance of its origin. *But I would like* to do the same with the acclaim too, by using this moment as a pinnacle from which *I might* be listened to by the young men and women already dedicated to *the same anguish and travail,* among whom is already that one who will some day stand here *where I am standing.*[7]

In this famous address William Faulkner concludes that "man will prevail." He has chosen a moment of triumph to call for action. The tone he projects might be called "urgent"—a bid for attention in a time of need. How many personal "tags" can you discover in this paragraph? What is the effect of words like *travail, commensurate, anguish, human spirit?* Comment on the nature of the "ethical appeal" here. (See pages 101 and 104 for additional information.)

---

[6]From "The Science Jungle" by Paul Saltman in *Harper's Magazine,* February 1967. Copyright © 1967 Harper's Magazine.

[7]William Faulkner, "Nobel Prize Acceptance Speech." Reprinted from *The Faulkner Reader.* Copyright 1954 by William Faulkner (Random House, Inc.).

G.

> The School System has much to say these days of the virtue of reading widely, and not enough about the virtues of reading less but in depth. There are any number of reading lists for poetry but there is not enough talk about individual poems. Poetry, finally, is one poem at a time. To read any one poem carefully is the ideal preparation for reading another. Only a poem can illustrate how poetry works.[8]

The thesis statement at the end of introductory Paragraph *G* asserts firmly what this poet-critic will be discussing. Although the "voice" you hear is authoritative, it doesn't have quite the sense of personal argument that most of the previous paragraphs have. Of all the paragraphs, it is probably the most clearly *expository,* setting up a thesis and then supporting it in a fairly long paper. The writer decides to use the personal "I" very sparingly (there are only two or three, and they appear later in the discussion). Does he write in a way to create interest? What is the effect of the *parallelism* and *antithesis* in the first two sentences? (See page 86 for some hints.) Although there is no "I" in the paragraph, could you call it "impersonal"? Why not? (See page 48 for some comments about challenge and strength in thesis statements.)

To summarize. The questions you must ask yourself when thinking about tone in a work include at least the following:

1. What specific response does the writer want from his reader? "I understand"? "I agree"? "I sympathize"?
2. How does the writer create interest?
3. What kind of person does the writer sound like? An authority? Objective commentator? Involved participant? A lively human being?
4. Are the words strong and expressive or weak and colorless? Is their effect "negative" or "positive"? Personal or impersonal?
5. Are the sentence patterns simple or complex? What effect do they have on the tone?
6. How serious is the thought presented? Is there any attempt to tone down the seriousness with humor or sarcasm?

If you look back at the diagram on page 278, you should see immediately how these questions apply to your writing and to the decision you make *before* you begin writing. The diagram shows that you, as writer, decide on the "voice" or tone *before* you begin to write the paper. If you are clear on "who you are," how serious, how informal,

---

[8]"Robert Frost: The Way to the Poem" by John Ciardi from *Saturday Review,* April 12, 1958. Copyright 1958 by Saturday Review Inc. Reprinted by permission of the author and publishers.

how personal, how assertive, you should be able to carry this attitude into the paper itself giving it the *unity of tone* a good paper must have (see the two shaded areas in the diagram).

exercises on tone

A. Here is a simple exercise that will make you aware of some of the limitations most of us have when we grab words from our vocabularies in a hurry.

The list below consists of words you probably learned before you went to school. Look at them quickly and decide their meanings.

arm	knife	dish
eye	nose	cup
worm	chair	can
elbow	finger	egg
spoon	hand	table

You probably thought of them as nouns (names of things), just as you first learned them. But these "baby" words can become strong *tone verbs* if you think about them. For example: *Arm* yourself with strong verbs; don't *finger* your hair that way; she *wormed* her way into my affections; *spoon* out the chemicals carefully; can you take it as well as *dish* it out?

List another ten words that you consider preschool words (hint: think of pets, body parts, furniture, food, things around any home, including kitchen, dining room, and bathroom).

Now write ten short sentences which turn these common words into strong tone-creating words you can use.

B. Come to class prepared to discuss *denotation* and *connotation*. Why are these two words important clues to tone? (Recheck Exercise *C* on page 153.)

C. Recheck Exercises *C* and *D*, pages 169 and 170. Using Exercise *C* as your model, write three different paragraphs on one of the subjects listed for you in Exercise *A*, page 124. Your instructor may want you to repeat the assignment with other topics in the list to practice creating tone.

review exercises

A. On the basis of the material in this chapter, revise these sentences in any way necessary.
1. World War II was over, and he was coming in on a wing and a prayer.
2. Majorie Ann is gorgeous, but to hear her tell it, she is plain, unless she is too modest, as not many of her age group are.

3. He was on Cloud 9 when he inherited enough money to live in the manner to which he had become accustomed.

4. They knew, moreover, that the malady was to be a lingering one and that insidiously it would increase in seriousness until the dear one's life itself would be snuffed out, as a candle is suddenly relieved of its light-giving pleasure when its usefulness is ended.

5. They were too tired to move, but they walked home, slowly as though they resented every step of it, but they did not have bus fare, and they did not know what else to do but to walk.

6. His own father, who was to Paul a financial wizard, and whom Paul hoped to imitate, knew now that the cards were down and that it would be tough sledding and uphill all the way from now on along the road to Wall Street.

7. To whom should she appeal for funds for the Scouting outing, she asked herself. Who cares enough to give, and from whom can I seek aid?

8. They hurried to church fast, because they knew that the choir director would not be happy if they came into rehearsal late again, and they did not like to walk the full length of the building up to the choir loft while she looked at them with anger in her eyes.

9. At least we can say with certainty that nobody can deny Charles the praise he deserves for making the organization run more smoothly than Tommy was able to, or Buster, either.

10. You haven't lived until you've sat at the lake's edge while the sun goes down, with a hired hand to mix up the refreshments and swat away the mosquitoes.

11. Freddie refused the invitation due to the fact that his aunt was expected, whom he had not seen since her third marriage, which was three years ago.

12. Nothing is more charming than Delilah with an armful of tulips and a smile on her face.

13. The doorbell had been loudly rung, and it was too late for anything but hope.

14. The figs preserved by Mrs. Wenglar, the ceramics painted and baked by Mrs. Hill, the doilies embroidered by Mrs. Pearl—all were truly lovely and all well deserved the blue ribbon.

15. The large family, including innumerable in-laws, showed interesting characteristics and aspects in lots of ways, especially as pertained to the various occupations and different hobbies they were involved in.

B. Study the cartoon on page 277. Decide on two or three words to describe the *tone* of each statement in the cartoon. Write a paragraph to show how the contrast in diction is used to create humor. What assumptions by the sender cause the message to go astray?

10

revising
your paper
–sentences

ore than any other animal, human beings seem to need to communicate with each other. They build complex communities that demand a subtle mixture of freedom and control. They invent machines, buildings, and ideas in response to their environment. They develop elaborate social systems and governments and territories that play on the harmonious interaction of natural hostilities. Cities, skyscrapers, computers, planes, love, democracy, country, war—without an efficient, effective communication system, these products of man's labor wouldn't be possible. If you think about it, you'll see there are three basic ways people communicate:

1. Through physical touch—a handshake, a pat on the back, a kick in the shins
2. Through body movement in space—pointing a finger, smiling, winking, nodding the head
3. Through visible and audible symbols—words and sentences, written and spoken

The subject of this book has been *written* communication—a complete paper, paragraphs, words, sentences.

But you have already seen from the discussion of tone in the previous chapter that one major problem in writing is to make the written message represent the "voice" you have in mind and—equally important—to make sure that readers of your message receive what you want them to in thought and tone. The tone of voice, the wave of the hand, the pat on the back are absent in the sentences you write. One aim of your sentence revision should be to compensate for the loss of these in written communication; another is to choose sentence patterns that give the most important ideas the strongest position.

SENTENCES IN GENERAL   Good sentences are not born automatically. Not for anyone. They are created, with patience and skill, out of the accumulated knowledge of many years, out of the thoughts, feelings, words, and word patterns you *have available to you.* But unless you—and, in fact, anyone who wants to improve his writing skill—consciously study how to improve, you may find that what is "available to you" are the simple sentence patterns of your childhood. This chapter should help you recognize these basic patterns and improve them, and encourage you to experiment with them to gain new strength and emphasis.

You already know much about sentences. *Length,* for example.

287

Short sentences move fast. Long ones, on the other hand, tend to move somewhat more slowly toward their final destination. You need them both in your writing, and you need to know when to use them. You know also that there are many *kinds* of sentences, depending on how you classify them:

1. Grammatically—simple, compound, complex, compound-complex
2. Rhetorically—loose, periodic, balanced, antithetical
3. Functionally—question, command, statement, exclamation

Why so many "kinds"? Each performs a specific job in communication. Because of their structures, some keep the reader involved by withholding the full meaning until the end of the sentence (as this one has done). Others make their point at once. Still others balance part against part, meaning against meaning. The five sentences immediately preceding this one, for example, illustrate five kinds. Which are they? Using different kinds of sentences gives your writing *variety* and prevents monotony. You can gain variety in sentence patterns in four basic ways: (1) *balance* (which you learned about on page 86 in the chapter on coherence); (2) *inversion* or unusual word order, a pattern different from the one a reader might expect; (3) *repetition* of phrases or clauses for effect, for emphasis; and (4) *omission* of certain words supplied by the sense of preceding passages. (Meaningful sentence fragments are an example: "How do you feel?" *Sick.*) Most of the material on revision in this chapter can be studied under the three broad headings just discussed: *length, kind,* and *variety.*

THE SIMPLE SENTENCE

A sentence isn't necessarily *a group of words containing a subject and a verb and expressing a complete thought.* Modern grammarians are cautious in defining a sentence, for the pat, conventional definition doesn't always fit. Perhaps it is best to think of a sentence as just a complete thought. Thus, single words like *help* and *incredible* can be sentences, when properly capitalized and punctuated, without our having to be concerned about what is understood; they are both units of expression.

Sentences come in all *lengths:* minute, medium, and mammoth. Some of the most effective in English are quite brief. For instance, the famous, shortest verse in the Bible, *Jesus wept,* expresses in its context more feeling and emotion than a longer sentence might. Similarly, at the end of *Hamlet,* Shakespeare uses four words, *The rest is silence.* On the other hand, sentences can be quite long. But extremely long sentences are used infrequently and only for a special effect that might not easily be conveyed by a series of shorter sentences. For instance, Ernest Hemingway tried to give the feeling of a bullfight in 151 words.

> Cagancho is a gypsy, subject to fits of cowardice, altogether without integrity, who violates all the rules, written and unwritten, for the conduct of a matador but who, when he receives a bull that he has confidence in, and he has confidence in them very rarely, can do things which all bullfighters do in a way they have never been done before and sometimes standing absolutely straight with his feet still, planted as though he were a tree, with the arrogance and grace that gypsies have and of which all other arrogance and grace seems an imitation, moves the cape spread full as the pulling jib of a yacht before the bull's muzzle so slowly that the art of bullfighting, which is only kept from being one of the major arts because it is impermanent, in the arrogant slowness of his veronicas becomes, for the seeming minutes that they endure, permanent.[1]

Ordinary sentences are much shorter than this one, for the reader has trouble following long involvements. Shorter units of thought, cast for the most part in normal, expected English word order, are more desirable; the reader can recognize such sentences almost automatically. Lewis Carroll, the author of *Alice in Wonderland,* recognized this fact long ago when he wrote the nonsense poem "Jabberwocky":

> *'Twas brillig and the slithy toves*
> *Did gyre and gimble in the wabe;*
> *All mimsy were the borogoves,*
> *And the mome raths outgrabe.*

Even though you don't know what *toves* or *borogoves* look like, or what *brillig* and *slithy* mean, you can still easily recognize that this verse is made up of English sentences. You can spot these unknowns as parts of speech: *brillig, slithy,* and *mome* are obviously adjectives: *toves, wabe, borogoves,* and *raths* are nouns: *gyre, gimble,* and *outgrabe* are verbs.

Any group of nonsense words arranged in the patterns of English sentences can be recognized as sentences, as long as articles and prepositions are real. Look at these different sentence patterns using nonsense nouns, verbs, and verbals:

---

[1] Reprinted with the permission of Charles Scribner's Sons from *Death in the Afternoon* by Ernest Hemingway. Copyright 1932 Charles Scribner's Sons; renewal copyright © 1960 Ernest Hemingway. Used also by permission of the executors of the Ernest Hemingway Estate, and the publishers in the British Commonwealth, Jonathan Cape, Ltd.

The junbig cranned a biglou.
A biglou was cranned by a junbig.
Cranned by a junbig was a biglou.
After cranning a biglou, the junbig
zlon up the donnen.

Each of these represents a recognizable English sentence pattern. The first uses the basic word order of all English sentences, the normal SVC pattern.

Subject . . . . Verb . . . . Complement (Object)
or
Actor . . . . *Action* . . . . *Goal*
(The boy . . . . hit . . . . the ball.)

It is "normal" and "expected" because the *subject-verb-complement* pattern is by far the most common and because it is probably the one we all learn first. When you study style at the end of this chapter, you will see that special sentence effects are possible *because* we are so accustomed to expect the "normal" one.

Most English sentences are written in this "normal" order with these parts, though there are often modifiers (words, phrases, or clauses) of any one or all the parts. For emphasis and sentence *variety*, the normal word order can be varied: *Into the room ran the girl* reverses normal word order, with the subject in last position. Used rarely, this type of sentence is acceptable, but overused, it draws attention to itself, as most unusual word order does.

To be called complete, in the grammatical sense, a sentence must have at least two of the parts indicated above—a subject and a verb. The subject may be understood (*you*); the verb may not. A complete sentence expresses ONE complete thought. If it has more than one, it is probably not unified; that is, it does not move in one direction but in as many directions as there are topics in the sentence. Look at this sentence:

My car broke down twice on the way to the campus, and I spent all day Monday at registration.

Here there are two complete thoughts in two independent clauses. One complete thought has no necessary relationship to the other. In effect, they move in different directions. This sentence, then, has MORE THAN ONE complete thought; consequently, it is not a good sentence.

On the other hand, a group of words without a complete thought is a sentence fragment. Look at these groups:

We arrived at 8:00 o'clock. Before the game started.

The first of these is one complete thought. The second is not. The presence of *before* turns this group of words into a dependent clause and demands the addition of an independent, complete unit. We can add this dependent element to the end of the other group of words by replacing the period with a comma. Then the dependent clause (with its incomplete thought) is attached to a complete thought:

We arrived at 8:00 o'clock, before the game started.

Look at these two groups:

He preached against three sins. Cards, whisky, and tobacco.

The second group is made up of three nouns and one conjunction, but it is missing a verb to express action. It has LESS THAN ONE complete thought. Because the first group of words is a complete sentence, the second group can be attached to it, as it obviously should be:

He preached against three sins: cards, whisky, and tobacco.

Some "sentence fragments," however, do communicate complete thoughts because the context supplies the missing meaning. Here are some examples:

No one can write well without practice. *No one.*
Now for the second point.
What did he do? *Nothing, as usual.*
And the result? Chaos.

exercise

Try your hand at spotting which of the nonsense word groups are complete sentences. Write *F* for fragments, *C* for complete sentences.

1. The junbig cranned a biglou.
2. The junbig cranning a biglou.
3. After the junbig had cranned a biglou.
4. There is the biglou the junbig cranned.
5. Since cranning a biglou, which was done by the junbig.
6. A biglou was cranned by the junbig.
7. The biglou being cranned by the junbig.
8. The biglou cranning junbig.

Ideas and words gain emphasis if they are placed in strong positions within the sentence. In normal word order of English sentences, the opening and the closing positions are usually the most emphatic. For instance, look again at this simple sentence:

Actor	*Action*	*Goal*
The boy	hit	the ball.

The most important words in this sentence are in the most important positions. Boy (the actor) and the ball (the goal) are the important key words. In this normal English sentence, *boy* opens the sentence, and *ball* closes it. The key words are then in the emphatic positions— the beginning and the end. The end position is stronger, however, because words and ideas in that position are the last ones the reader sees.

This diagram will illustrate the importance of sentence positions.

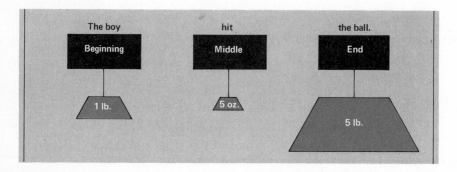

Here the three sentence positions are assigned weights to indicate their relative importance. The beginning position has been given a weight value of one pound; the middle position, five ounces; and the strong end position, five pounds. Now, by applying these weight values to the key words in a sentence, we can assign a weight to the whole sentence to indicate the strength of its emphasis. Look at this group of sentences.

1. However, *she* was an excellent *cook.*   5 lbs., 5 oz.
2. *She* was an excellent *cook,* however.   1 lb., 5 oz.
3. An excellent *cook she* was, however,   1 lb., 5 oz.
4. *She* was, however, an excellent *cook.*   6 lbs.
5. An excellent *cook,* however, was *she.*   6 lbs.

These weights are assigned by taking the key words (*she* and *cook*) and giving them the value of the position in which they appear in the sentence. Thus, in the first sentence, *she* is in the middle position and gets a weight of only five ounces. *Cook,* in the end position, gets a weight of five pounds. Altogether, the whole sentence has a value, then, of five pounds, five ounces. In this sentence, one of the important positions, the beginning of the sentence, is taken by the unimportant word *however,* suggesting that this transition word might be better buried in the middle of the sentence. The second has even less emphasis. *She* is in the beginning position for one pound, the *cook,* the other key word, is lost in the middle position and can be assigned an importance of only five ounces. The whole sentence, then, has a weight of only one pound, five ounces. In the third sentence, the position of the key words is reversed, and the value of the sentence remains the same as for the second sentence. The fourth sentence, however, has a different arrangement. *She* is in the beginning position and weighs one pound, whereas *cook* is in the end position and weighs five pounds. The whole sentence weighs six pounds, more than any other so far considered. The reason for this is that the two key words come in the two important sentence positions. Note that the transition word, *however,* is in the middle position where it does not detract from the impact of the sentence on the reader. The fifth sentence also puts the key words in the important positions, but the difference is that the positions have been switched. The sentence emphasis remains the same on the surface because it is assigned the same weight as the fourth sentence. But the two sentences differ considerably.

The fourth sentence is in normal English word order, which indicates that we ordinarily use this arrangement of sentence parts in writing. The fifth sentence reverses the arrangement, and the very oddness of this switch will make it more emphatic if it is mingled in a context of sentences arranged in the expected normal order. Only occasionally would you rely on a sentence like the fifth one—only when you want an unusual emphasis on the sentence. Although sentence variety is important, most of your sentences will have the same arrangement of sentence parts as that in the fourth sentence.

the periodic sentence

In any writing, the most powerful position for an idea—the one that gives the idea most emphasis—is usually at the end. In this respect, a sentence is no different from any other piece of writing. *The power spot in the sentence is at the end.* The main idea in a sentence, then, should come logically in this power spot. A sentence withholding its main idea until the end is called *periodic.* Look at this sentence:

Just as he bent over to tie his shoelace, *a car hit him.*

Here, the main idea, *a car hit him,* is at the end of the sentence. Certainly the other idea in the sentence is of less significance. In periodic sentences, important modifiers precede the basic SVC pattern; in loose sentences the modifiers come after the basic SVC pattern.

the loose sentence

More common in English, the *loose* sentence ends with a dependent sentence element—a subordinate element or a modifier. Rearranging the sentence just used as an example produces a loose sentence:

A car hit him, *just as he bent over to tie his shoelace.*

The main clause (the independent SVC pattern) containing the main idea comes first in the sentence, whereas the subordinate element (the dependent clause) is at the end. Take care to keep the main idea in the main clause. If you do not, sentence emphasis goes askew. In this sentence, for instance, the insignificant idea is in the main clause, and the main idea is in a dependent clause:

He bent over to tie his shoelace, just as a car hit him.

The first part of the sentence is the main clause; the second part, the dependent clause. Such a sentence can have no logical emphasis.

Here are two more examples of a loose and a periodic sentence; the main idea (the independent SVC pattern) is italicized in each.

(Periodic) Having passed his house every day and knowing that it had been unoccupied for years, I *was surprised to see smoke coming from the chimney.*
(Loose) I *was surprised to see smoke coming from the chimney,* because I had passed his house every day and knew that it had been empty for years.

Periodic sentences build suspense to gain emphasis for the main idea. If the main idea is held to the last in the sentence, and modifying elements are built up in the first part of the sentence, real suspense can be achieved that makes the main idea hit the reader with force. For instance, a simple sentence of this type makes little impact on the reader:

The old woman fainted.

But we can add a dependent element before this sentence, make it periodic in tone, and increase its impact:

> As *confetti showered her head,* the old woman fainted.

We can increase its impact even more by adding another dependent clause:

> As *the laughing crowd swirled around her* and as confetti showered her head, the old woman fainted.

To heighten the impact yet further, add another dependent element:

> As *the band blared louder,* as the laughing crowd swirled around her, and as confetti showered her head, the old woman fainted.

This type of periodic sentence is not as natural to the English language as it is to the modern Germanic languages. Most English sentences are loose in structure. That is, they are likely to be "strung" along with dependent elements at their end. They do not build to their point as the illustrative sentence above does. In English, the best sentences, then, are *periodic in tone but loose in structure.* You can achieve a periodic tone in three ways:

1. Suspending the subject
2. Suspending the verb
3. Suspending the complement

To suspend an element, delay its appearance in the sentence.

1. suspending the subject. Here is a sentence, simple in structure and English in word order:

> The man hurried down the street.

Here the subject is *man.* To suspend this subject and give the sentence a periodic tone, delay the point where it appears in the sentence. Just add simple adjective modifiers before the subject:

> The *gray-haired old* man hurried down the street.

Or you can add adjective phrases modifying *man:*

> *Limping on his wounded foot,* the gray-haired old man hurried down the street.

You can suspend this subject even further by adding another phrase:

Limping on his wounded foot and *staggering from side to side,* the gray-haired old man hurried down the street.

The sentence now has become periodic in structure as well as in tone. You can change the structure by adding modifying elements at the end:

Limping on his wounded foot and staggering from side to side, the gray-haired old man hurried down the street *that was littered with tin cans and shattered glass.*

2. suspending the verb. Using the same sentence and the same modifiers, you can delay the appearance of the verb in the sentence and create a periodic tone:

The man *hurried* down the street. (verb italicized)
The man, *old and gray-haired,* hurried down the street. (modifiers italicized)
The man, *limping on his wounded foot,* hurried down the street. (modifiers italicized)
The man, *limping and staggering,* hurried down the street. (modifiers italicized)

3. suspending the complement. In this same sentence, you can also suspend the complement. The phrase *down the street* is not actually a complement in the strictest sense. It is not a noun construction but an adverbial prepositional phrase. The word *complement* is used to mean a completer of the verb. *Down the street* fits this definition. Here it is suspended:

The old man hurried *down the street.* (complement italicized)
The old man hurried *limping and staggering* down the street. (modifiers suspending the complement italicized)

Caution: The process of suspending sentence elements can be overdone. If every element in the sentence is suspended, the subject, verb, and complement become too separated for the reader's quick comprehension of the thought. In the same way, take care not to separate any two elements enough to interfere with the flow of thought. The student who wrote this sentence, for instance, put too much space between the verb and the complement:

Chris attempted, even though his foot hurt him so much that he staggered as he ran, to reach the rifle.

In this sentence, the verb *attempted* and the complement (a verbal phrase), *to reach the rifle,* are separated by a long dependent clause. The result is a clumsy sentence so involved that readers can lose sight of the verb before they reach the completer. (If you have difficulty with this section, review pp. 220–22 on sentence components.)

the periodic-loose sentence

Consider these two sentences:

The ball soared toward the goalposts, which were fifty yards away from the kicker's toe. It wobbled end-over-end, but arced high and true.

Both sentences are concerned with one action, so they can easily be combined into one sentence. The second sentence can be reduced to two modifying phrases and worked into the first sentence. The first sentence would be improved by deleting the *which.* As the basic independent clause in the sentence, take this one:

The ball soared toward the goalposts.

Now, suspend the subject *ball* and the verb *soared* by adding modifying elements to the basic SVC pattern.

Arcing high and true, the ball, *wobbling end-over-end,* soared toward the goalposts fifty yards away.

Or, you can suspend the verb and the complement with these same modifiers:

The ball, *wobbling end-over-end,* soared *in a high and true arc* toward the goalposts fifty yards away.

These last two sentences are periodic-loose sentences because they have a periodic tone through the suspension of two sentence elements in the basic independent clause. The structure is loose because of the modifier *fifty yards away* at the end of the sentence.

exercise

Your teacher may ask you to review pages 220–22 before doing this exercise. From each group of sentences, make one sentence by suspending two elements in the basic independent clause (italicized in each group).

1. *Bertha labored to secure bait to hook.* She winced as the worm tried to escape her uncertain grasp, and she hoped none of the other fishermen noticed her squeamishness.

2. *Ralph transported his aching jaws straight to the dentist's chair.* He held himself aloof with his shoulders erect as he marched through the reception room.

3. *The car coasted to a stop.* Its motor was dead. It bumped on one flat tire. It was long, shiny, and black.

4. *The legislature finally revoked the law.* The law had been impossible to enforce because the people held it in contempt. The legislature met in special session.

5. *The puppy barked at the cat.* He pranced and dodged back and forth. He was an excited puppy. The cat spat and hissed at him.

6. I hesitated for two weeks before making my choice, but I finally decided to attend Glory University. *I think I made the best choice.* I had to choose between Glory and Primitive University.

7. *Fleance broke up the rehearsal.* He entered from stage right. His wig was askew and his mascara was running. Lady Macbeth had just urged the assembly to "Take seats."

8. *The children giggled and cavorted.* They chanted "The one-eyed flea keeps bugging me." They marched out of step and ill-aligned.

9. The English teacher looked the Salutatorian straight in the eye. She was angry. *She said, "When you chose that topic for your research paper, I told you it wasn't worthy of you."* The Salutatorian was embarrassed and crestfallen.

10. *Grandfather inched up the stairs.* He grasped the handrail with one hand. He leaned on his cane with the other. He firmly planted both feet on each step.

SECONDARY SENTENCE PATTERNS: COORDINATION AND SUBORDINATION So far in this chapter we have dealt mostly with one type of sentence— the simple sentence with normal order (subject—verb—complement) and phrase and single word modifiers for one or more of the elements. In effect, we have been dealing with this pattern:

I see the puppy. (S . . . V . . . C)

The idea expressed is approximately on the first-grade level and is appropriate for a primer. But educated writers need to communicate more complicated ideas than this sentence pattern can express. For this purpose, English provides secondary sentence patterns. The two most useful types of secondary sentence patterns are: (1) coordination (the simplest) and (2) subordination.

Coordination is joining together similar grammatical constructions with a connecting word called a *conjunction.* In its simplest form, two nouns or two verbs or two adjectives, for instance, can be joined by the conjunction *and.*

Chris and Jane
bacon and eggs
read and write
happy and carefree

Signal words for coordination (conjunctions), Group 1:

and	or
but	so
for	yet
nor	

Conjunctions in this group can be used to join *equal* grammatical structures only. That is, they can join together two independent clauses, two noun clauses, two prepositional phrases, two participles, or two of anything, as long as they are the same grammatically. They cannot join together, however, an independent clause and a dependent clause.

Caution: Group 1 signal words, especially *and,* are sometimes inappropriately used to string sentences together. This relatively short sample uses *and* four times:

I asked Dad for the car *and* then I picked up the corsage *and* got my date, *and* we went to the dance *and* had a wonderful time.

Although this sentence does have coordination, it defeats the purpose of coordination. Certainly there are no complicated ideas here that could not be expressed in the simplest sentence pattern.

Signal words for coordination, Group 2:

consequently	nevertheless
hence	nonetheless
however	then
in fact	therefore
moreover	thus

These signal words are used as conjunctions *only* to join two independent clauses. They have no other use as conjunctions.

To illustrate the use of this group of conjunctions, here are two sentences (two independent SVC patterns):

Marriage and hanging go by destiny. Matches are made in heaven.

Because these two are connected in idea, they may be joined grammatically into one sentence by making them independent clauses and by using a conjunction:

Marriage and hanging go by destiny, *but* matches are made in heaven.

The Group 1 conjunction *but* is used here because a contrast is being drawn and this conjunction is the appropriate one. (Remember, too, the section on transition words.) Or a Group 2 conjunction can be just as appropriately used:

Marriage and hanging go by destiny; *however,* matches are made in heaven.

Or, the two basic SVC patterns can be joined without a conjunction, if their ideas are closely enough related and if emphasis is needed:

Marriage and hanging go by destiny; matches are made in heaven.

punctuation of coordinate elements

Perhaps as much as 60 percent of your punctuation problems can be solved by knowing the Group 1 and Group 2 conjunctions and by understanding how they work.

1. Group 1 conjunctions *(and, but, for, or, nor, so, yet),* when they join two independent clauses (SVC patterns), take a comma before them. See the diagram below.

(Independent clause)	but	(Independent clause)
A		B
—————————— ,		—————————— .

2. Group 2 conjunctions *(however, then, thus,* for instance) join two independent clauses together with a semicolon, in this way:

(Independent clause)	thus,	(Independent clause)
A		B
—————————— ;		—————————— .

3. Two independent clauses may be joined without a conjunction if a semicolon separates them:

(Independent clause)   (Independent clause)
A   B

_____ ;   _____ .

For additional information on punctuation, study pages 236–44.

exercises

Supply the best mark of punctuation in the blanks of these sentences.

1. Great-grandfather would not refrain from chewing his noontime wad of tobacco_____nor would great-grandmother give up dipping snuff, no matter how often we complained.
2. Santa brought Robin three dolls, a swing set, a Cinderella watch, and a plug-in refrigerator_____but Bobby seemed satisfied with his new socks and corduroy jeans.
3. The veteran scholar took her first degree in the history and literature of Persia_____the next step was to master the Arabic language.
4. From 6:00 to 10:00 in the evening he supplemented his income by teaching local teens to bowl_____so for eighteen hours a day he was on somebody's payroll.
5. Just before school opened, Old Hat found her way to Rita's doorstep_____and before Thanksgiving, Jet wandered in_____then, on Easter Sunday morning, the cat they call Peeps made it a threesome.
6. Sandra seemed to sense that her partner held the trump ace_____yet she deliberately underbid the hand.
7. No one claims that the red rambling roses are more attractive than the New York Pinks_____I simply state that they are a showier flower.
8. Yaupon and poison sumac grew on the upper ten acres_____elsewhere over the ranch grew mesquite and huisache.
9. She tried first tape, then glue, and finally staples_____however, Frances' Man in the Moon shadow box fell apart before fifth period.
10. The young wife insisted that air conditioning in that two-room west-side apartment was essential_____her husband called her an extravagant simpleton.
11. If students live in Duncan Hall, or Dorms 11, 12, or 13, their laundry problems are solved_____if they live in Milton Square or close to the Quadrangle, they practice the do-it-yourself system.
12. Bill bought shares in two local banks and spent two weeks fishing in Mexico_____therefore his parents assumed that he could scrape by without further loans from them.
13. Mrs. Anderson embroidered icon after saintly icon_____but she would not part with one of her collection, although they lay yellowing in the trunk of heirlooms in the parlor.
14. Six, seven, and eight come first_____eleven comes somewhat later.

When more than two coordinate elements appear together, they are a series. Any three or more *equal grammatical elements* can appear in a series—nouns, verbs, participles, noun clauses, prepositional phrases, or any part of a sentence. For instance, this sentence shows verbs in a series:

Cathy *ran, skipped,* and *jumped.*

Or this one has three noun clauses in a series:

Herb never stopped to consider *that the weather was not favorable, that the boys did not want to go,* and *that the highways would be too crowded for comfortable travel.*

1. When coordinate elements are used in a series, a comma separates each element from the others. The two sentences just used as examples illustrate this punctuation. It may be diagrammed this way:

(First element)   (Second element)   and   (Third element)
A   B   C
————————— ,   ————————— ,   ————————— .

The comma before *and* between the second and third elements is commonly left out. This practice is acceptable as long as the reader has no chance of assuming that the last two elements are linked together to the exclusion of the first.

2. The coordinate elements in a series must be parallel (that is, the same grammatically). The elements here are italicized:

Jo did the job *quickly, competently,* and *hardly working at all.*

In this sentence, three adverbs are supposedly in a series; but one element in the series is not an adverb. This can be seen in a diagram.

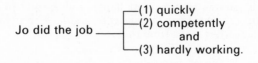

The third element will have to be changed to make it parallel with the other two, that is, it must be grammatically the same. This sentence makes that change.

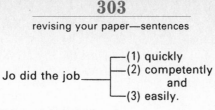

Jo did the job quickly, competently, and easily.

Or look at this sentence:

The instructor told them *to study Chapter IV, to make notes on it,* and *that they would have a quiz next period.*

A diagram will expose the elements in this sentence that are not parallel.

The instructor told them
—(1) to study Chapter IV
—(2) to make notes on it
and
—(3) that they would have a
quiz next period.

The first two elements of the series here are infinitive phrases (that is, *to* plus a verb plus a noun), but the third element is a noun clause (with *that* as the subordinating conjunction, *they* as the subject, and *would have* as the verb). Because these elements are not the same grammatically, the third element must be changed to make it an infinitive phrase starting with *to* plus a verb.

The instructor told them
—(1) to study Chapter IV
—(2) to make notes on it
and
—(3) *to prepare* for a quiz
next period.

The instructor told them to study Chapter IV, to make notes on it, and to prepare for a quiz next period.

Here is a different one:

Although not many of the class went, those who did found the lecture heavy, dull, and the acoustics in the lecture hall adequate, although not everything could be heard.

This sentence appears to have a series of three. In truth it does not, because it has two subjects—*lecture* and *acoustics.* Look at this sentence in diagram form.

Although not many of the class went,

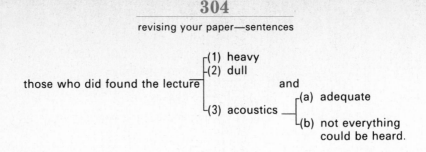

Acoustics (a noun) is not parallel with *heavy* and *dull* (adjectives), nor can these three be changed to make them parallel. But the sentence can be improved by making *lecture* parallel with *acoustics* (both nouns).

Although not many of the class went,

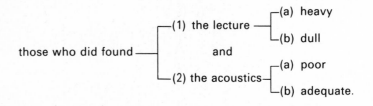

Although not many of the class went, those who did found the lecture heavy and dull, and the acoustics in the lecture hall poor but barely adequate.

All coordinate elements in a sentence must be clearly grammatically parallel, whether there are more than two elements or only two. Sometimes a fuzzy parallelism will confuse the reader temporarily, as in this sentence:

The lawyer begged that the accused be judged insane and committed to a mental hospital.

Momentary confusion may result here because the reader may want to insert *be judged* before committed, because apparently *insane* and another adjective are being joined by *and*. A diagram illustrates the possible confusion.

The lawyer begged that the accused —(1) be judged insane
                                          and
                                    —(2) committed to a
                                         mental hospital.

The solution is simple: The parallelism is made clear if *be* is put before *committed*, as well as before *judged.*

The lawyer begged that the accused ⎰ (1) be judged insane
and
(2) be committed to a
mental hospital.

The lawyer begged that the accused be judged insane and be committed to a mental hospital.

This sentence is similarly confusing:

He said he had read the poetry of Thomas, Spender, and the novels of Updike.

Here the writer has attempted to create a series of three coordinate elements, but there are only two. Look at a diagram of this sentence as the author wrote it.

He said he had read the poetry of ⎰ (1) Thomas
(2) Spender
and
(3) the novels of Updike.

Obviously, *Thomas, Spender,* and *the novels* are not parallel. *Poetry* and *novels* are, however. Then there is a better construction for the sentence:

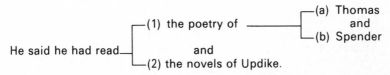

He said he had read ⎰ (1) the poetry of ⎰ (a) Thomas
and
(b) Spender
and
(2) the novels of Updike.

He said he had read the poetry of Thomas and Spender, and the novels of Updike.

The comma is placed before the second *and* for clarity. Otherwise the reader might expect the material following Spender to be a third element in a series. The comma specifies that it is not.

Here is another example of faulty parallelism:

His musical career, unlike most students who played in the band, continued after he left high school.

The fault here is one of logic. Careers and students are being compared, but they cannot be compared. It is like attempting to make a comparison between apples and wood splinters; they have nothing in common.

So they cannot be made parallel in this way. A diagram of this attempted parallelism looks like this:

> His musical *career*
>   unlike   (continued). . . .
> most students

This sentence can be made logical and parallel.

> His *musical career*
>   unlike   (continued). . . .
> the *musical careers* of most students

Now careers are compared to careers, and the sentence is logically parallel. But a substitute, a pronoun for *career,* is more suitable than repeating the noun so soon after it is first given. The sentence then looks like this:

His musical career, unlike *those* of most students who played in the band, continued after he left high school.

---

exercise

Correct any nonparallel elements you find in these sentences.

1. He studied the grouping of the stars in their constellations and how close Saturn is to Pluto.
2. The desk had a scratched top, a sticky drawer, and one leg wobbled.
3. Slicing away at the Winesap and whistling as he pared, Eric knew that the first cucumbers were already spoiled on the vine, how he would have to rebuild the chicken roosts tomorrow, and his son had asked him twice to repair his toy truck.
4. She bought a pound each of nails, woodscrews, and a gallon of red paint.
5. Dr. Payne's tests, like all the other professors', were complex, detailed, and offered great difficulty.
6. Since he had already ruined his chances to recover the money and recouping his loss, Ronald shrugged, grinned, and, turning away, sauntered whistling down the hall.
7. Pete was quite slow in discovering that he had no singing voice, could not act, and his personality did not project well.
8. The gold plastic bracelet from the local dime store, added to Ruthie's talent on the dance floor and appreciating the excellent dance band, made the evening a mad memory.
9. Despite his aversion to seafood and liquor, he ate oysters, catfish, and drank beer.

10. Although the house was dark and because he knew the family was out of town, Greg went ahead with his plan to repair the television set in the living room and resetting the loose tiles on the kitchen floor.

subordination

In considering matters of sentence structure, *superior* constructions are independent clauses; they carry the main thought of the sentence and are complete in themselves. Words, phrases, and dependent clauses are *inferior,* or subordinate, because they do not consist of a complete thought; they are used most often as modifiers of some part of the independent clause. Sometimes they are used as the subject or verb or complement in an independent clause. The process of subordination, then, is changing what might be stated in an independent clause into an inferior or subordinate construction and attaching it to a part of another independent clause. Consider these two sentences:

John completed his final examination. Two hours still remained in the examination period.

One of these independent clauses (independent clauses and basic SVC sentences are the same structurally) can be subordinated to the other and the two combined into one sentence. First, you must decide which idea in the two sentences is the more important one, because it should come in the independent clause. Because the writer put it last, he apparently considers the idea of the second sentence the more important of the two. Then subordinate the first independent clause to the second in one of these ways:

When John completed his final examination, two hours still remained in the period. (Independent clause reduced to a dependent clause. Note that the only difference between an independent and a dependent clause is the presence of a subordinating conjunction, *when* in this sentence, at the beginning of the dependent clause. Other subordinating conjunctions are *while, that, since, although, until, which, who, because, as if, if, when, before.*)

Upon completing his final examination, John discovered that two hours remained in the period. (Independent clause reduced to a prepositional phrase.)

Completing his final examination, John discovered that two hours remained in the period. (Participial phrase)

His final examination completed, John discovered that two hours remained in the period. (Absolute construction)

John discovered *upon completing his final examination* that two hours remained in the period. (Prepositional phrase)

John discovered that two hours remained in the period, *although he had already completed the final examination.* (A dependent clause with the subordinating conjunction *although.* The addition of the dependent clause makes the sentence loose in structure.)

Here is a more complicated example:

> [1]Our best quarterback was caught stealing Primitive University's mascot. [2]This happened at the beginning of the football season, and so [3]he was not allowed to play after the first game, [4]thus causing us to lose the championship.

This sentence is written in a primer style; it is a string of independent clauses, except that the main point—we lost the championship—is in a participial phrase at the close of the sentence. Because it is the most important idea in these sentences, this point should be in an independent clause to give it the most emphasis, whereas the other inferior material should be subordinated. *This* (at 2) and *thus* (at 4) should be deleted. In this sentence, *this* is a pronoun with vague reference. It does not refer the reader to a single noun, as it should, but to action expressed in the preceding sentence. *Thus* is used as a conjunction. As one of the Group 2 coordinating conjunctions, it joins two independent clauses. But here it does not serve this function; instead, it joins an independent clause to a phrase. *Thus* can then be deleted without affecting the meaning of the sentence, and there is no structural problem. Here is a revision with the main idea in the independent clause and with other ideas subordinated to it. The ideas are numbered for comparison with the unrevised version.

> [4]We lost the championship because our best quarterback, [1]caught [2]at the beginning of the season stealing Primitive University's mascot, [3]was not allowed to play after the first game of the year.

In revising, remember to select the main point in your sentences and subordinate all others to it by casting them in dependent clauses, phrases, or single-word modifiers.

exercise

Make one sentence from each of the following groups of sentences. Cast the main idea in an independent clause and subordinate all other material.

1. It was dark and the night was cold and rainy. Emily started cautiously down the path. It was slippery and clogged by roots and weeds.

2. The chair had one broken leg. It was old and its upholstery was tattered. It collapsed with Pete when he sat in it. A loud noise resulted.

3. The secretary ripped the paper from the typewriter roller. He gave a sharp exclamation and slammed his pencil on the desk.

4. The gringos crowded the Mexican streets. They all appeared overfed, and they were all underdressed.

5. The book lay by the window. The window was open. Wind flipped and tore the book's pages, and they had been soaked with rain.

6. The university rates high scholastically. It has a library of four million volumes. Its teachers are internationally recognized, and its students are the best from quality high schools.

7. The American elk is a relative of the red deer of other continents. Its scientific name is *Cervus canadensis* of the family *Cervidae*. It is occasionally attacked by cougars.

8. They had loved their home. It had three bedrooms, a sun parlor, and impeccably kept gardens. But now the West Church Street School had been built across the street. It housed the first graders who could not be accommodated in the old elementary school.

9. Nancy waltzed proudly around the floor. The hem of her stylish, black-sequined dress had come loose in two places. A lock hung limply from the back of her upswept hairdo. People were tittering. She did not know all this, of course.

10. Jordan was only three and a half when it happened, but he can still remember Uncle Jake shooting the largest elk the state had recorded. The elk stood five feet, nine inches tall and weighed 1100 pounds.

STYLE   Style is the last of the major rhetorical subjects discussed in this book (the other two are organization and discovery). By now you are probably aware that nearly everything you have studied to this point is in some way related to style. The ideas you discover to write about, for example, may not be original; still, *how* you use them, what you decide to include or to omit, what illustrations you use as support—these may very well be original, and, because of this, have something to do with what we call style. Similarly, the organization you choose for these ideas is also probably your own, unlike the organization someone else might use for the same set of ideas. In revising diction and sentences, again the *choices* you make will probably distinguish your writing from that of others. *How* you decide to get your reader interested, *how* you create a tone or "voice" that will win your reader, are probably your own too. For no two writers solve the same communication problem in the same way. The resulting differences in the works may be explained as a matter of style.

To discuss style means trying to separate *what* is said from *how* it is said. Strictly speaking that's not possible. But for purposes of discussion it's useful to think about *the message* and *how it is sent* as if they were separate. Look at the following sentences:

1.

> That such a life is likely to be ecstatically happy I will not claim. But that it can be lived in quiet content, accepting resignedly what cannot be helped, not expecting the impossible, and thankful for small mercies, this I would maintain. That it will be difficult for men in general to learn this lesson I do not deny. But that it will be impossible I will not admit since so many have learned it already.

Because this writer chose to use balance for his sentence patterns, he has given the passage a special effect (see page 87 for a discussion of parallelism, antithesis, and coherence in this passage). You notice it immediately because the word order is unusual; you know it's unusual because it departs from the "normal," expected pattern, *subject-verb-complement.* You notice, too, that he uses no simple, loose sentences; all are periodic and complex. Another writer might have done it differently:

2.

> I will not claim that such a life is likely to be ecstatically happy. But I would maintain that it can be lived in quiet content, accepting resignedly what cannot be helped, not expecting the impossible, and being thankful for small mercies. I do not deny that it will be difficult for people in general to learn this lesson. But I will not admit that it will be impossible since so many have learned it already.

Version 2 carries exactly the same meaning as the first; yet the *effect* is different. The "expected" word order moves the reader quickly to each main point: "I will not claim . . .," "I would maintain . . .," "I do not deny . . .," "I will not admit. . . ." The effect is one of directness and strength. Version 1 suspends each main statement, making the reader wait for it until the end of each sentence. The effect on the reader is probably a "sense of expectation," but this would depend on the kind of ear that was listening. Still, though different readers might argue about the exact effects of the two versions, they could hardly fail to see that they were intentionally different. Expected (or unexpected) *word order, directness* of movement and meaning, heightened *reader expectation*—these are matters of style.

    But style is also a matter of *sound.* Read Version 1 aloud and listen for the effects that parallel structure, antithesis, and inversion create. Some listeners would say the passage sounded "formal," "heightened," "elevated," perhaps too "contrived." Others might say, simply, that the passage was "hard to read." Their disagreement would be about the effects of writing styles. But if both readers had stored in their memories the same basic sentence patterns, the same vocabularies, the same sounds, they would disagree far less. For judging the effects of differing writing styles depends largely on what a reader has "inside" to use as a sounding board.

Suppose, further, that we altered Version 2 by changing some of the words, still keeping the meaning of the passages the same. For example:

3.

> I won't say that such a life will lead to great happiness. However, I would say that it can lead to contentment and quiet, stoically accepting what can't be helped, not expecting the impossible, and being thankful for small mercies. I don't deny that people will generally have a hard time learning this lesson. But I will not admit that it will be impossible since many men have already learned it.

The addition of contractions to Version 3 adds some *informality* to the *tone*; simpler balance adds to directness. Most of the word changes increase the informal tone (*say, great, happiness, contentment, hard time*). The use of *however* plus a comma slows down the movement (compare the sound of "However, I would say . . ." with the sound of "But I would say . . ."). All these choices are also a matter of style. Considering the possibilities suggested by the three versions, trained writers would choose patterns and sounds and words that they felt their *readers would like*. Style, then, also includes *audience consideration*.

You can see that the writing style you decide to use in a particular situation involves many decisions, only a few of which have been suggested in this discussion. What matters most is that you see style as conscious *choice* and realize that there are many solutions to each problem in communication. If, for example, you chose to write all your sentences in the style of Version 1, you would probably lose most readers quickly. Similarly, extended passages in the style of the second or third versions, with all sentences marching forward in the "normal" *subject-verb-complement* pattern, would tend to sound monotonous. One solution to this problem would be to vary sentence patterns and lengths, though variety for its own sake shouldn't be your only aim. A study of style will increase the number of choices available to you and greatly expand the "sounding board" you have "inside"; it should also add to your sense of "play" and discovery, for you should become increasingly aware of the power and richness of language. Some changes in style you can probably strive for in your rough drafts, but it is during the careful process of revision that you'll be able to discover the need for stylistic changes.

Style, then, is a matter of *personal choice*—of ideas, of words to carry the ideas, of sentences, of organization, of appropriate tone, of paragraphing. And because it is personal, your style is limited by who you are, by what knowledge and vocabulary you have, and even by the subjects you habitually write about (since they probably will appear repeatedly in your work). In this sense, style *is* the person; your style is *you*. In fact, you already have many writing styles of your own which reflect the limits just described. But just because style reflects your personality does not mean you're stuck with one way of writing.

Style is also the result of conscious *choice*, something you can therefore improve and change. If you let habit dictate your choice, as many beginning writers do, you'll find yourself tied to the diction

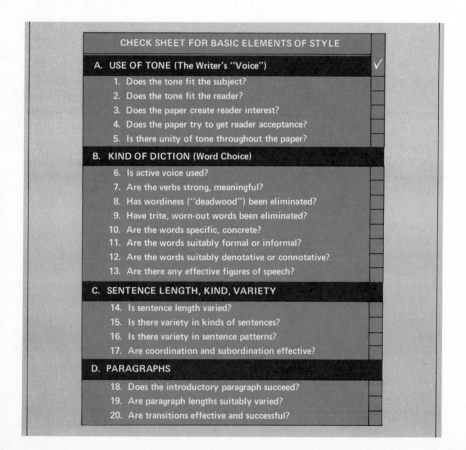

CHECK SHEET FOR BASIC ELEMENTS OF STYLE	
A. USE OF TONE (The Writer's "Voice")	✓
1. Does the tone fit the subject?	
2. Does the tone fit the reader?	
3. Does the paper create reader interest?	
4. Does the paper try to get reader acceptance?	
5. Is there unity of tone throughout the paper?	
B. KIND OF DICTION (Word Choice)	
6. Is active voice used?	
7. Are the verbs strong, meaningful?	
8. Has wordiness ("deadwood") been eliminated?	
9. Have trite, worn-out words been eliminated?	
10. Are the words specific, concrete?	
11. Are the words suitably formal or informal?	
12. Are the words suitably denotative or connotative?	
13. Are there any effective figures of speech?	
C. SENTENCE LENGTH, KIND, VARIETY	
14. Is sentence length varied?	
15. Is there variety in kinds of sentences?	
16. Is there variety in sentence patterns?	
17. Are coordination and subordination effective?	
D. PARAGRAPHS	
18. Does the introductory paragraph succeed?	
19. Are paragraph lengths suitably varied?	
20. Are transitions effective and successful?	

and sentence patterns of your earliest training. (Remember the exercise on preschool words? See page 284.) To change your writing habits, however, you will first have to recognize what they are. That means putting to work everything you have learned in this book—as you discover and plan, as you organize and write, and, most important, as you revise. It also means studying the ways in which other writers (students and professionals) use words and sentences to solve their communication problems. That is the basic approach: *Know your own style,* and *study the styles of other writers.*

To summarize, *style can be defined as the individual, personal way in which you use your own knowledge and language to present your chosen subject to a specific audience in an appropriate "voice."* The full implications of this definition are seen in the check sheet (page 312) on style; its questions will help you look for qualities in your own style and in the styles of other writers.

You should now be able to put this check sheet to work. First, use it to analyze the two student selections below; take notes on each of the twenty questions on the check sheet and be prepared to support and illustrate your impression of the style. Both selections are by the same student writing on the same subject; the difference between them is that in the first the tone is supposed to be "confident," while in the second it's supposed to be "angry and disgusted."

A. THE FIRST DAY
(Tone: Confident)

Tackling the closed door with her foot, she conquered the hallway. It was the noncommittal green used in military installations. But most of this color was obliterated by the thundering herd of students. The width of the hall was equal to six students, shoulder-to-shoulder. The length, about thirty students. And the hall held its capacity at this time. But she made room. Among the masses, she stood out. Marching down the hall, heel first, she carried herself with confidence and authority.

Similar to Moses, she parted the sea of students, enabling her to go from the left side of the hall to the right. She grabbed for the door. The doorknob was cold and uninviting. She tried to force the locked doorknob to turn, then finally forced the slightly ajar door all the way open.

B. THE FIRST DAY
(Tone: Angry)

Rammming the glass door with her foot, she stormed the hallway. It was the repulsive light-green used in military installations. But this color was obliterated by the screeching mob of students. The width of the hall could only be measured in terms of

students--six students, shoulder-to-shoulder. The length, about
thirty students. And the hall was bursting at the seams at this
time. Forced to make room, she was caught up in the sweating,
flowing current of bodies.

Only through struggling and pushing and griping did she manage to get across the hall. She grabbed for the door, only to find
the doorknob shockingly cold and uninviting. She struggled
with the doorknob, only to find the lock frozen and the door
already slightly ajar. Infuriated by the wasted effort, she swung
the door completely open.

Do you think this student has succeeded in creating the two tones?
Are there any differences in detail? Compare the verbs in the two
versions; are they consistently different? Make a list of the words
in each selection that seem to you most appropriate to the tone the
student tried to create. Are the sentence patterns similar in both
selections? Do you think they should be similar? If you didn't know
that both versions were written by the same student, what evidence
could be presented to show that they probably were, that they are
stylistically similar, despite some difference in tone? Do you think
the two passages are aimed at different audiences? Point to specific
words or phrases that support your conclusion. How would you change
the passages to make them appeal more clearly to two different
audiences?

exercises on style

A. One way to become conscious of sentence patterns unlike your own
is to imitate sentences written by others. Here, for example, is a very
famous sentence from Henry David Thoreau's *Walden:*

I went to the woods because I wished to live deliberately, to front
only the essential facts of life, and see if I could learn what it had
to teach, and not, when I came to die, discover that I had not lived.

Although you should try to match the model in its major parts (phrases,
clauses, balance, inversions), you may depart in minor ways, as a student
has done in this imitation:

I questioned the system because I wanted to see how it worked, to
determine its bad points, and see how effective it was, and then after
thorough analysis, propose a system that would work better.

Here are some additional models with student imitations:

Model: The cat shivered in the barnyard, wet from nosing her way
through the dew-filled grass and covered with damp cockle-spurs.

Imitation: The man ran in the race, wet from perspiring at every step and panting with laboring lungs.

Model: Disobedience, the rarest and most courageous of the virtues, is seldom distinguished from neglect, the laziest and commonest of the vices.

Imitation: Friendship, a rare and marvelous gift, is sometimes killed by hypocrisy, a shallow and worthless imitation.

Model: The human species, according to the best theory I can form of it, is composed of two distinct races, the men who borrow, and the men who lend.

Imitation: Friendship, as I see it, is based on two concepts, the idea of communication, and the idea of covenant.

Model: The apple tree never asks the beech how he shall grow; nor the lion, the horse, how he shall take his prey.

Imitation: The professor never asks the department head how he should teach; nor the gambler, the bookmaker, how he should place his bet.

1. Write imitations of the five models given above (include Thoreau). First write down the model; read it carefully and listen to the sound and the rhythm; then write your imitation of it.
2. Write imitations of the first two sentences in Paragraphs *F* and *G* on pages 282 and 283 (Faulkner and Frost).
3. The following three sentences come from the paragraph by E. B. White on page 148. Write a coherent, three-sentence imitation.

New York should have destroyed itself long ago, from panic or fire or rioting or failure of some vital supply line in its circulatory system or from some deep labyrinthine short circuit. Long ago the city should have experienced an insoluble traffic snarl at some impossible bottleneck. It should have perished of hunger when food lines failed for a few days.

B. 1. Use the style check sheet to analyze one of your own papers written earlier in the course. Take notes and be prepared to write a one-paragraph commentary on your style.
2. Using the style check sheet as your guide, analyze the style of the two paragraphs in the section "Sentences in General" (pages 287–88). Take notes. Be prepared to discuss and write about the four major subjects on the check sheet (tone, diction, sentences, paragraphs). If, for example, you think that the tone of these two paragraphs does *not* fit you (the reader), you should try to discover why. What can you discover about the length, kind, and variety of the sentences used?

C. Choose any five of the sentences you wrote for the exercise on page 309. Rewrite each sentence twice, changing the *kind* of sentence (see page 288 for kinds of sentences) or the sentence pattern; keep the meaning and details of your originals. (You may get some additional ideas by rereading pages 294–98.)

summary exercises

A.

Monte Alban in period IIIb was a nearly incredible enterprise. It occupied not only the top of a large mountain, but also the tops and sides of a whole range of high hills adjoining, a total of some fifteen square miles of urban construction. Human labor may be characterized as cheap under some circumstances, but a man's time is never cheap in a pre-industrial economy, where what he eats has to be produced by hand labor. Except for the possibility of catching more or less rainwater during four or five months of the year, the population of Monte Alban had to drink water carried up the mountain—as much as 1,500 feet—in jars. This alone would be costly; but the quantities of water required in building construction make the location of a large city on this high ridge even more astonishing. In addition, the maintenance of a major religious capital such as Monte Alban would necessarily require the services of thousands of specialists: priests, artists, architects, the apprentices of all these, and many kinds of workmen, including servants for the dignitaries and their families. [2]

1. What is the pointer in the topic sentence (the first sentence)?
2. What method of paragraph development does the author use to support the topic sentence? Why might you have difficulty deciding which method is used?
3. Does this paragraph have coherence? Is there any point where the coherence might be improved? Why?
4. What is the purpose of *this alone would be costly* and *In addition*?
5. Explain the use of commas in the second sentence.
6. Why is a comma used after *circumstances* in the third sentence?
7. Why are dashes used in the fourth sentence?
8. In the fifth sentence, why would an author choose a semicolon rather than a comma?
9. Why is a comma used after *in addition* in the sixth sentence?
10. Explain the punctuation in the last sentence, particularly the use of the colon.
11. Comment on the length, kind, and variety of sentences used. How many kinds of balance can you find?
12. Are the verbs strong and meaningful? Are the words specific and concrete?
13. How does this writer try to gain and keep your interest? Do you think he succeeds?

B.

Spacecraft that produce immediate, tangible benefits are a fact of life. Weather satellites continually track weather over the entire earth,

---

[2] John Paddock, "The Cloud People of Monte Alban," *Stanford Today*, October, 1966. Reprinted by permission of *Stanford Today*, Leland Stanford Junior University, Stanford, California.

and communications satellites relay messages and pictures between continents. Soon there will be a third type of practical spacecraft, another tool to help man understand and control his environment—the natural resources satellite. In its effect on the billions of persons who inhabit this planet, it may be the most important space program yet undertaken. [3]

1. This introductory paragraph skillfully introduces a broad topic and narrows it to a specific thesis statement. What is the broad topic?
2. What means does the author use to narrow the broad topic to one of its parts?
3. What is the specific thesis statement introduced in this paragraph?
4. What would you expect the author to discuss in the remainder of the paper?

C.

More communications satellites are sure to be launched over Southeast Asia. Comsat is already planning for a second Pacific satellite to be placed in orbit this year. Later, there are plans for an even bigger satellite with a capacity for 1,200 two-way telephone circuits or four television channels—five times the capacity of Intelsat II and a lifetime that is two years longer. Nor is that all. Specifications have already been drawn by Comsat for an even more versatile, high-capacity communications satellite that could accommodate 6,000 to 8,000 two-way telephone circuits, 12 to 20 television circuits, or perhaps a dozen circuits for communication between flying aircraft and ground stations. Even this huge, excess capacity over current needs is not expected to be too great, considering the future communications requirements of the area. [4]

1. What is the topic sentence?
2. What method has the author used to develop the topic sentence?
3. What coherence devices has he used?
4. One number, *five*, is spelled out. The others are not. What is the difference?
5. *Higher-capacity and two-way* are hyphenated. Why?
6. Account for the use of a dash before *five times.* Would a comma be as effective here? Why or why not?

D.

If Man has benefited immeasurably by his association with the dog, what, you may ask, has the dog got out of it? His scroll has, of course, been heavily charged with punishments: he has known the muzzle, the leash, and the tether; he has suffered the indignities of the show

[3] Louis F. Slee, "Coming: A Natural Resources Satellite," *Electronic Age*, Autumn, 1966. Reprinted by permission of *Electronic Age*, Radio Corporation of America.

[4] Mitchell Levitas, "Communications Boom in Southeast Asia," *Electronic Age*, Autumn, 1966. Reprinted by permission of *Electronic Age*, Radio Corporation of America.

bench, the tin can on the tail, the ribbon in the hair; his love life with the other sex of his species has been regulated by the frigid hand of authority, his digestion ruined by the macaroons and marshmallows of doting women. The list of his woes could be continued indefinitely. But he has also had his fun, for he has been privileged to live with and study at close range the only creature with reason, the most unreasonable of creatures.

The dog has got more fun out of Man than Man has got out of the dog, for the clearly demonstrable reason that Man is the more laughable of the two animals. The dog has long been bemused by the singular activities and the curious practices of men, cocking his head inquiringly to one side, intently watching and listening to the strangest goings-on in the world. He has seen men sing together and fight one another in the same evening. He has watched them go to bed when it is time to get up, and get up when it is time to go to bed. He has observed them destroying the soil in vast areas, and nurturing it in small patches. He has stood by while men built strong and solid houses for rest and quiet, and then filled them with lights and bells and machinery. His sensitive nose, which can detect what's cooking in the next township, has caught at one and the same time the bewildering smells of the hospital and the munitions factory. He has seen men raise up great cities to heaven and then blow them to hell. [5]

1. These two paragraphs fit tightly together. Explain why by commenting on the first and last sentence of the first paragraph and the opening sentence of the second paragraph.
2. What is the major method of development used in both paragraphs?
3. What is the function of the second sentence in the first paragraph? What is its relation to the word *but* that introduces the last sentence of this paragraph?
4. Comment on the major effects of balance in these two paragraphs (include parallelism and antithesis).
5. What is the main function of the first paragraph? Does it contain a thesis statement where you would expect to find it?
6. What has been added to the thesis statement in the second paragraph?
7. How would you characterize the tone of these paragraphs? Point to specific words and phrases that illustrate this tone.
8. Is the main subject of these paragraphs presented in the thesis statements or in the last sentence of paragraph two? Explain.
9. Comment on the length and kinds of sentences. Can you explain the writer's strategy of development?

E.

The cultural fallout from television has been astounding. Critics may, of course, debate the level of musical discrimination shown by an audience that applauds on sight. Yet, the significant thing here is

[5] Copyright 1955 by James Thurber. From "An Introduction" in *Thurber's Dogs*, published by Simon & Schuster, New York.

television's incredible ability to increase the awareness of a vast public. The opening of the Lincoln Center for the Performing Arts is a case in point. Some 25.6 million television viewers saw and heard some part of the two-hour concert; in contrast, 2,600 attended the concert that night in Philharmonic Hall. Television attracts the biggest and most heterogeneous audiences in the history of communications. It can attract 16 million people to a program like "Bonanza," and it can interest another 16 million in Leonard Bernstein's "Young People's Concert." Consider the social impact of a program such as Lou Hazam's NBC production, "The Louvre," which drew 15 million viewers when first shown in November, 1965. In 1966 it was run again before an estimated audience of 15 million people. That is a total of 30 million Americans— more Americans than visited the Louvre in Paris since George Washington was President.[6]

1. This paragraph is developed chiefly by reasons supported by illustrations. Outline it using this form:

   Topic Sentence: . . . .
     BECAUSE:
       Reason 1: . . . .
         Supporting illustration . . . .
     BECAUSE:
       Reason 2: . . . .
         Supporting illustrations:
           A. . . . .
           B. . . . .

2. What coherence devices are used in the paragraph? List examples of several methods.

3. Why has the writer inserted *of course* at the beginning of the second sentence? How does it affect the tone? How is it related to the argument presented? Why is the phrase set off by commas?

4. Comment on the relation between "astounding cultural fallout" and "increase in awareness" as "pointers" for this paragraph. To which of these is the support more closely related?

5. Find two examples of antithesis. How does the writer tag them?

6. Why is *yet* (third sentence) followed by a comma? What function does *yet* serve in the sentence? In the paragraph?

7. Why is a semicolon used after *concert* (fifth sentence)?

8. Why is a dash used in the last sentence?

F.

The uncanny ability of video to involve the viewer deeply is well known. For example: KQED, a San Francisco educational TV station, ran a half-hour program about Japanese brush painting. Since it was a "how to" program, a young woman producer bought 300 painting kits in anticipation of a moderate viewer response. The station eventually sold

[6]Desmond Smith, "The Social Impact of Television," *Electronic Age,* Summer, 1965. Reprinted by permission of *Electronic Age,* Radio Corporation of America.

a staggering total of 14,000 sets at $3.00 each. And when the H. J. Heinz Company offered a salad recipe book on a single daytime commercial, more than 112,000 viewers wrote in for a copy. When Leonard Bernstein reported the reception the New York Philharmonic Symphony received on one of its recent tours, he said there was "an explanation other than musicianship to explain the extraordinary enthusiasm" of the audience. "You can't imagine," he said, "how we have been gathered in by audiences that obviously know about us through television." There were places where the audiences stood and cheered for minutes before the orchestra even played a note. [7]

1. What is the topic sentence of this paragraph?
2. What is the pointer in the topic sentence?
3. What basic method of development does the author use in this paragraph?
4. Is this paragraph unified? Does any sentence fail to support the pointer in the topic sentence?
5. What means of achieving coherence are used in this paragraph?
6. Why does the author place a colon after *For example*?
7. Why does he quote *how to*?
8. Why is *half-hour* hyphenated?
9. Why does the author start the quotation, *an explanation other than . . .*, without capitalizing *an*?
10. At the end of the Bernstein quotation, the period is put inside the final quotation mark. Is this practice correct? Which marks are put inside the quotation marks and which outside?

G.

Though they are not produced in wide-screen Cinemascope, have never won an Oscar, and cannot be viewed on "Saturday Night at the Movies," electronic films are already smash hits in many important sectors of modern electronics technology. Increasingly, they are being "booked" into television equipment, computer logic and memory circuits, two-way communications systems, missile and spacecraft controls, and of course, pocket radios. In fact, if present trends continue, they may yet make the electronics industry the new "film capital" of the world.

As distinguished from photographic film, electronic films are delicate tattoos of electronically active material condensed, for the most part, from hot vapors onto cold, hard, insulating surfaces such as glass. Depending on the materials used and the manner in which they are deposited, such films—many of them 10 times thinner than the shimmering coat of an ordinary soap bubble—may act singly or in combination as whole electronic circuits or simply as components thereof from transistors, diodes, and oscillators to resistors, capacitors, and interconnection paths. [8]

---

[7] Smith, "The Social Impact of Television."

[8] Bruce Shore, "Electronic Films," *Electronic Age*, Summer, 1966. Reprinted by permission of *Electronic Age*, Radio Corporation of America.

These are beginning paragraphs from a long article. The first is an introductory paragraph, and the second is a paragraph of definition. Together they form the necessary introduction to the article.

1. What point is to be established in the article? What is the specific thesis statement for the article?
2. Is the introductory paragraph a good one? Why or why not?
3. In the second paragraph, is definition by classification used? If so, where is this definition found?
4. The author uses two other methods to make his definition clear. What are they?
5. In the first paragraph, why does the author use quotation marks around *Saturday Night at the Movies*? Why around *booked*? Why *film capital*? Would any of these be just as effective without the quotation marks?
6. In the first paragraph, why are commas placed after *Cinemascope, Oscar,* and *Movies*? Is the comma inside the quotation mark after *Movies* properly placed?
7. In the second paragraph, explain the comma after *film*; after *condensed* and *part*; after *cold* and *hard*.
8. Why are dashes used after *films* and *bubble*? Would commas serve just as well here?
9. What coherence devices are employed in these paragraphs?
10. Analyze sentences for suspension of the subject, verb, or complement.

H.

The different international attitudes toward action and violence in children's programs were pointed out when NBC Enterprises co-produced an animated series with Mushi Productions in Japan. It seems the Japanese can comfortably separate reality from fantasy and do not object to a children's program in which death is presented. In one of the co-produced "Astro-Boy" episodes, the story included a highway accident in which a hot-rod driver kills a pedestrian. For syndication in the United States, the plot of the program was softened by skilled translators. Instead of being killed by a hot-rod driver, the pedestrian was slightly hurt in an unavoidable accident. The audience could then identify with the young driver of the automobile and sympathize with both the driver and the pedestrian.[9]

1. What is the topic sentence?
2. What is the pointer in the topic sentence?
3. What is the chief method of developing the topic sentence? What other method is used in combination with it?
4. Can you see any objection to beginning the second sentence with *It seems . . .* ? If so, what might you substitute?

[9] Al Husted, "American Television Abroad," *Electronic Age,* Autumn, 1966. Reprinted by permission of *Electronic Age,* Radio Corporation of America.

5. Explain the use of a comma after *episodes* in the third sentence, after *United States* in the fourth, and after *driver* in the fifth.
6. Why is *hot-rod* hyphenated?
7. Why is a comma not used before the first *and* in the last sentence?

The next selection is excerpted from an article of about 2500 words. It is, in effect, a five-hundred-word paper within the longer paper, and it establishes one point in support of the thesis of the longer article. Here, in other words, the five-hundred-word paper serves the same function in a 2500-word article as the paragraph does in the shorter paper.

I.

All of this is by way of saying that the computer will eventually have no less impact on engineers and engineering than gunpowder had on archery. It will be registered in several ways.

For one, the computer is going to intellectualize the practice of engineering to a degree inconceivable until now. In the past, the engineer has resorted to pencil, slide rule, and T-square to fashion his new designs; a machine shop and mechanical skills to develop his prototypes; and a pilot line to evolve their manufacture. Now, in theory, all but the conception of the idea can be accomplished by computer in tandem with automatic tools. Thus, instead of plotting his design on paper, the engineer will reduce it to a mathematical program. Instead of developing a physical prototype, he will construct a mathematical analogue and let it stand for his prototype. In addition, this analogue will take into account not only engineering matters but technological, operational, economic, and environmental factors that may be pertinent. The computer will then be asked to decide, in effect, whether the design is worth building. Waste and inefficiency in the design process will shrink to a minimum, hopefully, and ill-conceived products will never emerge from the computer.

There will be more to it than this, however. The computer will also make it possible for the engineer to consider the whole context in which his new design is to function. It will compel him consciously or unconsciously to think in systems rather than component terms. A greater emphasis on systems design will be in the inevitable result. More and more, the engineer will conceive the system and let the computer work out the components.

Finally, there is the somewhat imponderable but intriguing matter of the modifications and innovations in design which will stem directly from the man-machine interaction that results when he works with a computer. There is a modern anthropological theory that progress is the result of man's interaction with his own tools. It holds that the evolution of civilization has been and is a great boot-strap operation that has seen man invent tools, which experience then causes him to modify and differentiate until ultimately they inspire the invention of still more tools, which then are modified by experience and lead to yet newer tools, and so on.[10]

[10] Bruce Shore, "Computers and Engineers," *Electronic Age*, Winter, 1966/67. Reprinted by permission of *Electronic Age*, Radio Corporation of America.

1. What is the thesis statement of this selection?
2. What is the topic sentence of the second paragraph?
3. What methods of paragraph development are used in the second paragraph?
4. What point is made in the third paragraph? Do you consider this paragraph to be well-developed? Why or why not?
5. What point is made in the fourth paragraph? How is it established?
6. Note that this selection has no concluding statement because it is part of a longer article. Add a concluding statement.
7. How does the author achieve coherence between paragraphs?
8. What coherence devices does he use within paragraphs?
9. In the second sentence of the second paragraph, the author uses two semicolons. Why has he not used commas here?
10. Wherever commas have been used in this selection, explain their use.
11. How would you describe the tone of this selection? List your supporting evidence.

The next selection is about twice the length of a five-hundred-word paper and is more argumentative than most expository essays. Read it carefully once to get the main thought; then reread it for tone and other elements of style. After you are through, use the two check sheets (for the whole paper, for basic elements of style) to analyze the selection more closely.

J.

ON WHOSE SIDE ARE THE UNIVERSITIES?[11]

(1) Ten years ago college kids resented being called kids. Today they call one another kids with pride and solidarity. Today students have power; they do not need to play pretend.

(2) What happens in the colleges today may be decisive for the next 30 years. Small but articulate groups of students have attained an astute political consciousness and are promising disruption and rebellion. The Congress—that band of old men two generations removed from reality—is threatening reprisal. A nation founded by an armed revolution and still pledging allegiance to unfulfilled revolutionary principles—like liberty and justice for all—does not wish to educate rebellious students.

(3) What, then, is an education for? In the minds of many, a kid who "turns out right" moves into the social network of American industry with an affable smile, an easygoing manner and the reliable, efficient, pragmatic style on which our technological society depends. Hardheaded, realistic and committed to the demands of the present order of things, such a promising young man is encouraged to indulge in sentimentalities about defending freedom.

(4) One sees his friends in combat: crew-cut, clear-eyed, soft-spoken,

---

[11] Michael Novak, "On Whose Side Are the Universities?" Reprinted from *Christianity and Crisis*, October 14, 1968. Copyright 1968 by Christianity and Crisis, Inc.

determined. One sees them everywhere in the universities: clean-shaven, hard-working, bright, smooth. These are the "silent students," not represented by the radicals who dominate the news; for there is nothing new about them. The American educational system has been geared to turning out millions of them.

(5) What is an education for? To keep the clocks ticking, the factories humming and the planes flying? To keep American democracy strong? To keep the young loyal? To teach them to be happy with bread and circuses?

(6) The liberal answer to that question during the past 30 years has been to use the schools as agencies of progressive political and social enlightenment. And, indeed, public opinion polls regularly show a marked correlation between length of education and progressive views. But the liberal solution was a compromise with the ongoing system. Against utopianism and apocalypse, liberalism under Franklin D. Roosevelt chose pragmatic adjustment from within the system. The fruits have been many. But the compromise appears, now, to have broken down. The evidence is the malaise felt almost everywhere.

(7) The public schools are supported by public money and the private schools are supported by industry and government. How can such schools prepare students to be revolutionaries? How can any system prepare young people to transcend itself? The problem is even more vexing than the problem the institutional church must face: how to catechize prophets. For in the society at large, all the wealth, power and force of arms of the social system are preserving the system on its present course.

(8) Where revolutionary criticism is neither promoted nor heeded, moreover, those who strike the revolutionary pose for its own sake—desiring neither power nor its responsibilities but inner exaltation—are difficult to distinguish from genuine men of power. Without the hot-blooded, the romantic and the profoundly confused, on the other hand, no revolution can proceed. A revolution is not an act of reflection but of passion. Tom Paine's instability is not an argument against the validity of 1776, and it is unfair to discredit the present revolution merely by denouncing its tactics or the personalities of some of its leaders.

(9) Do we want a political revolution in the United States, a serious rearrangement of the bases of power, wealth and prestige? That is the fundamental educational question. If we do not want a serious revolution, then we should allow our various educational systems to function as they are. The logic of such a political choice would lead us to: (a) squash the student revolutionaries forcibly, or (b) co-opt their energies in pseudo-revolutionary programs (place them on committees). Generally, it is the liberal administrator who is the slowest to grasp the force and the origin of such logic. That is why he is the most hateful in the student's eyes.

(10) There has not been much serious revolutionary passion in the U.S. since the days of Reinhold Niebuhr's *The End of an Era.* But the doors of the Pandora's box closed by World War II have again flown open. Can a capitalistic democracy possibly serve the ideals of "freedom and justice for all"? Or is the whole system inherently contradictory?

(11) When young radicals close down one or another university during this school year or next, it would be a mistake to imagine that merely procedural issues are at stake. A streamlining of the administrative process or functional adjustments that relieve the pressure at concrete points of protest will not meet the issue. (In liberal pragmatic theory, issues are swiftly reduced to functional, operational terms.) The revolution that has begun on the campuses is not raising a procedural issue; it is substantive.

(12) That revolutionary issue has two parts. In the first place, the crew-cut, affable American is not an attractive human type. He is repressed, empty, quietly and blindly savage, without an interior life, boring and bored. The first substantive issue has to do with inhibitions, repressions and diminished imaginative and affective capacities.

(13) In the second place, the revolutionary issue is concerned with economics, technology, the mass media and political machinery. What is good for Texas money does not, clearly, promote "freedom and justice for all." The "law and order" that police forces now defend does cruel and arrogant violence to too huge a number of human beings; it is not tolerable. The interests that dominate social and political decision-making in the U.S. are unfaithful to the revolutionary ideals on which this country is founded.

(14) Faced with such a revolution, on whose side are the universities? And do they dare to say so? There is no other basic educational issue.

1. This paper should be compared with the "Law and Order" paper at the end of Chapter 2 (page 32). Their methods of arrangement and development are quite different. Make a list of similarities and differences. (Check the rest of the questions in this exercise for ideas.)

2. In what ways is the first paragraph designed to gain reader attention and agreement? Does it succeed for you? Why or why not? (See also Question 10.)

3. What is the purpose of the last sentence in the second paragraph? What is the purpose of Paragraphs 12, 13, and 14 at the end?

4. Make a list of modifiers and judgment words (for example, *disruption, soft-spoken, loyal, hot-blooded*) that give away the basic tone of the paper. How would you describe this tone? (List at least three or four descriptive words and be prepared to support your list.)

5. How could you combine the first two paragraphs into one strong unit? Would it be possible to combine the third, fourth, and fifth paragraphs? What, if anything, would you omit?

6. According to paragraph 3 on what kind of young man does "our technological society depend"? Do you agree with the statement? Why or why not? Can you find a similar problem in the fourth paragraph?

7. Does the paper contain any unsupported generalizations? List five, together with suggestions for making each more specific. (Be sure to consider stereotypes.)

8. Is the topic sentence in Paragraph 9 an accurate restatement of the thesis statement of Paragraph 1? How are these two sentences similar? Different?

9. This writer places the "system" on one side in a fight for change. Whom does he place on the opposing side? Do you agree with this two-part

division? Why or why not? (Be sure to consider the paper's title and last paragraph.)

10. List some of the psychological and ethical appeals used by the writer. (Refresh your memory by rereading pages 101 and 104.) Do these appeals work for you? Why or why not?

11. Using the check sheet for style as a guide, comment on the diction and sentences in this paper. List your observations and be prepared to support them.

12. Use the simplified check sheet for the whole paper (page 158) to evaluate the thought, organization, tone, and mechanics of this paper. Does this evaluation fit your first impression of this paper? Why or why not? List your observations and be prepared to support them.

Also about twice the length of a five-hundred-word paper, this next essay presents special problems in meaning and tone. Even a quick reading should tell you that the "writer's voice" in the essay does not *directly* present the author's meaning. Read it carefully to decide what its main points are; then reread for tone and other elements of style using the two check sheets as a guide (for the whole paper, for basic elements of style).

K.

UNSOLICITED OPENING DAY ADDRESS BY PREXY[12]

(1) Ladies and gentlemen, welcome—and welcome back—to Diehard University. I shall start the academic year by describing the contract you have entered into by the act of enrolling in this university. That contract is clearly set forth in the university catalogue, but since literacy is no longer prerequisite to admission, let me lip-read the essential points of our agreement. As you emerge from this convocation you will be handed a digest of these remarks in attractively prepared comic-book form with all dialogue limited to basic English and with the drawings carefully designed to help you over any grammatical difficulties. Those of you, moreover, for whom the requirements of Sub-Literacy One have been waived, may dial AV for Audio Visual, followed by 0016, and a dramatized explication will appear on your TV sets.

(2) Diehard, as you know, is no longer dedicated to excellence. The trustees, the administration, the faculty, and the federal government—not necessarily in that order—have concurred that excellence has been outnumbered. The restated policy of Diehard University is simply to salvage what it can from what little it gets from the too much being thrust upon it.

(3) We recognize that the achievement of any given intellectual standard is no longer prerequisite to a bachelor's degree. The insistence of any educational institution is defined by its minimum standards, and Diehard

---

[12]John Ciardi, "Unsolicited Opening Day Address by Prexy." First appeared in *Saturday Review,* September 28, 1968. Copyright 1968 by Saturday Review, Inc. Reprinted with permission of author and publication.

no longer has any. As a contractual agreement, the faculty undertake to confer a bachelor's degree upon you in acknowledgment of four years of attendance.

(4) If you are willing to settle for that degree, I suggest you do not waste money on textbooks. The presence of a textbook may tempt you to open it. The psychological consequences are obvious: if you must actually open a textbook in order to meet nonexistent minimum standards, how will you ever be sure you are not a moron? Your whole future career could be warped, in such a case, by guilt and uncertainty. Our educational activities, let me say, are so organized that any member of the in- or out-group of the affluent society can stroll through them in the intervals between political rallies, draft-card burnings, love-ins, water fights, sit-ins, sit-outs, sympathy marches, student elections, anti-raids and generalized adolescent glandular upheavals. These programs have been carefully constructed to assist your social development as students. I urge them upon you as the social duty of every minimalist. Diehard would serve no purpose were it to allow an intemperate emphasis on learning to deflect its minimalists from the fullness of their undergraduate social development and thus, indirectly, from future computerization.

(5) To further that social development, Diehard imposes no rules of extracurricular behavior. We shall not act *in loco parentis.* With a mild shudder of revulsion, we return that function to your legal parents. We have problems enough with our own failures and cannot accept as ours the genetic failures of others.

(6) This university has eliminated dormitories. Where you live, with whom you live, and what you do off campus are matters between you and your parents, or between you and the police, as the case may be.

(7) You are free to demonstrate on all matters of conviction, or, simply, on all matters. For your convenience we have set aside a fireproof, waterproof, open-occupancy convention center called Hyde Park Hall. You are free to occupy it and to harangue in or from it at your pleasure. You have full license for all noncriminal acts that occur in Hyde Park Hall. Any criminal actions you may engage in there will be, of course, between you and the police.

(8) Should you choose to act unlawfully in any of the otherwise assigned buildings of the university, you will be warned once that your actions are unlawful, and the police will then be summoned to take normal action against a breach of the peace.

(9) The university will seek your advice on all matters of student organization, social development of the university, and community relations. We shall seek that advice temperately and with as much open-mindedness as we can achieve in our senility. In seeking it, however, we do not pledge ourselves to be bound by it. Where your views seem to be reasoned, they will be honored in reason; where they seem intemperate or shortsighted, they will be rejected in reason. A faculty-student board will be elected to study all grievances.

(10) In no case, however, will that board, or any body of this university, consider a general amnesty as a condition for ending a demonstration that violates lawful procedure.

(11) Diehard will not consider any request made by a minimalist for changes in the curriculum, faculty, or academic qualification. On these matters we ask nothing from you and we will hear nothing.

(12) We do confess to a vestigial nostalgia for the long-honored and now outmoded idea of the university as a bookish community of learning. While most of you are pursuing your social development, therefore, the faculty will direct such students as are inclined to volunteer for it, in a course of study leading to the degree of Laureate in Arts or in Science. We shall continue to grant the Bachelor's degree in Arts or in Science without requirement, though to assist your social development we do invite you to attend various discussion groups to be held at carefully spaced intervals.

(13) With those who elect the Laureate program, the university insists on a different contract. It insists that in the act of electing such a program, the student will have submitted himself to the faculty as candidate for a degree to be conferred at the discretion of the faculty. The faculty, having already thrown away minimums, must insist on reserving to itself the right to formulate maximums for those who are willing to reach for them. It is the student's business to qualify, or to revert (without prejudice), to the social development program leading to the degree of Bachelor.

(14) I ask all those who are interested in a course of study to return tomorrow to start our further discussions. The rest of you may now return to your pads to drop out, turn on, and tune in. If you are arrested between now and your graduation, the university will credit the time up to your conviction toward your attendance and will do its best to readmit you upon completion of your sentence. By decision of the board of trustees, days of attendance completed while out on bail pending an appeal will be counted toward a degree.

(15) If the police, that is, are willing to let you out of jail, and if you are willing to check in on the roster, we are willing to keep the attendance records and to grant appropriate degrees upon satisfaction of the requirement.

(16) We are not willing to have our reading and discussion time interrupted by protest, no matter how passionate, that breaks the law. Nor are we willing to police the law. Criminality is the proper concern of the police; ours, we believe, is reasoned discussion. When the discussion goes beyond reason and to the point of interfering with the curriculum of those who have chosen one, we reserve the right to suspend or to expel you from the hazy premises of our failing venture into education for those few who are interested in the unlikely.

(17) Hello. Goodbye. And may your standardization be your fulfillment.

1. What "role" has the poet-critic John Ciardi assumed as he writes this essay? If you didn't have the essay title, how could you tell?

2. List a number of reasons for Ciardi's use of the name "Diehard University." Is the "speaker" within the essay "for" or "against" Diehard U.? How can you tell? Is Ciardi "for" or "against" Diehard U.? How can you tell? (See Question 4.)

3. What is the effect of the *I-you* relationship established at the beginning and carried throughout? List other words and phrases that add to the conversational tone. (Consider the shift from *I* to *we*.)

4. Irony is a device used by writers who want to say one thing but mean another. How can you tell that Ciardi is using irony? (Consider such things as overstatement, understatement, and departure from the reader's expectations.) When writers are being ironical, how can you tell what they mean? Is it possible that the president of Diehard U. (the "speaker") is also being ironical? Explain your views.

5. List as many words and phrases as you can that seem to be overstatements (for example, *comic-book form, four years of attendance, moron, minimalist, diehard, full license, senility, without requirement*).

6. What is the function of the first three paragraphs? (Consider problems of introduction, tone, and thesis statement.)

7. What are the main points made in Paragraphs 4 through 13? Could you justify the use of so many short paragraphs? Could some of them be combined?

8. How do Paragraphs 14 through 17 tie the paper together? Are they a conclusion?

9. List a number of reasons why the last sentence in the essay may be considered its most important one.

10. Does Ciardi depend on stereotypes to make his exaggerations clear? List some examples.

11. When you are through reading this essay, do you "identify with" the speaker ("I"), the students addressed ("you"), or the writer (Ciardi)? Or none of these? Explain your views.

12. Using the check sheet for style as a guide, comment on the diction and sentences in this paper. List your observations and be prepared to support them.

13. Use the simplified check sheet for the whole paper (page 158) to evaluate the thought, organization, tone, and mechanics of this essay. Does this evaluation fit your first impression of this paper? Why or why not? List your observations and be prepared to support them.

14. This selection is neither expository nor purely argumentative. The irony makes it *satire*. Check the word *satire* in a good dictionary and be prepared to write an extended definition of this kind of writing.

INDEX